To all the people who inspired me to write this book, who, unfortunately, have now passed away, so will never read it.

I'LL TAKE THAT ONE

WILLIAM B GREEN

1 3 1769429 5

Matador
9 Priory Business Park,
Wistow Road, Kibworth Beauchamp,
Leicestershire. LE8 0RX
Tel: 0116 279 2299
Email: books@troubador.co.uk
Web: www.troubador.co.uk/matador
Twitter: @matadorbooks

ISBN 978 1789016 550

British Library Cataloguing in Publication Data.
A catalogue record for this book is available from the British Library.

Printed and bound in Great Britain by 4edge Limited
Typeset in 12pt Adobe Garamond Pro by Troubador Publishing Ltd, Leicester, UK

Matador is an imprint of Troubador Publishing Ltd

I'll Take That One

Prologue

～≈～

The Second World War brought with it a global cataclysm that resulted in the death of more than 60 million people.

In September 1939, Britain's Prime Minister Neville Chamberlain announced that Britain was at war with Germany. In the days and months following that announcement, 3,000,000 people were relocated from towns and cities across England as part of an evacuation scheme code named 'Pied Piper'.

A committee was set up in May 1938 and local billeting officers were appointed to find suitable homes for the evacuees. For months they interviewed possible hosts, who, once selected, were compelled to take one or more evacuees. Anyone refusing faced the threat of a fine. For some, this threat prompted them to take in an evacuee to avoid being fined, rather than a desire to foster a child. Hosts were paid by the government, which again could be more an incentive for the money than a moral obligation.

In 1940, during the onset of this grim period in history, one boy began his own journey; one that would irrevocably change the course of his life.

Authors Note

⌒

In this memoir I have tried to recreate events and conversations from my memories of them. In most instances I have changed the names of individuals and identifying characteristics. In some instances I have omitted people and events, but only when my memories of them were insufficiently clear, or the omission had no impact on either the veracity or the substance of the story.

William B Green

Chapter One

'Where is everybody going?' I asked my dad that chilly morning in November 1940. World war two had been raging for some fourteen months and things were getting worse with each passing day. Amongst all the turmoil, my older brother and I were taken to Bristol railway station after being told by our parents that we were going on our holidays to the seaside.

What little clothing we had was packed into a cardboard box and secured with a length of rope. Labels, stating our name and destination, were fixed to the lapels of our jacket. Around our necks hung a brown cardboard box containing our 'Donald Duck' gasmask, so called because the exhaust flap was a flat piece of rubber which resembled a duck's beak.

The station was a hive of activity, with teachers, police, and railway staff bustling everywhere. As a four-year-old boy I found it all very exciting, but the real significance completely passed me.

'Maybe they are also going on their holidays,' my dad replied.

The thought of going to the seaside was uppermost in my mind as I excitedly boarded the train. My dad placed our cardboard box on the overhead luggage rack and re-joined my mother on the platform. Only when the railway guard closed our carriage door and my parents were still on the platform did I realise something wasn't right. Wedging my head through the crowded carriage window, I called out.

'Mum, dad, come on, you'll miss the train.'

'You go on. We're not coming with you,' replied my dad.

As the train began moving, I suddenly remembered my dad had not given me my pocket money.

'Dad, dad, you didn't give me my penny,' I shouted.

'I'll give it to you next week when we come down to see you,' he called back. I continued waving until they were out of sight before sitting down.

My parents didn't come to see me the next week, or the week after. It was more than two years before I saw either of them again.

My disappointment that my parents were not coming with us soon passed, the excitement of going on holiday to the beach filling my mind. But with nothing to do but listen to the clacking of the train wheels, or watch the countryside whizz by, I soon became bored. To break the monotony, I whispered to my brother.

'I want to go to the toilet.'

'There's no toilet, you will have to wait until we get to the next station,' he replied.

The third-class carriage we were in had no corridors. Passengers who needed a toilet break were expected to hop out when the train stopped at a station. At each station, the guard announced the station name, which had been removed to prevent enemy planes using them for navigation purposes.

Glad to be off the train, I skipped along the platform. Sighting the tea trolley, which had been wheeled onto the platform when the train pulled in, I asked my brother to buy me a cake, but he said he had no money.

Minutes later, when the train was ready to depart, I was not onboard. Oblivious to any urgency, I came sauntering out of the toilet to see my brother frantically calling out the window. As the guard ushered me onto the train, an irate man shouted out the window, 'If he does it again, leave him behind.'

After what seemed like an eternity, the train arrived in Exmouth, Devon. Blackout regulations had been imposed on 1 September 1939, so the station was in complete darkness. These regulations required that all windows and doors were covered at night with a suitable material, such as heavy curtains, cardboard, or paint, to prevent the escape of the tiniest glimmer of light that might aid enemy aircraft.

A council appointed billeting officer met us at the train. Shielding the torch with her hand, she checked our labels, before leading us to a bus.

Chapter Two

After a short ride, we arrived at a small hotel requisitioned by the Government to house evacuees. A figure, barely visible in the dim light of the hooded headlights of the bus, was waiting at the top of the steps.

As soon as we were gathered on the pavement, the bus pulled away, taking with it the only source of light. Across the road, I could hear the sound of waves breaking on the beach.

'Do you think we'll be able to go to the beach tomorrow?' I asked my brother.

'Maybe,' he replied, his voice holding very little conviction.

Only when we had been hustled inside and the door closed, was the light switched on.

'Welcome everybody,' said the woman. 'I'm Sister Heppel, the matron. Leave your belongings in the hall and take a seat in the dining room.'

We all jostled for a seat, but before I could join my brother at his table the other seats were taken. An early indication that in future I would need to be on my toes.

The cook moved between the tables ladling out soup. It was my first food since breakfast and I was starving. Several of us immediately picked up our spoons.

'Do not start until you are told; wait until everybody has been served.' My soup-filled spoon was already on its way to my mouth.

Taking a tiny sip of the hot liquid brought a disapproving look from the matron.

'Right, you may begin,' she said. One child complained she didn't like soup.

'Well there's nothing else. It's soup or nothing,' she was told. She picked up her spoon.

When everyone finished eating, we were shown to our beds. The rooms, normally for hotel guests, had been converted into small dormitories, with four single iron beds on each side of the room. There was a small locker between them.

My brother began unpacking our box, claiming his stuff. What was left in the box was mine, although I had no idea what I was supposed to have. The matron came to check on us. Totally confused by the whole experience, I was still dressed.

'Come along, get ready for bed. Where are your pyjamas?' she asked.

'Don't know.' I replied.

Pushing me out of the way, she rummaged through my box and handed me a pair.

'Here put these on,' she said, turning down the sheets.

The starched sheets smelled of carbolic soap, and the bed was cold and impersonal. This was nothing like the holiday I had imagined.

'Right, settle down everyone.'

The matron turned off the light and closed the door. An eerie silence descended upon the darkened room, emphasised by the tightly drawn blackout curtains across the windows. The only visible light was the small amount coming in under the door. I called across the small space to my brother.

'Frankie, Frankie.' He didn't answer. As my eyes became accustomed to the dark, I could see he was already asleep.

I was just dozing off, when someone began crying. The door opened, and a woman entered.

'What's the matter?' she asked.

'I want my mum,' replied the sobbing child.

'Don't cry, I'm sure she'll be coming to see you soon. Now go to sleep.'

Another figure entered the room.

'Stop that crying, we will have none of your nonsense, now get to sleep.' The woman stepped away from the child's bed.

'You mustn't be too soft with them, otherwise they will take advantage of you and you will be in here all night,' said the Matron. Both women left the room; the child's sobs continued. I soon fell asleep.

Chapter Three

It seemed I had only just fallen asleep, when the lights were switched on, and a voice called out, 'Time to get up.'

My 'impersonal' bed was now warm and comfortable. So comfortable, I dozed off. Suddenly, the bedclothes were pulled off me, the cold air bringing me to life as a hand grabbed my foot.

'Come on, up you get, we have a very busy day ahead.' The woman tugged me towards the edge of the bed, before leaving me shivering in my pyjamas and taking her annoying voice off to harass someone else.

Still half asleep, I dressed and went downstairs to look for my brother. I found him in the dining hall, but the table he was seated at was already full.

Porridge was being served, as it was most mornings. There were no fussy eaters, most just happy to get anything at all.

After breakfast, we were ushered into the play area, a converted lounge off the entrance hall. Except for a large cardboard box of toys donated by the local community, the room was devoid of furniture. There were never enough toys to go around, so it was first-come first-served. This meant the older children took what they wanted, leaving the younger children to sort out what was left.

Often, unable to secure a toy, I just sat on the lino covered floor gazing out the bay window. I spent many hours each day watching the people passing by, whilst hoping that one of them would be my mother come to take me to the beach.

I could see the beach not far away on the other side of the road, and wondered when I would get there. The Matron had warned us not to leave the building unless accompanied by an adult, so I couldn't see how I was ever going to get to the beach. Apart from her and her staff, there were no other adults, and they were always busy.

Inevitably, a quarrel broke out between two boys. They were squabbling over a toy lorry. The bigger boy wrested it away from the smaller boy, hurting his fingers. He ran crying from the room. Within seconds, the matron stormed in dragging the boy with her.

'Whoever hurt this boy had better stop, right now, or there will be trouble,' she shouted, in no uncertain terms.

Being one of the youngest and smallest children in the room, I had little chance of getting a toy. I asked my brother to get one for me. He was two and half years older than me, so I saw him as one of the 'big boys'.

'What for?' he said. 'Someone will just take it off you.'

Soon, another argument broke out. Within minutes, the matron was back and pulled the boys apart. Giving each a quick clip around the ear, she ordered them to stand in the corner and face the wall.

During the scuffle, the toy lorry the two boys had been arguing over fell to the floor. Seeing a chance to get my hands on a toy, I scampered over and picked it up. One of the boys spotted me, quickly snatched it back, and placed his foot on it. As soon as he turned to face the wall again, I pulled the toy from under his foot and ran to the other side of the room. Furious at being caught unawares, he chased after me and tried to snatch the lorry back.

I hung on for as long as I could, until finally, fingers aching, I let go. The sudden release caught him off balance, and he staggered backwards into a group of children playing on the floor. The commotion had the matron storming back into the room.

Snatching the lorry from the boy, she threw it to the ground, and propelled him into the corner of the room, giving him another clip around the ear.

I retrieved the lorry and proudly showed it to my brother. He was not impressed.

'You only got that because the matron took it from him,' he said.

Chapter Four

～~～

Each evening after supper, usually bread and soup, we all lined up in our underwear outside the bathroom. At the command 'next', we entered. One woman gave us a wipe down with a wet flannel, whilst another gave us a rub down with a towel. I don't remember brushing my teeth, or even if I had a toothbrush.

Our underwear and pyjamas were all washed together, so only those whose clothing was marked with their name were sure of getting the right things back. I often ended up with odd pyjamas and underwear. Because the hostel was a holding centre until foster homes were found, nobody really cared what you were wearing, just as long as you had something on. We would soon be someone else's problem.

Friendships in the hostel didn't last long either. No sooner had you met someone, and they would be off to a foster home. That was normally the last you saw of them, unless the foster parents found them unsuitable and brought them back to the hostel.

One evening, I was getting ready for bed, when I was hit on the head with a pillow, the blow catching me unawares.

'That's for taking my lorry,' said the boy, laughing and running from the room.

Grabbing my pillow, I was about to give chase, when I was grabbed by one of the staff and told to keep the noise down. By the time she released my arm, 'lorry boy', for want of a better name, was nowhere to be seen. Then I spotted a figure huddling under the blankets at the end of the room. Sneaking up, I gave the figure an almighty wallop. Immediately, the blankets were thrown back, only for me to discover I had hit the wrong boy. Jumping out of bed, he grabbed his pillow and began swinging at me. Moments later 'lorry boy' appeared. Soon all three of us were in full flight, with pillows raining in all directions.

Suddenly, a hand grabbed both me and 'lorry boy' and pulled us apart. The third boy quickly jumped into his bed.

'Get back here.' ordered the matron.

'It wasn't my fault, he started it,' he blurted out, pointing at me.

'No, I didn't,' I shouted, 'he did.'

'Quiet the lot of you. I don't care who started it. It's the same every night; shouting, screaming, fighting, and if it's not you, it is someone else. All I ask is that you get into bed, now is that difficult?'

She released 'lorry boy' and sat on his bed. Bending me over her ample lap, she brought her huge hand down onto my backside. My thin pyjamas gave me very little protection, my cries having no impact on her. By the time she stopped, my backside was well and truly warmed. Releasing me, she handed out the same treatment to the other two boys.

'Let that be a lesson to you, all of you.'

She turned off the lights and left the room. My backside was still tingling. To ease the pain, I rolled onto my stomach and sobbed into my pillow. I'd never felt so lonely in my life, completely unable to understand why my parents had sent me here.

Sister Heppel was a strict disciplinarian, but she also had a softer side. Often, she would be seen hugging a child.

'Hope she never hugs me,' said my brother.

'Why? it's better than being smacked,' I replied.

'Yeah. But if she hugs you it means your mum or dad have been killed.'

At that stage in the war casualties were a daily occurrence. Sister Heppel had the unenviable job of breaking the news to the child.

Chapter Five

Early in December, not long after we arrived, I was aimlessly wandering around the hostel when I spotted the front door was open. With no adults in sight, I just walked out. I could see the beach on the other side of the road. So, with very little traffic, I soon crossed over. The barbed wire deterrent, strung along the beach to keep the enemy out, presented little problem to me. Wriggling through it, I was soon on the beach.

Quickly removing my shoes, I ran to the water's edge. As each wave approached, I ran up the beach laughing and giggling. It was a cold day and the water was freezing, but was the best fun I'd had since arriving at the hostel.

Suddenly, the sound of aircraft caught my attention. I looked up to see a number of German aeroplanes, the markings plain on the wings and fuselage. I later learned they were heading for Plymouth, a large naval dockyard. Oblivious to their significance, I watched them disappear into the distance before going back to my game.

The next thing I know, I was plucked from the sand. The Air Raid Precautions warden tucked me under his arm, ran up the beach, and dumped me down in an air raid shelter. After gathering his breath, he said.

'Don't you know when the siren sounds you must run to the shelters?'

'Yes,' I replied, having been told many times.

'So, why didn't you?'

'I didn't hear the siren.'

'Didn't you see the planes overhead.'

'Yes.'

'So why…oh never mind.'

I squeezed myself onto the crowded wooden bench. My bare feet, now quite cold, a reminder I'd left my shoes on the beach.

The 'all clear' sounded and the shelter emptied. By the time we reached the hostel, the matron had already despatched members of staff to try and find me. The ARP warden told her that he would need to make a report. She invited him into her office, and told me to stand in the corner and face the wall. Tea and biscuits were served, and I could hear the satisfied munching as the ARP warden and the Matron tucked in. Biscuits were not on the menu for evacuees, and it didn't look as if things were about to change.

As they enjoyed their afternoon tea, the Matron was busy convincing the warden it was a one off, and was it really necessary to take the matter any further. The tea and biscuits worked. As soon as the warden agreed to let it pass, the Matron began easing him into the hall. Through the door jamb, I could see he was in no hurry to leave. Spotting the remaining biscuits lying lonely on the plate, I quickly snaffled one, stuffed it into my mouth, and put my jaws into overdrive as I saw the Matron returning. Her chair creaked as she eased her ample backside into it.

'You can turn around now,' she said. Putting my hand to my mouth and coughing, I hoped I had wiped any tell-tale crumbs from my mouth.

'So, what have you got to say for yourself?' she asked.

What could I say? I remained silent. She, on the other hand, was soon into full swing, lecturing me on all the do's and don'ts. I was sure it was leading to a good hiding. Finally, she stopped. Grasping my arm, she led me into the hall.

'Face the wall. You are not to speak to anyone. Do you hear?'

'Yes matron,' I mumbled.

'And, if we don't find your shoes you'll have to walk around in your bare feet, as there are no more,' she added. She sent one of the staff to see if they could find my shoes.

The hall floor was cold on my bare feet. I tried warming them by rubbing them up and down the backs of my legs. When this didn't help, I eased myself onto the hall carpet. My brother saw me and asked where I had been. Before I could answer, the matron chased him away.

'I told you not to speak to anyone. Now get back over there, and face the wall.'

'But my feet are cold.' I complained.

'You should have thought of that before you lost your shoes.'

A few minutes later, my brother sneaked back. Still facing the wall, I told him where I had been. Suddenly, my head exploded, the blow bringing tears to my eyes.

'Now perhaps you'll do as you're told,' said the matron, leaving me sniffling in the hall.

The smell of food as the evening meal was prepared reminded me how hungry I was. Soon, the other children started filling the dining hall and I could hear the clatter of cutlery. No one came for me. Worried I would miss my supper, I began easing myself towards the dining room.

'Where do you think you're going?' The Matron's voice stopped me in my tracks; I returned to the corner.

'You're such a disobedient boy aren't you?…Go on, get your supper.'

My shoes were never recovered. Each day I just ran around in my socks until someone from the community donated a pair. They were not new, were too big, but there was still plenty of wear in them. It was them or nothing. One of the staff tied the laces as tight as possible, but even curling up my toes didn't stop them from coming off. In the end, I only wore them when we lined up for fostering out. After all, who's going to pick a boy with no shoes.

Chapter Six

Each day, when a potential foster parent called into the hostel, the staff would usher us into the hall. I had no idea why, as they never explained the reason. Even a child being selected and whisked away, meant nothing to me. After a selection was made, those children not chosen were sent back to the playroom to await the next time. Even when a woman pointed at my brother and said, 'I'll take that one', meant nothing to me.

Only when our cardboard box was packed, and we left the hostel with our new foster parent, did I realise something was going on.

Excited to be out of the hostel, I pointed out to my brother where I had lost my shoes. Apart from that walk on the beach, this was the first time since arriving in Exmouth I had been outside the hostel.

After a short bus ride, we reached our new home and were introduced to the rest of the family. A boy about my age, his older brother, and their grandfather. Their father was away in the army. One of the boys showed us to our room. As we passed the dining room I noticed the table was laid.

'Did you see all that food?' I excitedly whispered, once we were in our room.

'Yes,' replied my brother, smacking his lips and rubbing his hands with glee.

They were a nice family, and fed us well. Then, a couple of weeks after Christmas, like unwanted Christmas presents, they took us back to the hostel. No explanation was given or considered necessary. That was the last I saw of that family.

Whilst we had been away, a number of new children had arrived at the hostel. I soon slotted in, as if I had never been away.

A few days later, around 2 am on the morning of January 18th, 1941, we were all sound asleep in our beds, when the air raid warning sounded. We were quickly hustled into the shelter at the back of the hostel. The air raid shelter was cold and damp, with the only light coming from a couple of candles and the hooded torches the staff carried.

Still half asleep, I wrapped my blanket around me and huddled with the rest of the children on one of the cold benches. I was just dozing off, when a tremendous bang shook the very foundations, startling us out of our slumbers. Several of the children began crying, but for the life of me I was unable to muster a single tear. Several hours later the 'All Clear' sounded.

'Everyone stay where they are until I have checked that it is safe to go outside,' ordered the matron.

Dawn was just breaking as we emerged and were able to see what had caused the bang. Three high explosive bombs had hit the built up area around The Cross and Chapel Street, which was just at the back of where we were living.

See Eric R Delderfield's note dated 18 January 1941. Nine adults and three children lost their lives.

The blast had blown all the windows out of the back of the hostel, and broken glass was lying everywhere. As we entered, a fireman was handing out boiled sweets. It seemed to me that only the children who were snuffling received a sweet. My 'sham' fit of crying had the fireman saying.

'You can stop now, you've got your sweet.'

We had been evacuated to Exmouth to get away from the bombing. It turned out to be anything but. The incident I referred to in this chapter was the one listed on the 18th January 1941.

Eric R. Delderfield took an interest in all things to do with Exmouth. He was a local councillor and wrote several books about the town. I gratefully acknowledge the careful notes he made about the air raids on Exmouth. He wrote: 'Who will ever forget the air raids of 1940 – 1943. For a town of its size, Exmouth suffered very severely, both in lives and in property, during those years.'

Here is a summary of the raids which caused the greatest loss of life:

18 January 1941: *In the early hours of the morning, three high explosive bombs hit the built-up area around The Cross and Chapel Street. Nine adults and three children lost their lives.*

25 February 1941: *Three high explosive bombs fell in the St. Andrew's and Victoria Road areas. A visitor to the town (Arthur John Harding Hill) was killed by a direct hit.*

1 March 1941: *Five bombs were dropped at 8.0 in the evening, only two of which exploded – the one in the Parade caused four fatalities but the one at the back of Phear Park Lodge caused damage but no casualties.*

28 May 1941: *Bombs were dropped in the Woodville Road area, demolishing three houses, and killing six adults and three children. A further 8 people were hospitalised.*

12 June 1941: *During the evening, a British plane returning from patrol was attacked by a Messerschmitt over the town. The British plane crashed in flames on a house in Cranford Avenue which was destroyed by fire. The inhabitants of the house escaped but the two crew members were killed.*

12 February 1942: *Just after 8.0am, three bombs were dropped in the area of the Beacon. One exploded in Bicton Place where there were five fatal casualties and seven were injured.*

26 February 1943: *Around mid-day, eight enemy planes attacked with high explosive bombs, cannon and machine gun fire. Eight bombs were dropped and all exploded. One demolished a row of shops in the Strand killing people who were working or shopping in them as well as a queue of people waiting at an adjacent bus stop. A total of 25 people died on this occasion and a further 40 were injured, some seriously. During the same raid, a man working on his allotment on Albion Hill (Thomas Maxwell) was killed by cannon fire.*

There were many other air raids which caused damage to property and we may never know why Exmouth was targeted so consistently.

With thanks to the Devon Heritage Internet site for the above information.

Authors note. In my opinion the German planes returning to base after attacking the Royal Naval Dockyard in Plymouth would have been low on fuel. To lighten the load, they would have jettisoned any bombs they had left. It just happened that Exmouth was under their return flight path and was a soft target.

Chapter Seven

Although the bombing was a setback, the windows were soon boarded up, and it was soon business as usual. Within days, we were again lined up in the hall to be eyed by another potential foster parent. She quickly walked along the assembled faces, pointed to my brother and said, 'I'll take that one'.

The matron explained that he had a younger brother, so we were both on our way to our second foster home. Our belongings were again packed into a cardboard box, and moments later we silently followed her to the bus stop. She didn't speak or ask us anything about ourselves during the short bus journey. Her only words were, 'this is it', when we arrived at our stop. Making no attempt to help us carry our cardboard box, she led the way towards a block of houses. I didn't like the look of them one bit, becoming more apprehensive the nearer we got. Opening the front door of a two-storey terraced house, she was immediately greeted by two children.

'Mum, mum, did you get somebody?' they yelled.

She pushed past them without answering, leaving my brother and me, *the somebodies*, on the doorstep, being surveyed by the two children. One was a boy about my age, and the other a girl, possibly a couple of years older. From within the house, the woman called out, 'Come on then, in you come.'

The girl moved down the passage. As my brother and I struggled with our box, the boy blocked my path. His mother saw him and called out.

'Now John, don't be naughty. Where are your manners?' He reluctantly moved to one side. As I passed, he sneered into my ear.

'I don't like you.'

On hearing that I knew that my initial misgivings were justified. It was bad enough arriving at a strange home, without the added trauma of being greeted in this way.

The house smelled of stale cooking and unwashed bodies, and did not appear to be very clean. A woman, the next-door neighbour, gave us a cursory glance and excused herself.

'So, you're Frankie, and you're Billy,' said the woman, addressing us for the first time. We both nodded.

'John,' she said to the boy. 'Take them upstairs and show them to their room.'

'Don't want to,' he replied.

Janet, the girl, said she would do it. John placed himself on the landing and watched as we struggled up the stairs with our cardboard box.

'This is my room, so keep out,' he said.

Janet showed us into the smaller room next door. Seeing the double bed, which took up most of the space, I was not happy. Sharing a bed with my brother didn't appeal to me.

The foster parent, who we were told to call 'Auntie', went to work each day. This didn't help my relationship with John. He was unruly and made it plain that he didn't like me. Every time we had a dispute, which was every day, he reminded me that this was his house and that I was an evacuee.

My brother and Janet seemed to get along well enough, but I spent a lot of time on my own.

Then one day, things really came to a head. Completely bored, I aimlessly wandered into my bedroom just in time to see John peeing in the corner.

'Ugh, you dirty thing, I'm telling on you,' I said.

'Go on then, see if I care, I'll tell them it was you.'

He pushed past me and went into his own bedroom. I ran down stairs and told my brother, showing him the puddle of yellow urine in the corner.

Later that day, as if nothing had happened, John asked me to play 'hide and seek'. He may have forgotten his disgusting act, but I hadn't. However, in the hope I could get my own back on him, I agreed.

Pretending to cover my eyes whilst counting to ten, I watched him hide in the wardrobe in his bedroom. The key was in the door, so I silently locked it and sat on his bed.

Some moments later he realised I was not looking for him, and tried to open the door.

'Billy, let me out, I know you're there,' he called. I ignored him.

'Let me out, let me out,' he shouted, kicking the door. I left the room and went into the back garden where I wouldn't hear him.

He was still banging and screaming when his mother arrived home. She was livid when he told her what had happened.

'Did you lock John in the wardrobe?' she said, angrily looking at me.

'No auntie, I've been in the garden all the time,' I innocently replied.

'You're a liar. He locked me in because I caught him peeing in the bedroom,' shouted John. I couldn't believe my ears.

'It wasn't me, it was you,' I protested. 'Ask Frankie.' My brother supported my story.

Auntie rushed upstairs followed by the four of us. The last dregs of John's pee could still be seen on the lino. Too livid to speak, she pushed us out of the way, got a cloth and wiped it up.

That incident passed, but the conflict between John and I continued. I really hated living in that house, unable to see an end to the misery of living there.

Then, the following week, to my never-ending relief, we were called into the kitchen and told we were being taken back to the hostel.

I didn't much care for the hostel, but anything was better than that stinking house.

Chapter Eight

The first few months of our evacuation had been eventful, to say the least. My brother and I had been fostered out twice and returned to the hostel. But within days, we were again lined up in the hall whilst a woman slowly wandered along the row of upturned faces. After giving me a cursory look, she moved on. To my surprise, she returned and said.

'I'll take that one,' indicating me.

The Matron told her I had a brother and where possible they liked to keep families together. The woman said she couldn't take two children. After a slight pause the Matron agreed to let me go on my own.

My few articles of clothing were packed into a cardboard box, and within moments I was ready to leave. This time without my brother.

Whilst I waited for the Matron to sort out the paperwork, I looked into the playroom to wave goodbye to my brother. The fact that I might not see him again never crossed my mind. He saw me, but immediately looked the other way pretending not to see me. I joined my new foster parent in the hall.

'Now remember Billy,' said the matron. 'Be a good boy and do as you are told.'

'Yes matron,' I dutifully replied.

'I'm sure you won't have any bother with him,' she continued. 'He has such a placid nature.' Giving me a sly grin, she steered me towards the door.

During the bus journey, my new foster mother asked me lots of questions, quite different from my previous foster parent. I couldn't tell her much, except to say I thought I was from Bristol.

The first thing I noticed when we arrived at her house was how quiet and peaceful it was after the continual noise in the hostel. She showed me to my room and I couldn't believe my luck. It was like opening Aladdin's cave.

I had a set of drawers, a wardrobe, and a single bed. This was the first time I'd had a room to myself. Even when I lived with my parents I shared a room with my brother. Auntie helped me unpack.

'Are these the only clothes you have?' she asked. I nodded.

'And what about your shoes? … they don't seem to fit very well.' I told her about my walkabout on the beach and how I had lost my shoes.

'Well, we will have to do something about that won't we?' Again I nodded, not sure what I was expected to say.

'Are you hungry?' she asked.

I was always hungry. In fact, I can't remember a time during the war years when I was not hungry.

She called me to the table in the dining room and I surveyed the sandwiches and cake. Not wanting to risk being seen as greedy, just in case I was taken back to the hostel, I quietly waited until I was told to start.

'Come on, don't be shy, help yourself,' she said.

Help myself. This was something new to my ears. I didn't need a second invitation. Keeping one eye on Auntie for any signs of disapproval, I demolished several sandwiches. She then cut me a slice of cake which she had baked herself. As I sunk my teeth into the more than generous serve, I didn't really care who had baked it.

Lying in bed that night, I thought how lucky I was to have been chosen to live here. For the first time in months my stomach was full, and my room was beautifully silent. It was complete contentment. I momentarily wondered if I should ask 'Auntie' to go to the hostel and get my brother. But not wanting to spoil a good thing, or give her a reason to take me back to the hostel, I rolled over and went to sleep.

Over the next few weeks my wardrobe grew as Auntie came home with articles of clothing from the second-hand clothing shop.

'Yes, that's not a bad fit,' she would say. 'Do you like it?' I always said yes, grateful for anything.

She took me for walks in the park, and I had a garden to play in. Life was good, and this was the happiest I had been since leaving Bristol.

After about three months of my good life, 'Auntie' told me she was expecting a visitor. She told me to play in the garden whilst she was here. I didn't ask who the visitor was. Young children were not encouraged to question adults as it was seen as being cheeky.

The visitor arrived. The window in the dining room looked out onto the back garden where I was playing, but because of the net curtains I was not able to see who it was. The following day, I was given the news that I hoped I would never hear.

'Billy, I'm sorry, but I have to take you back to the hostel.'

The news hit me in the back of the throat and I felt the tears welling up in my eyes.

'Why?' I asked, choking up.

'Something has come up and I am no longer able to look after you.'

'But why?' I cried.

Until now she had been so loving, often cuddling me, but today she kept her distance. I was sure she also had a tear in her eye as I repeatedly asked why I had to go back. In the end she said.

'I can't tell you why. But it's nothing you have done.' It didn't make it any easier knowing that.

After breakfast, I gazed out my bedroom window as Auntie packed my belongings, which had increased during my stay. I took one last look around the room I had come to love and followed her downstairs. Minutes later, we left the house, which for a few brief months had been my happy home.

We both remained silent as we boarded the bus. To avoid my woeful 'cow eyed' look, she spent most of the short journey looking out the window.

The matron met us on the pavement. I stood next to Auntie, not wanting to go into the hostel just in case there was a last-minute change of plans. But no such luck. When the matron finally told me to go inside, I knew it was not going to happen. I despondently headed up the steps.

'Aren't you going to say goodbye?' asked the matron.

I turned and came back down. Auntie gave me a peck on the cheek, which did nothing to allay the parting or the thought that she could have kept me if she had really wanted to. At the top of the steps I gave her one last wave, but she was talking to the matron and didn't notice.

The noise from the playroom at once caught my attention. Slowly wandering in, I was delighted to see my brother. I ran over and greeted him, although he had not much been in my thoughts for the last few months. He noticed my new clothes and told me that he had also been to a foster home, and was brought back to the hostel the previous day.

I spent the next few days gazing out the window at the spot on the pavement where I had last seen Auntie. She never came back. A year or so later, I was wandering around Exmouth, when something about my surroundings seemed familiar. I realized I was in the street where I had had such happy times. I chanced knocking on 'Aunties' door, but she was not at home. Disappointed, I wandered off and never tried to see her again.

Chapter Nine

Within days of returning to the hostel, my brother and I were on our way again. This was the fourth time we had been fostered out. But on this occasion we were not alone. There were six of us. Two brothers, my brother and me, and two boys unrelated to each other.

But instead of being picked up by our foster parent, we were collected by a billeting officer. All six of us had been fostered out before and returned to the hostel. Maybe the authorities were getting desperate! After a short bus ride, we arrived at our 'new home'.

'This is it,' said the billeting officer. 'Now remember to be on your best behaviour, you don't want to be sent back to the hostel again do you?'

She led the way through the small front garden of a two-storey terraced house as we silently shuffled behind her. Seconds later, her knock was answered, as if the woman had been sitting waiting for our arrival. She looked nice, and I thought this may not be so bad after all. We followed her down the entrance hall, but on entering the living room my moment of euphoria evaporated.

Six children, seated on the floor, plus two older adults seated in arm chairs either side of the fire, turned and looked at us as we entered. We were told to sit on the floor. Children were only allowed to sit on a chair if not needed by an adult.

The billeting officer introduced the two older adults as our new foster parents. She told us we were to call them Pop and Ma. She then introduced the woman who had opened the door as Aunt Gladys, and the boy sitting on Pop's knee as her son Raymond. He looked about my age, and I hoped he would not be like John from my previous foster home. The children seated on the floor, one of them a girl, were also evacuees.

She then instructed us to hold up our hand when she read our name from her check list.

Satisfied she had done her job, the billeting officer left, and Ma wasted no time in laying down the rules. The front door, which we had all just come through, was for adults and visitors only. In future, we were to use the back door. The upstairs toilet was only to be used at night, any other time the outside toilet was to be used. Everyone was to be on time for meals, or no food. Given I was always hungry, I couldn't see me being late for a meal.

She then explained the sleeping arrangements. The house had three bedrooms, and there were fifteen of us to be bedded down. Ma and Pop had the master bedroom which overlooked the front road, whilst Aunt Gladys, her son Raymond, and the girl were in the next biggest room. Four boys would sleep in two single beds in the back bedroom. The other six boys would be sleeping in the dining room. The dining suite had been pushed up against the window and a double bed placed against the main wall. A camp bed took up what was left of the floor space.

I had no idea how the bed allocations were made, but my brother and I ended up with the camp bed. The four other children, one of them the younger brother of the girl, were in the double bed. He wasn't happy about being separated from his older sister, but was told boys don't sleep in the same room as girls.

Having to sleep in a camp bed was bad enough, but there was only one pillow, which my brother, ever the generous one, claimed for himself. Not only did he take the pillow, but he claimed the 'head end' of the bed. I was left to fit in around his legs as best as I could. When I asked Ma if I could have a pillow, she told me there were no more. She didn't offer an alternative solution.

Each night there was a lot of kicking, arguing, and pulling of the blanket, which was never going to be big enough to cover the both of us. Not having a pillow, I rolled my clothes into a bundle. A few more creases wouldn't make any difference. I awoke each morning with a stiff neck.

Fed up with not having a pillow, I took one from the double bed. The boy whose pillow it was whinged, so Ma took it from me and gave it back to him. As soon as she left, I pulled it from under his head. His cries had Ma back in the room. Despite my complaints that it was not fair, and why couldn't I have a pillow, she snatched it from me and gave me a clip around the ear. I again slept on my rolled-up clothes.

It seemed the only way I was going to get a pillow was to sort something out for myself. The next night, as soon as Ma returned to the living room, I sneaked into the parlour and took one of the cushions from the settee. I had a lovely sleep, so good in fact I was still snoozing soundly when Ma came in to wake us up. She spotted her precious cushion crumpled beneath my head and blew her top. My head bounced off the floor as she wrenched the cushion from under me.

'Who told you to take my cushion?' she yelled, clutching the cushion to her ample bosom like a small child.

'No one,' I mumbled, staring up her skirt from my position on the floor.

'Don't you ever touch my cushions, or for that matter anything else, from my parlour again. You are not allowed in that room, do you hear?' She brought the cushion down onto my head.

'It's not fair, everyone else has a pillow,' I whined.

'One more word out of you and you'll get it from Pop.'

She flounced out, returning the cushion to its sacred place on the settee with the other cushions.

Soon after, 'whinging boy' and his big sister moved out. Their parents visited one weekend and were not happy with the crowded conditions. Not long after that, another boy moved out. With three less people to bed down, Ma changed the sleeping arrangements. My brother moved into the double bed and I got the camp bed to myself, complete with the luxury of my own pillow.

Chapter Ten

Not long after that, I arrived home from school to find two men assembling a steel table, about the size of a king size bed, in the living room. It was called a 'Morrison Shelter'. It had steel mesh on all four sides, and was designed to protect the occupants if the house collapsed during an air raid. They were supplied to houses without gardens. Those with gardens had an 'Anderson shelter'.

The new Morrison Shelter slept four, two at each end. Now I had a pillow, I was quite happy sleeping in my camp bed and wanted to stay where I was. But Ma wanted her dining room back.

Pop told us that the shelter was named after the home secretary Herbert Morrison who introduced it, not that it mattered to me. I would be sleeping in it and that was that. Ma was a lot happier now her dining room was returned to normal.

We still didn't eat in the dining room. Each week it was dusted and polished and the door closed, only to be opened for visiting parents to take tea with their children. As soon as the parents left, the dining room was closed until the next visitors arrived. My father only visited a couple of times in the years I was there, so I didn't get to take tea at the 'hallowed' dining table very often.

Raymond, the grandson of the house, slept in his mother's room. His dad was in the army so was not home much. Raymond often played alone in his bedroom. His mother would sneak him a biscuit, which we evacuees were not supposed to know about. But we did, and quickly sussed out that if you played with Raymond you could score a biscuit. I often went to his bedroom, stayed long enough to get a biscuit, then found an excuse to leave.

In the winter, when it was too cold to play in the back alley, we played in the living room, the only room with any heat. Nine kids, one living room, and a shortage of toys, was a recipe for arguments. Every night there would be squabbling, until Ma could stand it no longer.

'Right, get to bed the lot of you.'

We couldn't all get into the bathroom at once and I always seemed to be last. I would have a pee, wipe my face with a cold smelly flannel, and brush my teeth with a toothbrush which I hoped was mine. I was never sure if we had a brush each, or whether we were supposed to share. I know the toothbrush I used was always wet by the time I got to use it.

There was no toothpaste, just a 'Gibbs Block', which we scrubbed with a wet toothbrush until a small amount of the block stuck to the bristles. When it was not available we used salt, which scoured the teeth but was not good for the taste buds.

'Have you washed behind your ears?' Ma always asked when I came down from the bathroom. I'm sure she picked on me because I was last and gave the impression I was not too keen on personal hygiene.

'Yes Ma,' I would sigh.

'Come here and let me look.' When I got close, she would grab my ear and say.

'You could grow potatoes in your ears.'

Aunt Gladys would then drag me to the bathroom, where my ear would be pulled into all shapes as she forced a cold flannel into it. My ears glowed like a couple of beacons by the time she had finished.

Some of the children, those with parents who cared, had pyjamas. Frankie and I wore what we could get, usually something Ma brought home from the used clothing shop. One time I was given a pair of really long 'Long Johns'. Even pulling them up to my armpits didn't help.

I asked Ma to cut the bottoms off, but she said that would fray the legs, so she just tied a knot in them. I would hobble around with the knotted part trailing behind me, causing great laugher when someone stood on one of them and I stumbled over. I probably looked ridiculous in them, but pride was the least of my concerns. In winter, I would tuck my arms in them to keep warm, a bit like a chrysalis. It was them or nothing.

Being the last to get into the 'Morrison Shelter' each night, I had to climb over my brother to get to my side of the bed. He always chose to sleep on the outside of the bed, and deliberately made it difficult for me to get in by holding the blankets close to his body. I responded by kneeling on his stomach as I climbed over him. The resultant squabbling disturbed the other two boys, who would then kick out. Soon, we were all kicking one another, until Ma sorted us out with her slipper.

Mornings were pandemonium. Aunt Gladys and Ma would be banging and clattering in the scullery as they prepared breakfast. The cutlery would be banged on the table top right above our heads, which made sure we were well and truly awake.

Dressing was straightforward enough. I just dressed in the clothes I had taken off the night before lying on the floor alongside the bed. Morning ablutions were equally straight forward. Go to the bathroom, wipe face with a wet flannel, pee, and go back downstairs.

Porridge was the staple diet for breakfast. It was cooked in a large pot on the fire in winter, and the stove in the scullery in summer. We were always hungry, eyeing each other's plate in case anybody got more than you. My porridge never took me long to eat. I was never sure if I was a quick eater, or because there was so little food on my plate. Or, because I lived in hope there might be seconds, which were only handed out if you had finished. The pot being taken back to the scullery was the signal that there were no seconds and that breakfast was over.

Due to rationing, there was never enough to eat. Nobody ever needed to be coaxed to eat, and nobody was fat. I can't ever remember leaving the table feeling full. As a result, withholding food was a favourite form of punishment. Like being sent to bed without any tea. I hated it. I much preferred a walloping as it was over and done with, while the hunger gnawed away at your stomach all night.

Food wasn't the only thing in short supply. Clothes and shoes were just as scarce. To obtain either, you needed both money and coupons, which was why all our clothes came from the second-hand shop. Colour, style, or whether it fitted, was secondary. You took what you were given. Check the photo of my brother and me taken in 1942.

The author (L) with his brother in 1942. By the look of our hands and jumpers it looks like we had been playing in the coal bunker. But this was pretty much how we were dressed each day.

The alley where I spent many years playing. During the war years it was teeming with children.

Chapter Eleven

Every so often someone had a birthday. The more fortunate ones might have received a present from their parents. When this happened, the 'birthday person' was told to show their present to the rest of us. I always looked on enviously as we sang 'Happy Birthday to you'.

After one such event, I asked Aunt Gladys when it was my turn to have a birthday. She said she would find out, but as my parents didn't send presents or even acknowledge my birthday there was not much point knowing and getting excited for nothing. As a result, birthdays and Easter held very little meaning to me. They came, and they went.

Christmas was the same. Presents received from parents were put away. On Christmas Day we all sat in a circle on the living room floor as each child unwrapped their present and showed it to the group. So that my brother and I were not left out, Aunt Gladys would get us something.

One Christmas, she handed me a present. It was wrapped in brown paper, Christmas wrapping paper not being available. I carefully unwrapped the present after being told not to tear the paper, so it could be used again.

'Show everyone your present,' Aunt Gladys said.

I was not comfortable showing my present when it was something I didn't want. I would much rather have waited until I was on my own before opening it. Disappointed by what looked like clothing, I quickly showed it around without unfolding it.

'Do you like it?' Aunt Gladys asked.

'Yes,' I said, choking back my disappointment as I felt my eyes fill.

The rest of the children opened their presents and showed them around, their excitement obvious by the big smiles on their faces.

I was envious of them, even becoming annoyed that they had received a nice present. *Why*, I thought, *had they received presents from their parents and I had not? All I had received was a piece of clothing, and that was from 'Aunt Gladys.' I wanted to throw it away. I wanted a real present, like a gun or a racing car. It was not fair. I hated Christmas and just wanted it to go past as quickly as possible, so things could get back to normal.*

Later, when things had quietened down, I decided to check out my present. I picked it up from the corner where I had laid it. Now that no one was watching, I examined it in more detail. To my surprise, I found it was not a piece of clothing at all, but a 'despatch rider's' outfit. Pouch, shoulder strap, and belt. I put it on and strutted around in front of the other children.

'Look what I got,' I said, proudly showing off my present.

From then on, each time we played war games, I was the 'despatch rider', dashing from place to place on a make-believe motorbike with top secret messages.

Chapter Twelve

~⌒~

When it came to religion, foster parents were expected to ensure that children under their care went to church on Sunday. I couldn't remember ever going to church with my parents, but as my brother and I were sent to the Catholic school I assumed we must be Catholics. As a result, I spent the next few years living in fear of nuns and priests.

My brother was taught by nuns, but being two years younger, my teacher was an 'ordinary person'. This didn't stop the nuns from coming into our classroom to get in some early Catholic brainwashing. I was terrified of them, shrinking into my seat, and looking out the window when they asked a question. I believed that if I could avoid eye contact they wouldn't ask me anything.

It didn't always work, being reduced to a nervous heap as I mumbled, 'I don't know' to yet another religious question. It seemed that everybody, except me, knew religious things. I was always glad when they left.

Church on Sunday was an absolute nightmare for me. I would do anything to avoid going. My brother, on the other hand, always appeared more comfortable. He liked to sit at the front, so the nuns saw him, whilst I preferred being at the back in the hope I wouldn't be noticed.

The collection plate always fascinated me. I would stare at the money as I passed it on, wondering what my chances were of stealing a coin or two. I'd seen in a movie someone pretending to put money in by flicking the bottom of the plate with their thumb, whilst actually taking some out. I wondered if I could do the same, but hadn't worked out how to avoid the verger's beady eye.

Then one Sunday, the opportunity came my way. The verger was momentarily distracted, so I tried flicking the bottom of the plate with my thumb. It didn't work, resulting in several coins spilling onto the floor. The verger gave me a look which suggested I was going straight to hell. I quickly picked up the coins and handed him the plate. Moments later we were all on our knees, with our eyes supposedly closed, praying. But, as we knelt, I spotted one of the coins had rolled under the seat in front. This was truly 'manna from heaven'. All I had to do was retrieve the coin without being seen. Gingerly looking around, I eased the coin under my knee. I figured that if anyone saw me, I could say I was going to turn it in. Minutes later we stopped praying, at least those around me did. As we returned to our seats, I prised the coin free of my knee, and in one swift movement pocketed it.

Knowing there was every chance I had a hole in my pocket, I kept hold of the coin. Feeling its knurled edge with my fingernail, I hoped it was a shilling. I thought of all the stuff I could buy once I was clear of the church.

I waited for the congregation to move towards the door, before easing into the aisle. The priest was standing at the door thanking everyone for coming. Keeping my eyes on the floor, I sidled out the door, expecting at any moment to feel the 'Hand of God' on my shoulder.

I avoided the temptation to run off, hanging around until the congregation had dispersed. The coin, now warm in my hand, was a shilling. As I squandered my ill-gotten gains, I told myself that if God saw everything and he didn't do anything to stop me, then he must have wanted me to have the money. He knew my need was greater than the church's.

Then one Sunday, my brother was sick. I thought this would get me out of going to church, but I was sent on my own. Without my brother to keep an eye on me, I gave church a miss and went to the park. When I figured the service was finished, I put the frogs I had caught back into the pond, and went home. Ma asked me about the service and I told her it was just like any other Sunday. She was not a Catholic and thought no more about it. Until my brother piped up.

'Where's your Palm?' he asked. I had no idea what he was talking about.

'It's Palm Sunday,' he said. 'If you had been to church you would have got a palm.'

'Yeah I know, but they had run out by the time I got there,' I stammered, playing for time and hoping he would shut up.

'You weren't there were you? You didn't even know it was Palm Sunday. I'm going to ask the priest next week if you were there.'

'The priest won't know if I was there because I sat at the back, like I always do, so he wouldn't have seen me,' I replied.

'I'm still going to ask him.'

'You do that Frankie,' said Ma, who was listening to every word. 'And let me know what he says. You had better not be lying,' she said, looking straight at me.

I said nothing, but if looks could have killed, my brother would have died on the spot. I left the house wondering why he hadn't told me it was Palm Sunday. I could have made the effort to go.

But that wasn't my only problem. Each morning a Nun positioned herself at the school entrance to give each pupil the evil eye as they entered. This, in my opinion, was too scare the living daylights out of any of the pupils who had missed church on the Sunday. As I headed for the school entrance I could see her watching me, and quickly averted my eyes towards the ground. I was nearly past her, when she suddenly reached out, grasped my arm, and drew me to one side.

'I didn't see you at church yesterday,' she said. My heartbeat quickened and a feeling of terror came over me. It was obvious she knew I was not there.

'You know it's a mortal sin not to go to church on Sunday,' she continued.

'Yes Sister,' I mumbled, still staring at the ground.

'And what about your brother? He wasn't there either.'

'No Sister. He's sick.'

This seemed to appease her, so she released my arm thus saving me from lying to a nun. Lying to a nun was bad, but not as bad as lying to a priest, which was not as bad as lying to God himself. But God knows everything, so you couldn't really lie to him. From then on, each Sunday, I made sure the nuns noticed me.

I had a strange association with the Catholic Church, never really coming to terms with it. I was much happier when I moved from the Catholic school to a Church of England school.

Chapter Thirteen

Margaret and Eric, the sister and brother who moved out of our house, really landed with their 'bum in the butter'. Their new foster parents had a car, which equated to one thing. People with cars were 'rich'.

Often, they would wave to me as the car sped by. I'd never been in a car and always waved back in the hope I would get offered a lift. I never was. They were also picked up at the end of school each afternoon. The rest of us, come rain, hail, or shine, walked.

Eric was the boy whose pillow I tried to steal when he lived with us. For some reason he often asked the driver if he could walk home with me. I said I would swap, but the driver always refused.

Going home was fun each afternoon. Most of us took a shortcut through Lime Kiln Lane, or Watery Lane as we knew it. It ran at the back of several large homes, many with fruit trees, always a temptation to hungry school kids.

One day, we were passing a house which had a beautiful tree full of apples, just ripe for the picking. All fruit trees were fair game. Scrumping, as far as us kids were concerned, was not stealing. Being the smallest, I was usually the one given a 'bunk up' the wall. I'd hardly grasped the first 'Cox's Orange Pippin', when a hand grasped my ankle and pulled me from the wall. The rest of kids, caring little for my fate, ran off. Dragging me into his house, the man locked the door behind him.

'Right, now I've got you. I'm phoning the police. I'm sick of you kids stealing my apples.'

'Please mister, don't phone the police. If you let me go, I promise I won't do it again,' I whined.

'Too late now, you should have thought of that before you stole my fruit.'

We sat in his entrance hall silently eyeing one another. I really didn't think he would go through with it, and had told me he had phoned the police to scare me. But when a policeman on a bicycle arrived, I knew I was in big trouble. The policeman took one look at my pathetic figure and said.

'Do you really want to take it any further?'

When I heard that my spirits lifted, but were short lived. The house owner was adamant.

The policeman set off on his bicycle with me jogging by his side. I thought about running off down a side street. As if reading my thoughts, he dismounted and walked alongside me.

As we approached my house, I again pleaded with him to let me go. I promised I would never do it again.

'If it was up to me,' he said, 'I would let you go. But it's out of my hands.' Pop answered the policeman's knock.

'What's he been up to now?' he asked, a resigned look on his face.

The policeman told Pop what had happened, and left. Pop, without a word, shut the door in my face. I stood for a while on the doorstep puzzled, before realizing I was expected to go around to the back door.

Moments later, as I sheepishly entered the living room, Pop reached for the razor strop. I felt the panic rise in me, knowing he was not about to have a shave.

I turned to run back out, but Ma, who had been in the scullery was blocking the door. Desperately scampering to the back of the room, I took refuge in the pantry. The other kids scattered as Pop followed.

Cowering in the corner of the pantry, I pleaded with him not to hit me. Ignoring my pleas, his first blow deflected off the top of the cupboard making a loud bang and adding to my fear. Unable to get a good shot at me, he grabbed my arm and dragged me into the back yard.

Holding me with one hand, he swung the strop catching me on the back of my legs. The next blow deflected off my arm and caught me on the face, drawing blood. In a desperate attempt to fend off his blows, I let my legs buckle under me. As he tried to drag me upright, I wriggled free and ran to the gate. But before I could get to the safety of the alley, he kicked the gate shut.

I heard the strop whistle past my ear and smack into the gate as I ran to the corner of the yard. Making myself as small as possible, I cowered into the corner expecting to feel the strop hit my back. It didn't. After some moments, with no more blows, I carefully peeked out from under my arm. The yard was empty. Slowly easing myself into an upright position, I realised he had gone back into the house. A knocking on the back window caught my attention. It was Ma, indicating to me to come inside.

Warily entering the house, I paused when I saw Pop sitting in his favourite armchair. He didn't make a move as Ma ordered me to my room. Upstairs, I checked my legs. They were really sore, one of them showing a nasty welt, no doubt caused by the edge of the strop. Sneaking into the bathroom, I placed a wet flannel on it. Noticing the blood on my cheek, close to my eye, I decided to leave it for sympathy.

A few minutes later, Aunt Gladys called me down for my tea. Tea. I couldn't believe it. I had already resigned myself to 'no tea', thinking it was part of my punishment.

Downstairs, the table was empty, everyone else having finished. There was a tin of 'Lyles Golden Syrup' on the table, a rare treat. I didn't think I would get any and there was no way I dared ask.

'Would you like some syrup?' asked Aunt Gladys, as I tentatively took a bite from one of the two slices of bread and margarine that had been laid out for me.

As I slowly chewed my bread, savouring every drop of the sweet syrup, Ma wasted no time in reminding me how thankful I should be.

'Naughty boys don't get any tea, never mind syrup', she said. This was Pop's cue to give me, 'a piece of his mind'.

'You should think yourself lucky you're getting anything, after the showing up you gave us. A policeman at the door, what will the neighbours think? All the years I have lived here, and never once was there a policeman at the door. And now this.'

I kept my head down, occasionally lifting my eyes to see Ma nodding her head in agreement. By the time Pop ceased his tirade, the sweetness of the syrup was long gone. I was desperate to get out to the back alley and safety, but didn't dare ask if I could leave the table.

Finally, Pop left to get ready for work and Ma said I could go. Back in the comfort zone of the back alley, I showed off my 'welts' to the other kids.

My 'welts' healed, but were soon replaced with fresh ones.

Chapter Fourteen

One morning, I stepped into the alley just in time to see a couple of boys climbing onto the back of a coal lorry. I ran like a looney shouting 'wait for me', but by the time I got there, the driver was already pulling away. I made a desperate bid to climb aboard, but was left clinging to the tailboard.

As the lorry gathered speed, I shouted to the other kids to pull me on board, but they thought I was joking. Whether it was the panic in my voice, or the look of terror on my face, finally one of the boys leaned over the tailboard and grabbed my collar. But he was not strong enough to pull me on board. By then, my fingers were so cold, the pain of hanging on was excruciating. Falling into the road seemed the better option.

But that option soon disappeared when a car began following us. Noticing my predicament, the driver accelerated alongside the lorry and blew his horn, whilst his passenger gesticulated to the driver to stop. The lorry slowed, by which time my fingers had given up and I couldn't hang on a minute longer. My feet hit the road and I was instantly running like a 100-metre sprinter, coming to an abrupt halt in the bushes at the side of the road. For several moments I just laid there.

'Are you alright?' asked an anxious woman's voice. It was the lady passenger from the car.

'Fine,' I said. Helped by the woman, I slowly extricated myself from the bushes.

'Oh dear, just look at your knees and hands. They are skinned raw. Do you want me to take you home?'

'No thanks lady, I'll be alright.' I said. The last thing I wanted was for Pop and Ma to find out what had happened.

'It's alright I'll look after him. I'm his brother,' said Frankie. We headed for the school toilets desperate that no one should see me, especially any of the nuns. I cleaned myself up and took my seat in class. Nobody commented on my dishevelled clothing. But given my normal dress, it was unlikely anybody would even notice.

During the day, my legs stiffened up causing me to limp. I hoped Ma would not notice, but as soon as I entered the house she said.

'What on earth happened to you?'

'Nothing.' I replied.

'Don't say nothing. Look at your clothes. They weren't like that when you went out this morning. And look at your legs, they're all cut and scratched.'

I told her I fell over in the playground. I hoped none of the other boys would mention the coal lorry.

My injuries quickly healed and the stiffness in my legs disappeared. My clothes remained just as shabby.

Chapter Fifteen

Despite the fearful nuns, school became my favourite place. Possibly because we got a nice dinner, or because of my liking for the teacher. The night after she told the class she was leaving I woke up sobbing.

'What are you crying for?' asked my brother.

'My teacher is leaving,' I said.

'So why are you crying? You'll get another one.'

'I know, but another one won't be the same.' I cried long and hard when my teacher left, but didn't shed one single tear when my mother left me.

I just loved my teacher to bits. One day, out of the blue, she came over to my desk and said.

'Here. Try this on.'

She handed me a jumper. I had often seen her knitting at the front of the class, but not for one moment did I think it was something for me. It was so nice to receive something that was not a hand-me-down; even though the wool had been used for something else before being ripped out and re-knitted into a jumper for me. That afternoon, as soon as I set foot in the house, Ma noticed it.

'Where did you get the jumper?' she asked, pulling it with her fingers as she inspected it.

'My teacher knitted it for me.'

'Your teacher. Why?'

'I don't know. She just came up to me this morning and gave it to me.'

'Why, of all the children in the class, did she pick you?' Ma was obviously oblivious to the deplorable way I was dressed.

'Maybe because she likes me,' I innocently suggested.

'Likes you,' said Ma, a note of sarcasm in her voice. 'I doubt that's the reason. Are you sure your teacher knitted it for you?'

'Yes, honest.'

'Hmmm… You'd better not be lying.'

When the rest of the kids saw my jumper, they called me teacher's pet. I was unfazed; I was just happy to have a warm piece of clothing, although I had to keep a close eye on it when I took it off, which was not very often.

Clothes were always in short supply, although all my trousers must have come from the same tailor. They were always patched, usually with a different material to the trousers. At the time there was a comic strip in the *Beano* called, 'Jimmy and his Magic Patch.' When Jimmy rubbed the patch in the seat of his trousers he would be whisked away to a fantasy land. I would rub the patch on my trousers imagining I was 'Jimmy' doing something magical.

During the winter I wore boots. Come the summer, I wore whatever I was given. One summer, I was given a pair of second-hand sandals. I'm sure they were girls' sandals, because they had a strap that buttoned down. But it was them or nothing. Because I had a high instep, I couldn't fasten the strap. My brother tried fastening them, but they were too difficult, so I walked to school with the straps undone and asked the teacher if she could do them up. She was only able to button them up by using a hairpin as a lever, looped around the button. She told me they were too small for me and would damage my feet. I nodded, but knew it was those or nothing. By the end of the day my feet were so swollen I walked home barefoot.

The next day my teacher attached a piece of elastic to the strap. This stopped my feet from swelling and enabled me to button them up myself.

In later life I had my small toe on my left foot amputated. I also suffered from ingrown toenails because of wearing shoes that were too small.

Chapter Sixteen

Saturday was always a busy day. All the kids were given chores to do. My job was to save a place for Aunt Gladys in the early morning queue at the butcher's shop. Ma always reminded me not to dawdle, or 'we won't get any meat'. I would run like mad, but despite how early I was, there was always a queue. Often Aunt Gladys only managed to get a sheep's head or corned beef, there being nothing else available.

On the rare occasions she managed to get a piece of beef, it was so small there was only enough for the adults. The nearest we got to getting any beef was the dripping, a combination of the lard used in the cooking, and the fat from the meat. It was spread on a slice of bread for our Sunday tea, a treat I looked forward to, and so much nicer than margarine.

As soon as Aunt Gladys relieved me in the queue, I would dash home to do my other chore. Take the empty 'Stout' bottles back to the bar where Pop worked, and get a fresh supply. As it was such a precious cargo, he allowed me use his wheel barrow, a rare privilege.

It was not one of my favourite jobs. I was always worried I would get waylaid by 'bigger boys' who might try to steal the Stout.

Then one Saturday, I was trundling my way home listening to the rhythmical clink of the bottles, when, like many things in life, something pops into your head for no apparent reason. I began wondering what Stout tasted like. I was passing the school at the time, so quickly ducked into the toilets. I popped the spring top on the bottle and took a swig. It was not at all what I had imagined, and quickly spat it out.

I topped the bottle up with water, and was about to leave, when my brother and another boy came into the toilet. They'd spotted the barrow outside the toilet and said they also wanted a swig. Fortunately, neither of them liked it. From then on Ma and Pop got their Stout undiluted.

Because a crate full of Stout bottles was too heavy for me to lift, when I got home I would take each bottle out of the crate and carefully carry them one by one into the pantry. Ma often helped, worried in case I would drop one.

As soon as lunch was finished we were out. Nobody hung around the house on a Saturday afternoon. The attraction was the local cinema. Often, they would show free films, sometimes the same one for several weekends. 'No', we would call over our shoulder to the usherette when asked if we had seen the film. The film would finish, the cinema would empty, but we remained in our seats to watch the same film again. I watched some films so many times I knew every word of the dialogue, mouthing along with the actors.

Sometimes, we arrived at the cinema to be told we needed to pay to get in. When this happened, we resorted to a more lucrative way of passing the afternoon.

To put our plan into practice we needed at least one penny, normally provided by Raymond. Raymond was Pop's grandson and the apple of his eye. He always gave him two or three pence each Saturday, saying the same thing. 'Make sure the others don't take it off you.'

As soon as we got into town, despite his protests, Raymond was always cajoled into giving me a penny.

The town was always busy on a Saturday afternoon, so there were plenty of prospects. Young men, like soldiers on leave and women, were my favourites. They were usually the most generous. Elderly ladies were also good prospects, my scruffy appearance and pitiful expression appealing to their motherly nature.

Armed with Raymond's penny, I would approach a potential prospect and say.

'Got two ha'pennies (half pennies) for a penny, please?'

If they asked why I wanted two ha'pennies, I told them I had to give my brother a ha'penny. Because it was such a small amount of money, I hoped my pitiful expression would convince them to let me keep the penny. If they took my penny, as many often did, I'd start again, only this time I would say.

'Got a penny for two ha'pennies, please?' It was tedious work, with many people ushering me away without even looking.

Once I'd made a penny, I gave it to my brother. He then worked the same stunt on a different street. On a slow afternoon, we might only manage two or three pence each. We never took any money home, and usually spent it on something to eat, like cakes and fruit.

Then one Saturday we both did quite well. My brother then sprung a surprise on me. I was to give him my money so he could buy a cinema ticket. Once inside, he would open the toilet window and pull me in. The plan worked well, and for the first time I saw a film which I hadn't already seen several times.

The following weekend we did the same thing again. But by the third weekend I was fed up and told him I was not giving him my money. He loved the cinema, and tried all ways to talk me around.

'No,' I persisted. 'You give me your money and I'll go in and open the toilet window,' I said.

'You're too small, they wouldn't let you in without an adult. Even if they did, you're too small to open the toilet window,' he argued.

'Not if I stand on the toilet seat.'

'No, it's my plan. If I hadn't thought it up none of us would get in.'

'Well I don't care. I don't want to see the picture anyway,' I said, walking away.

Seeing his smooth talk wasn't working he became angry. Grabbing my hand, he pulled my fingers apart, snatched my money, and ran into the cinema. I chased after him, but was too late to stop him buying a ticket. Giving me a quick glance over his shoulder, he disappeared inside. I was furious, but went around to the toilet window anyway. Several minutes passed and he had not opened the window. I was sure he was going to leave me outside as spite for not giving him my money. As the minutes passed by without any sign of him, I became angrier and angrier. I was just about ready to leave, when the window opened, and he looked out. I jumped up and grabbed the window sill.

'What took you so long?' I snarled.

He said the usherette had been walking around and he had to wait until she left.

'I don't believe you, you did it on purpose.' I shouted angrily.

'No, I didn't. If I had wanted to do that I would have still been in there.'

'Liar, I know you. Don't just stand there, pull me in,' I shouted.

He leaned out the window as I expectantly waited for him to grab my arms. Then, instead of pulling me in, he pushed me back outside and shut the window. I was furious.

'Let me in, let me in,' I shouted, jumping up and banging on the window. Finally, he opened the window again.

'Shut up or someone will hear you,' he said, pulling me inside.

My shouting had already attracted several boys who were also hanging around the cinema. They saw my feet disappearing through the window and quickly followed. My brother pushed the first boy back, but he became so annoyed he said if my brother didn't let him in he would tell the manager.

'See what you've done,' Frankie said, angrily pushing me to one side and walking out of the toilet. I quickly followed him as another boy wriggled through the window.

We watched the first film without incident. But when the lights came on at the interval, the usherette spotted several faces she didn't remember showing to their seats. When none of them could produce a ticket, she chased them out.

'You as well,' she said.

'I've got a ticket,' my brother smugly replied.

I hoped when she saw his ticket she would assume I had one too and walk away. No such luck.

'And you. Where's your ticket?' I made a show of looking through my pockets and under the seat.

'I must have lost it,' I said.

'Out.'

'But I had a ticket, didn't I.' I looked pleadingly at my brother.

'Did he?' she asked.

'I don't know, he came in after me,' he replied.

'Right, out you go before I call the manager.'

She grabbed my arm and pulled me out of my seat. I was furious. He had taken my money and now he was just going to sit there and let her put me out. Wriggling free, I threw a punch at his smirking face.

'It's not fair, he used my money to get in,' I protested, as she dragged me towards the exit. When we reached the foyer, she asked me how I had got in. I was so angry, I told her that my brother had pulled me in through the toilet window.

She went back into the cinema, returning a few minutes later dragging a protesting Frankie by the arm. He was livid. As soon as we got outside, he punched me. Soon we were rolling around on the ground punching one another, with me coming off worse. After that, the toilet window was permanently secured.

We continued working the penny for two ha'pennies routine, but I kept whatever I made. The only films I saw after that were the free ones.

Another highlight on a Saturday was bath night. Raymond didn't bath with the evacuees; his mother bathed him separately, so he had the luxury of a bath to himself.

The rest of us bathed two at a time. As each pair finished, some of the water was let out and more hot water added.

Being the youngest, I was usually left until last, by which the time the water was quite scummy.

During the winter months I wore boots, often with no socks. This caused the top of my boot to chaff a permanently sore 'blue ring' above my ankle, which only healed up during the summer when I stopped wearing boots. So, when Aunt Gladys hoisted my skinny naked body into the bath, the hot water was sore on my ankles.

My ankles would still be smarting, when my head was vigorously pushed under the water and washed with a block of soap. Complaining

I had soap in my eyes only resulted in my head being thrust under the 'scummy' water, until I finally spluttered to the surface.

'Right, that's you done, out you get.'

As I dried myself on the 'driest' of the 'wet' towels, I often wondered what it would be like to have a bath to myself. One with clean water that I could lay in for as long as I liked, and a towel that had not already been used.

Chapter Seventeen

April 1942, the Americans arrived, creating a lot of excitement. We kids loved them, shouting, 'Got any gum, chum?' as they marched through the town.

They were billeted in 'Marpool Hall' in Phear Park before it was demolished in 1951. We knew it as 'The Mansion'.

We quickly learned that we could earn money or food by doing little jobs for them, like running errands. There was a lot of competition for work amongst the boys, and having a big sister was an advantage. I didn't have a big sister, but said I did, adding that I would bring her along the next time.

Sometimes I was asked to get things that were not readily available. One soldier asked me to get boot polish. It took me so long to find a shop that had any, he thought I had run off with his money. Often, at weekends, I spent the whole day running errands.

At first the Americans were not familiar with the English currency. One actually gave me a half-a-crown for running an errand, about fifty US cents. I couldn't believe it. It was amazing how much you could buy with half-a-crown. I'd always liked the advert on a 'bill poster' near the railway bridge reading, 'Zubes are good for your tubes'. So, not knowing what they were, I spent thruppence ha'penny of my half-a-crown on a tin of them. Another time I was given an American dollar bill. I asked him for real money, but he said that was all he had.

I didn't want Ma knowing I had money, so put it in my empty 'Zubes' tin and hid it by my favourite tree.

A few days later, I was on my way to school with a bunch of boys who were smoking Camel cigarettes. I tried a couple of puffs, but was not impressed. One of them then said he had taken a dollar into the greengrocers and got four shillings and sixpence for it. The correct exchange rate was five shillings, or four dollars to the pound. This resulted in a half-a-crown being nick named 'half a dollar'.

After school, I went to the greengrocer's shop. I'd always been fascinated by the plastic 'Fyffe's' bananas sign that hung in his shop, but didn't know what they were. He told me they were bananas, but he didn't have any.

Grapes, as far as we were concerned, were the preserve of the rich. I'd only ever seen them being eaten by actors in the free movie at the local cinema. I was desperate know what they tasted like, but he didn't have any of those either.

Grapes being hard to get, reminded me of a story I heard. Apparently, a Lieutenant in the Royal Canadian Navy was seconded to a Royal Navy destroyer during WW2. The Officer's Steward was laying up the table for dinner and placed a very small bunch of grapes in the centre of the table. The Canadian Lieutenant saw them, picked them up, and ate them all. 'Excuse me Sir,' said the Steward, those grapes were for everybody. Canada didn't have the same severe rationing we had in the UK.

Oranges, which were often not available, was my next choice.

He gave back me four shillings. I was delighted, even though he had charged me sixpence for the orange, and sixpence for his commission.

'If you get any more dollars son, be sure and bring them to me,' he said, as I left.

Sometimes the soldiers gave me a 'K' ration box instead of money. A 'K' ration box was an American soldier's daily rations for a particular meal. They generally contained meat, biscuits, cheese, sweets, and chewing gum, things we never saw. The amount of cheese one American soldier was issued with was about the equivalent of a week's cheese ration for a family of four. It was sealed in a tin and came with a small tin opener, which really impressed me.

Ma had heard about 'K' ration boxes, but was not too sure what they were.

'Do you ever get any of those 'K' Ration boxes people are talking about?' she asked.

'No.' I lied.

'But you know about them?'

'Yes. I saw one of the other boys with one, so I know what they look like.'

'Well, if you do get any, make sure you bring them home, do you hear?'

'Yes Ma.' *Some hopes*, I thought as I left the house.

Chewing gum was not allowed in school. I would stick mine under the lid of my desk and retrieve it at the end of the day. I also never entered the house chewing gum, as that would have been a dead giveaway I was getting 'K' ration boxes. Before entering, I would stick it between the brickwork of the back wall and retrieve it later, provided someone else hadn't found it first. Remarkable as it seems, if somebody found a piece of gum stuck to the wall, they would quite happily pop it into their mouth. I'd done the same thing many times myself and remained surprisingly healthy. It was also surprising how many arguments broke out over the ownership of a piece of well-chewed gum in the crevice of a brick wall.

I enjoyed having the American soldiers around, never thinking that one day they would leave. But just as quickly as they had arrived, they were gone.

One evening, I went to 'The Mansion' hoping to earn a few pence, and found it deserted. I couldn't believe it. The place was full of soldiers one night, and the next night they were gone. One of the windows on the ground floor had not been secured properly, so I climbed in. The floor was covered in general debris left behind when a building has been evacuated in a hurry. I spotted a 'K' ration box lying on the floor and gave it a kick. I immediately knew there was something in it, and was delighted to find it had a tin of cheese in it.

I quickly ate it. I was sad the Americans had left, not just because I wouldn't be getting any more 'K' ration boxes, but I genuinely liked them. Fortunately, I'd stashed a few 'K' ration boxes away. A few days later I threw away my last empty 'K' ration box. That weekend, it was back to the 'penny-for-two-halfpennies' scam.

Then, just as everybody was beginning to think the bombing had finished, it started again. On the 26 February 1943, around midday, eight enemy planes attacked Exmouth. A number of bombs were dropped demolishing a row of shops in the Strand, killing people who were working or shopping in them, as well as a queue of people waiting at an adjacent bus stop. A total of 25 people died, with a further 40 injured. I remember passing by and seeing the huge crater in the road. I was quickly ushered away by the police, as the bomb and mine disposal team attempted to de-fuse one of the bombs, which apparently had not exploded.

Chapter Eighteen

One sunny afternoon, during the summer of 1943, I was sitting at the window of one of the upstairs bedrooms watching the other kids playing in the back alley below. I'd been sent to my room for some 'trivial' little thing which I can't remember. As I watched, I noticed they were getting ready to leave.

'Where are you going?' I shouted. They said they were going to the beach.

'No, don't go,' I called back. It was bad enough being stuck in my room where at least I could see them. But if they went to the beach, I'd be left staring at an empty alley.

'I want to come too,' I said.

'How you going to get out?' called my brother.

'I can climb out the window.'

I was gambling on the fact that in all the times I had been sent to my bedroom, no one had ever checked on me. As I was in an upstairs room, I supposed nobody thought I would climb out the window.

I'd heard Ma and Aunt Gladys go out, which just left Pop, who was snoozing after a few lunch time 'Stouts'.

With no thought for safety, I climbed out the window and onto the scullery roof. After easing myself along the ridge, I slid down the slates, grabbing the gutter just in time to prevent me landing in the neighbours back yard. After working my way along the dividing wall, I dropped into the alley.

My brother took a pair of Pop's underpants from the clothes line, saying we could use them as a swimming costume. We could all take it in turns to wear them.

The sunshine ensured that the beach was crowded. I was to be the first to put on Pop's pants. They were far too big, so I knotted them at the waist. It helped hold them up, but made me look like a latter-day Ghandi, only paler.

The sea was unusually rough, causing the waves to crash onto the beach with some force. It was so rough, the man who operated the speed boats was having a hard time getting his customers in and out of the boats. When he saw me, he told me to go further up the beach where it was calmer.

I moved a few yards along the beach clear of the speed boats, and ventured in. The water was freezing, and I was having difficulty standing up as each wave sucked the sand from under my feet as it receded. Urged on by the others, I slowly ventured up to my knees. Then, before I knew it, a wave knocked me off my feet and dragged me out of my depth. I desperately tried to touch the bottom, but each wave took me further and further away from the shore. I went under, the water making a loud swishing sound as it washed over my head. Bobbing to the surface, I momentarily noticed my brother standing in the water trying to grab me. Then it went quiet and peaceful, as if I was floating on air. The next thing I know I was coughing and spluttering as I looked up at a group of people staring down at me.

'Anybody know who he is?' said a man.

'Yes, he's my brother, I'll take care of him,' said Frankie.

'Well make sure you do. It's too rough for him to be in the water.'

Someone rolled me onto my side. After a couple of good coughs, I was able to sit up, only to discover I was naked.

'Oh no, I've lost Pop's pants,' I said.

'It's alright, he doesn't know we took them, so it doesn't matter,' my brother assured me. I noticed his clothes were soaking. I later learned the young man who had saved me from a watery grave was one of the onlookers when I opened my eyes. Once he saw I was breathing, he wandered off. I never did get to thank him.

'What are you going to say to Ma when she sees your wet clothes?' I asked my brother as we headed for home. One of the other boys said he had a pair of trousers he could borrow. I was to throw them out the window once I was back in the room.

As soon as we arrived home, one of the boys went into the house and reported that Ma and Aunt Gladys were still not home. That was a good start. Pop, however, was up and getting ready for work. I hoped he hadn't looked into my bedroom when he got up.

Getting back into the bedroom was more difficult than getting out. I was too small to climb from the dividing wall onto the roof. My brother, now with a vested interest in getting me back into the room, climbed on the wall and formed a 'backy' for me. After much wobbling, with the two of us nearly falling into the neighbour's yard, I managed to clamber onto the scullery roof and into the bedroom window.

Minutes later, I threw the trousers to my brother and closed the window. Shortly after, I heard Aunt Gladys and Ma return. Moments later the bedroom door opened. I was laying on the bed facing the wall. Pretending to be startled by the sound of the door being opened, I turned and faced her.

'You can go out now,' said Aunt Gladys. 'I hope you've learned your lesson.'

'Yes, Aunt Gladys,' I replied. I followed her downstairs, with her none the wiser for my near drowning.

Chapter Nineteen

I loved the summer months, the long light evenings when it only got dark around ten o'clock. We virtually stayed out the whole day.

Most of the houses on our street had evacuees living in them, the alley at the back making a perfect place to play. There must have been about twenty kids at any one time running around. It must have been pandemonium for the people living there, but then, there was a war on.

Some of the local mothers weren't too happy about their children playing with evacuees. They thought we were a bad influence on their kids, with our 'big city' way of life. They didn't see us as 'casualties of the war', but an interruption to their peace and quiet.

One woman, the mother of a boy about my age, didn't like her son playing with me and made no attempt to hide it. I liked to play with him because he had a three-wheeler bike. His mother had forbidden him from letting anyone have a ride. This didn't deter me one bit.

One evening, I knocked on her front door and asked if her son was coming out to play. She told me he was not in, but hearing my knock he came to the window of the front room and was looking out at me.

'But he is in, there he is,' I said, pointing to the window.

'If I say he's not in, then he's not in. Now go away and don't come back.'

She slammed the door in my face. A few seconds later, she pulled him away from the window and straightened the net curtain.

He must have pestered her, because a little later he came out complete with his three-wheeler bike. His Mum, in a voice loud enough for all of us to hear, warned that no one was to get on his bike. As soon as she went inside I said.

'Give us a go on your bike.'

'No, you heard my mum. I'm not allowed to.'

'Your mum won't know, she's gone back in now.'

'But she'll see me out the window and I'll get into trouble.'

'Not if we move to the end of the road.'

He peddled off down the road with me running after him. As soon as we were out of sight of his house, I jumped onto the back of the bike and grabbed his shoulders.

'Give us a backy,' I called.

'No, get off,' he yelled, turning to push me off. The extra weight on the back of the bike, plus my pulling on his shoulders caused the bike to tip backwards, throwing the two of us to the ground. I was quicker to my feet than him. Grabbing the bike, I set off down the road laughing like a drain, with him crying and screaming as he chased after me. When I got to the end of the road, I turned and confronted him. I waited for him to get close and immediately peddled like mad, still laughing like a drain at his vain attempts to catch me. Suddenly, my laughter was cut short, as a huge hand grabbed me and threw me to the ground.

Picking myself up from the gutter, I was just in time to see his mother grab him with one hand, the bike with the other, and march into the house slamming the door behind her.

Sitting on the kerb, I rubbed my bruised knees, thankful she hadn't told Pop, or I would have been in trouble again.

Chapter Twenty

Then there was the Ireland family. They lived a few doors along the alley from us. There were three of them. Two boys, John and Tommy, and their older sister Jill. They were evacuees from London.

Their foster parent was a woman on her own. Her husband was in the army, fighting in the war. She worked full time, often leaving them in the care of their older sister, who had absolutely no control over them.

Whilst their foster parent was out, we ran around her house like wild things. I loved it, as I would never have got away with it in my own house. It was on one such occasion I spotted the two Ireland boys making themselves a sandwich.

'Won't you get into trouble?' I asked, knowing I was not allowed to touch any food in my own home.

'No, we're allowed to.'

'You're lucky, I wish I was.' I replied.

I licked my lips as I watched them pour a liberal amount of 'Daddies' sauce onto a roughly cut slice of bread and take a bite.

'Do you want one?' they asked.

I didn't need to be asked twice. Mouth watering, I 'hacked' myself a slice and poured a liberal amount of sauce onto it. Suddenly, catching us all off guard, a voice screeched.

'What on earth is going on? That's all the bread I've got.'

The voice stopped me dead in my tracks, my 'butty' inches from my mouth and dripping sauce onto my already grubby jumper.

Believing I was about to have my 'butty' taken from me, I quickly took a bite and headed out the back door and into the alley.

Now I was in the alley I thought I was safe enough to pause and take another bite of my 'butty'. Suddenly, a hand fell on my shoulder.

'Which house do you live in?' said the woman.

She marched me up the alley as I frantically stuffed the rest of my butty into my mouth. Ma answered her knock.

'What now?' she said, a note of resignation obvious in her voice.

The woman told her, pointing to the sauce marks on my jumper to support her story. Ma apologised, and the woman left.

'Right, get up to your room.'

'I don't have a room, I sleep under the table,' I replied, in a rare act of bravado. Grabbing my arm, she dragged me across the room and pushed me towards the stairs.

'I know where you sleep, you don't have to tell me; do you think I'm stupid? Now get up those stairs and into the back bedroom, and don't say another word.'

I went upstairs, popping into the bathroom to wash my hands and face and clean the sauce from my jumper. The bed creaked as I sat on it. Once again, I was left to gaze out the window into the back alley. I soon became bored.

Silently opening the bedroom door, I sat at the head of the stairs. Moments later, I crawled down stairs head first pretending to be a leopard sneaking up on its prey. I then crawled back up the stairs feet first; then back down again head first. Anything to alleviate the boredom. Finally, completely bored out of my skull, I decided to check out the bedrooms.

Creeping into Pop and Ma's room, I surveyed the comfortable double bed, resisting the temptation to jump up and down on it. Moving to the window, I eased the net curtains to one side and checked the front street. I was just in time to see Pop coming down the road. Quickly straightening the net curtain, I scooted back to my own room hoping Pop hadn't spotted me. Moments later, I heard him enter through the front door, breathing a sigh of relief as I heard him go into the living room and close the door. I sneaked back into his bedroom.

Ears tuned for the slightest sound, I carefully opened each drawer and rummaged. Finding nothing of interest, I moved into Aunt Gladys' room. I'd hardly begun nosing around, when the sound of the living room door being opened and Pop calling out he was going for a lie down had me scooting back to my bedroom.

Pop went into the bathroom, which was next to my bedroom. The sound of him peeing made me giggle, but when he let out an enormous fart followed by a satisfied 'ooh', I went into an uncontrollable fit of laughter. Thinking he might hear me, I buried my face in the pillow, nearly choking as I desperately muffled my hilarity.

Moments later, his bed creaked, and I knew he would soon be snoozing. Silently leaving my room, I snuck across the landing. Peering with one eye through the gap in the door jamb, I saw he was peacefully sleeping. I silently entered, and watched him sleeping as I listened to his steady rhythmical breathing. Leaning in close, I made a silly face at him, his beery breath warm on my cheek. Giggling silently, I stepped back, startling myself as I momentarily caught my reflection in the dressing table mirror. For one minute I thought someone had entered the room.

Spotting his shirt on the end of the bed, I picked it up and gently brushed his face with it. He waved it away with his hand. I did it again, and again he waved it away, before spluttering awake. Dropping the shirt on his face, I ran from the room and watched him through the door jamb. After giving the shirt a confused look, he threw it to the end of the bed and went back to sleep.

My moment of mirth over, I lay on my bed bored to distraction. Finally, Ma called Pop, and he went downstairs, blissfully unaware I was in my room, never mind his.

Soon the sound of cutlery and crockery being rattled below indicated that it was nearing teatime. As each hungry minute ticked away and I hadn't been called down, I guessed I wasn't being fed.

It was dark when I was awakened by the other kids coming into the room. I gave them their bed and went downstairs. Ma and Aunt Gladys briefly looked in my direction when I entered the living room, but made no effort to offer me anything to eat.

'I'm hungry, can I have something to eat please?' I asked.

'You should have thought of that this morning when you stole the neighbour's bread. You've had your food for the day. Next time you won't be so greedy. Go on, into bed,' ordered Ma. I silently climbed over my brother into the Morrison shelter.

The gnawing in my empty stomach, and the hours I had slept upstairs, ensured I was still awake when Pop came in from his work at the pub. He had brought home a couple of bottles of stout, which he shared with Ma and Aunt Gladys by the fire.

'How much longer do you think the war is going to go on for?' Aunt Gladys asked, expressing concern about her husband who was away fighting.

'I heard in the pub tonight that it could all be over in a few months,' answered Pop.

'I hope so,' said Ma. 'Then they can all go back to their parents and we can get on with our lives. I don't know how much more of this I can take.'

I silently listened to them 'putting the world to rights.'

Finally, they went to bed, leaving me to silently stare at the glowing embers in the grate. Moments later I heard the toilet flush and the bedroom doors close, and knew they were safely tucked up in their beds.

Being careful not to disturb my slumbering bed mates, I eased myself out of bed. As I climbed over my brother he moved, and I was sure he was watching me. I remained motionless, the light from the dying embers in the grate not sufficient to see if his eyes were open or closed. I put my face close to his.

Satisfied he was asleep, I crawled from under the table and crept into the pantry. My stomach was rumbling so loudly I was sure someone would hear it. The pantry yielded very little; what rations we got each day being eaten as quickly as they were bought. However, there was a near full loaf of bread and an opened tin of condensed milk, about two thirds full. I was so hungry, I could have eaten the whole loaf.

Scooping a finger full of condensed milk, I stuffed it into my mouth, unconcerned that my audible 'ummmm', as I licked my finger clean, might be heard. One finger full was never going to be enough. I took another, before ripping off a chunk of bread and sneaking back into bed.

The sound of Ma banging on the table top and shouting brought me and my three slumbering companions to life. She was obviously very annoyed. But as she always seemed annoyed, I was not too fussed. The four of us slowly crawled out of bed and stood sleepily looking at her.

'Who did this?' she screamed, pointing at the cause of her annoyance. There in the middle of the table was the condensed milk tin, and a scrappy piece of bread. The condensed milk tin was virtually empty. I knew when I left the pantry there was more milk in it. When nobody owned up, Ma turned her focus on me.

'It was you, wasn't it Billy? You were the one who said you were hungry last night. Did you get up in the night and take the bread and milk?'

I knew I had taken some of it, but so had someone else, and I was not taking the blame for them.

'No, it was not me,' I replied, giving her a glassy eyed stare.

She glared at me, looking me up and down for any tell-tale signs that might give me away. Luckily, I hadn't dribbled any milk down my front, but I might have had difficulty explaining why the finger I sucked the milk from was cleaner than the rest of them.

'Right, well there's nothing else, so we will all have to go without breakfast. You can thank whoever stole the bread and milk because there is nothing for anybody. Lord knows what Pop will say when I tell him there's nothing for his breakfast.'

I left the house, glad to get out before Pop got out of his bed. At school I was so hungry I couldn't concentrate, my mind occupied with my free milk and school dinner.

Apart from being permanently hungry, the conditions we lived and played in assured we regularly caught a dose of nits. As fast as one person got rid of them, someone else picked them up. So, each week, our scalps were raked raw with a fine-tooth comb.

Ma or Aunt Gladys would sit with a sheet of newspaper on their lap whilst each boy knelt in front of them with their head over the paper. As the comb was dragged through the hair, the nits fell onto the paper where we cracked them between our thumbnails. I can feel my head crawling as I write this.

Then one morning, I awoke with a different itch. Most days I had an itch of some sort, but this was not like anything I had had before. It worsened as the day went on. My brother, who shared the same single bed, had the same itch. We both had scabies.

We were taken to the local hospital, unceremoniously dumped into a bath of boiling water, and scrubbed with carbolic soap from the neck down. The nurse scrubbed each burrow, or sore, until it was red raw. If you complained, you were told not to be a baby.

After being dried with a towel that felt like coarse sandpaper, we were both liberally smeared with something akin to axle grease. We were then handed a 'Wee Willie Winky' night gown made of rough grey material. It was extremely prickly on our freshly scrubbed bodies. The whole painful process was repeated twice a day for several days.

When we were discharged, we walked home still covered in the thick grease. We spent the next few days in isolation, boringly looking out of the upstairs bedroom window at the kids playing in the alley below.

Chapter Twenty-One

The railway embankment, which ran alongside our house, was, to all intents and purposes, out of bounds. The signs, as far as we were concerned, were for everybody else, not a bunch of young boys. We daily wriggled through the fence, often playing in the parked railway trucks. Often, the trucks would move, forcing us to jump before the train gathered too much speed.

One day, by way of passing the time whilst improving our education, we decided to go on a rail excursion, courtesy of Great Western Railways. Six of us lay in the long grass awaiting the train. Finally, the sound of the train could be heard as it pulled out of Exmouth station, about five hundred yards away.

We were all adept at jumping on to moving trains, but there was only a small window of opportunity in which to get on board before it speeded up. It was everyone for themselves. Anyone who was too slow and missed their chance got left behind.

As the train drew near we all sprung up and closed in on one of the carriages. Timing your leap was essential. Miss the running board, and you could end up under the wheels of the train. Also, there was every chance the guard could be looking out of his carriage window, so there was no hanging about. The first onboard flung the door open, and the rest of us quickly followed.

The first stop, our intended destination, was Budleigh Salterton. As the train approached the station and began slowing, we threw open the door, and one by one jumped into the long grassy embankment. Not for the faint hearted, but quickly learned, or you wouldn't get to go anywhere.

After a few hours roaming around Budleigh Salterton filching whatever we could, it was time to leave.

The train approached, and we again dashed up the bank. Scrambling into an empty compartment, we fell about laughing. Moments later, we were jumping around the compartment like a pack of playful chimpanzees. I climbed onto the overhead luggage rack and lay in it like a bunk.

Suddenly, the train jerked to a halt. It was too soon to be in Exmouth. Before we knew it, the compartment door opened and the guard climbed in. After a quick look around the compartment, he leaned out the window and shouted to the driver, who was stood on the embankment.

'Okay, it's this one.' He turned and slowly surveyed the carriage.

'Right, who pulled the communication cord?' I had no idea what a communication cord was and remained silent.

He pointed. Six pairs of eyes followed his finger to a dangling cord above the door, and the sign below which read.

'IMPROPER USE OF THIS CORD CAN RESULT IN A FIVE POUND FINE'

I was still in the luggage rack looking down at him. 'Get off there,' he shouted, pulling me to the ground.

'Right, tickets all of you.' Nobody moved.

'I thought so. No tickets, and someone has pulled the communication cord. You are all in big trouble. The police will be waiting when we get to Exmouth.'

He left the compartment and the train began moving again. Before long we were all arguing about who had pulled the cord. Suddenly, one of them said.

'It was Billy, I saw him. When he was in the luggage rack he pulled the cord.'

'No I didn't, you're a liar, it was not me at all,' I shouted.

'Yes it was, I saw you.' I jumped off my seat and threw a punch at him, shouting.

'Liar, liar, it was not me.' We scuffled around the compartment, until my brother pulled us apart.

'What we going to say to the police?' someone asked.

'Nothing,' said my brother. 'Because we won't be on the train when it gets to the station. We always jump off before we get to the station anyway.'

'Yeah. But won't the guard be watching now?' someone else asked.

'Yeah, but if we all jump and make a run for it, what's he going to do? By the time the train gets into the station, we'll be gone.'

'I don't think we should. If we get caught it will be worse for us.' It was 'the liar'. His mate nodded in agreement.

'Well it doesn't matter who did it, we're still in trouble, cos we don't have a ticket, so we'll have to jump,' added my brother.

The train began slowing as it neared Exmouth station. Releasing the leather strap holding the window shut, my brother let it drop with a thud. Leaning out the window, he grasped the door handle.

Moments later, the door banged noisily against the side of the carriage as it swung open. After a quick look, he launched himself from the train. I quickly followed, joining him in the long grass. The guard spotted us and shouted something which I couldn't make out.

We immediately got to our feet and began jogging along the railway lines in the opposite direction of the train. Soon we came to the gun post situated on the railway embankment. It was made of sandbags in a circular shape, and covered with a camouflage net to hide the 'ack-ack' gun, so called because of the noise it made. The small entrance gave just enough access, without destroying the security of the post.

Three soldiers manned it 24 hours a day. Often, I would get hot water from a nearby house for them to make tea. In return they gave me boiled sweets, or dried milk cubes. They were supposed to be dissolved in a cup of tea, but I just ate them like sweets. It was not as rewarding as working for the Americans, but, 'beggars can't be choosers.'

On one occasion, I was in the post when the air raid warning sounded. The soldiers chased me out, telling me to go to the nearest shelter. Instead, I hid in the long grass and watched them. They quickly removed the camouflage, manned the gun, and opened fire on the German planes. The noise of the shells was deafening. From my position in the grass, I could clearly see the puffs of smoke in the sky as the shells exploded. I saw a plane go down, smoke billowing from its engine. Naturally, the soldiers claimed it was a hit for them.

Frankie and I approached the post. Stealthily pulling the camouflage netting to one side, we crawled in.

'Oh, it's you. You shouldn't come creeping in like that, you could get shot,' one of the soldiers joked.

'Did you think it was Jerry then?' Frankie said, laughing. We referred to the Germans as 'Jerry', picking it up from the adults.

We chatted with the soldiers for a while. We wanted to make sure they would remember we were there. I even volunteered to get the hot water for their tea from the woman in the house nearby. Later, as we headed for home we went over our story. We would deny we were on the train, and that we played around the 'ack-ack' post all day.

Immediately we entered the backyard, the figures of two men could be seen through the living room window. We knew instinctively they were the police.

'Now remember what we agreed,' Frankie reiterated. 'No matter what they say, just deny we were on the train. And don't let them trick you.' We entered the living room, and Ma was immediately onto us.

'Where have you two been? And before you say anything, I don't want any of your lies. The police are here, and I know all about it. So, what have you got to say?'

I avoided her gaze and looked out the window.

'Don't look out the window, look at me,' she shouted. I continued gazing out the window, leaving the talking to my brother.

'I don't know what you mean,' he said.

'Don't get clever with me. You know what I am talking about,' said Ma.

'No, I don't.'

'I'm talking about what happened on the train today.'

'What train?'

'Are you denying you were on a train today?'

'Yes'. One of the policemen interrupted.

'According to the four boys we have already questioned, six of you went to Budleigh Salterton on the train. It was them who gave us your address. Anyway, none of you bought a ticket, and you all boarded the train by jumping onto it a short distance outside the station. On the return journey from Budleigh Salterton to Exmouth, the communication cord was pulled. One of the boys said it was you.' He indicated me.

He paused and waited for my response. I could see by my brother's eyes he was virtually pleading with me to remember what we had planned.

'It couldn't have been me, because I was not there,' I said. Quickly sussing out that my brother was influencing me, the policeman said.

'Is there another room I can use?'

Ma showed him into the parlour, and he indicated to my brother to go with him. The remaining policeman turned his attention to me.

'You know it is a very serious offence to board a train when it is moving, not to mention a very dangerous practice. You could easily fall under the wheels and be killed. You wouldn't like that, would you?'

'No,' I mumbled.

'Do you know what the fine for the improper use of the communication cord is?'

'No,' I again mumbled.

'Five pounds. Have you got five pounds?'

'No.'

'Then how would you be able to pay the fine?' Choosing my words carefully, I said.

'I don't need to, because I was not on the train.'

'That's not what the other boys said. Now why would anyone say it was you if you weren't there?'

'I don't know.' I could see Ma's mouth working in anger, without actually saying anything.

A few minutes later, my brother returned. Ma watched as we exchanged glances. I knew from his expression he was again

71

reminding me to stick to the story. The policeman beckoned to me, and I followed him into the parlour, amazed when he dared to sit on the hallowed settee.

'Sit down,' he said.

'I'm not allowed to sit on the furniture,' I meekly replied.

'I think it will be alright this time.'

I had never sat in the armchairs; in fact it was the first time I had been in the room since using one of Ma's cushions as a pillow. I lowered myself into one of the armchairs, more concerned about what Ma would say if she saw me, than the policeman.

'Right, you can stop your lies now. Your brother has told me everything, so you might as well own up. I'll ask you one more time. Did you pull the communication cord?'

'No, I was not even on the train.'

'Your brother has admitted it.'

I knew he hadn't. If he had, why was the policeman questioning me. He continued with his questioning. I continued to deny.

'Well,' asked Ma, when we returned to the living room.

'He still denies he was on the train,' replied the policeman. Ma jumped to her feet.

'Liars, your nothing but a pair of liars, the both of you,' she shrilled, her mouth dribbling saliva. 'They've obviously cooked up a story between them.' She looked from me to my brother.

Suddenly Pop, who had been sitting quietly in his armchair, stood up.

'That's enough Ma. If they say they were not on the train, then that's it, they were not on the train.'

Ma looked at Pop in amazement. She was about to challenge him, but the look on his face indicated she should shut up.

'What happens now?' asked Pop.

'Well, we'll put in our report and see what happens.'

'But, if as they say they were not on the train, then what?' asked Pop.

'Sir, I genuinely believe that they were on the train. But I could never prove it. So it's their word against the other boys. If, as they say, they weren't on the train, then it must have been one of the four boys we picked up at the station. The guard said there were six boys, but he didn't get their names. If he had, we would have had something to go on. We'll talk to the other boys, and we may come back and speak to these boys again.'

Pop went with the two policemen to the front door, and returned to the living room.

'So, what was all that about?' said Ma. 'It's obvious they're lying. You know as well as I do they lie all the time.' She glared at my brother and me.

'Have you got five pounds to throw away?' Pop quietly asked.

'What do you mean, five pounds? What's five pounds got to do with it?'

'The fine for improper use of the communication cord is five pounds, which we would have to pay if they had admitted they had pulled the cord.'

'Their parents can pay it, not us,' volunteered Ma.

'And what chance would we have of getting five pounds from *their* parents?'

He turned his attention to the two of us sitting at the end of the room.

'I don't know what went on today, and I don't want to. But if I find out that you have been jumping on moving trains, I'll give you both the leathering of your lives. Don't think for one minute that you have got away with it. Only for the five pounds fine, I would have let the police lock you up and throw away the key.'

I began to breathe easier as I sensed we had got away with it. For one brief moment, I thought I may never jump onto a moving train again. But I knew I would. I just loved the excitement of it. How else would I get to go anywhere?

The next day, I was munching on my daily tea time ration of bread and margarine, when one of the policemen came back. From the front door, I heard him tell Ma that one of the other boys admitted to pulling the communication cord. She returned to the room, said nothing, but the look she gave me quickly removed the smirk from my face.

Chapter Twenty-Two

Due to the number of kids under one roof, come hail, rain, or shine, we were put out of the house early morning and left to our own devices. With time on our hands, and no supervision, it was inevitable we would get into trouble.

Most days, we headed for the park, passing the cake shop on the way. Like a magnet, the shop window drew us to it, where we would stare hungrily at the spread of cakes.

'If I had any money I'd buy one of those,' someone said, pointing to a tray of cream cakes.

'No, I'd have one of those,' someone else chipped in.

'Me too,' someone else agreed.

'Raymond, have you got any money?' asked my brother.

'No.'

'Turn out your pockets,' he ordered.

Raymond dutifully turned out his pockets. He was as broke as we were. When it was obvious no one had any money, we began drifting off towards the park.

'Wait a minute, wait a minute, I have an idea. I know exactly how we can get a cake,' ventured my brother, immediately grabbing everyone's attention.

'What we do is this. We all go into the shop at the same time. The woman can't watch us all. So, whilst she's not looking, me and Billy will grab a couple of cakes and scarper.' A couple of the boys were a bit unsure.

'Okay. If you don't want to, you don't have to,' said my brother. 'But don't expect any cake, right.' They changed their mind.

A chime rang out as we entered the empty shop. A few seconds later, a woman came out from the back.

'Yes, what can I get you today?' she asked, a pleasant smile on her face.

She seemed so pleasant, it was a pity we were planning to steal from her. It would have been far easier if she had been grumpy.

'What have you got for a penny?' someone asked.

'Well, the cheapest and most filling are these.' She pointed to a tray of 'Nelson' cake under the counter. It was cheap because it was made from the stale cakes of the day before. As she bent down to pick up the tray, my brother nudged me. I had deliberately stood at the back of the shop, keeping the others in front of me. Grabbing four cakes from the display in the window, I quickly walked out the door.

The hair on the back of my neck was bristling, and it took all my self-control not to break into a run. I breathed easier once I was out of sight. A few seconds later, my brother joined me.

'Come on, let's go,' he said.

'But what about the others? We were supposed to wait.' I said.

'They can catch us up in the park.' I wondered if he intended for us to eat all the cakes before they got there, giggling at the thought of it.

Reaching Phear Park, we headed for one of the pavilions. We were soon joined by the others, anxious not to 'dip out' on the cake. We laid out the cakes on the bench, now a little worse for wear after being in our pockets, and surveyed our haul. Raymond was first to make a move.

'Leave that cake alone. You're not at home now,' said my brother, pushing him away. Being family, Raymond always received preferential treatment at home.

'Right, as it was my idea I get first pick,' said my brother. 'Ummm... now... which one shall I have?' He made a move towards a cake. Raymond watched, smiling, when he saw it was not the one he wanted.

'No... I think I'll have this one,' he said, picking up the cake Raymond had chosen. Giving it a lick, he took a large bite. 'Ummm delicious,' he said, munching into Raymond's face.

'It's not fair. You knew I wanted that one,' Raymond whined. In the meantime, the rest of us grabbed a cake and tucked in. Raymond stared at the only cake left.

'I don't want that cake,' he shouted, close to tears.

'Oh well, if you don't want it, I'll have it,' said my brother, picking it up. Raymond burst into tears.

'I'm telling my mum that you stole cakes, and you'll be in trouble,' he shouted, storming from the pavilion.

'Raymond, Raymond, hang on, I was only kidding,' shouted my brother. 'You can have your cake.' Raymond ignored him, and continued walking away. 'Come on Raymond. Come back. You can even choose what game we play.'

Normally, Raymond had no say in what games we played. He either joined in our game, or played on his own. Hearing this, Raymond returned and chose to play 'hide and seek'. We all ran off to hide. Sometime later, the game finished, and we returned to the pavilion. Minutes later, Raymond was in tears again. The bench where his cake had been was clean, not even a crumb. My brother, being the oldest, immediately took charge of the situation.

'Okay, who took it?' he demanded to know. I knew by his face and the tone of his voice he was shamming. I guessed he knew exactly what had happened to the cake. Some of the others found it amusing, and began giggling. Raymond was convinced we were all in it.

'I'm going home, and I'm telling on all of you,' he whined.

'Hang on, hang on.' said my brother, 'I'll find your cake. Don't go.'

He strutted around the pavilion looking under the bench seat, even climbing on the seat and looking in the roof joists. It was obvious he was taking the mickey out of Raymond as he put on a fake voice and said, 'no not here'. Needless to say, Raymond's cake was not found. But, through a devious selection of threats and promises, my brother convinced him not say anything.

76

On the way home, later that afternoon, we again passed the cake shop. To our surprise, a policeman stepped out and called us into the shop. My initial reaction was to run, but when no one else made a move, I followed them into the cake shop.

'Is this them?' the policeman asked. The cake shop lady looked us over.

'Yes, that's them. They were in my shop this morning, and when they left I noticed some cakes had been taken from the window.'

'Couldn't have been us, we were nowhere near this shop today, were we?' said my brother.

'No,' we all replied.

'Are you sure these were boys?' the policeman asked again.

'Yes, I remember them well.'

'Right, where do you all live?' he asked.

My brother gave him an address, which was clearly not ours.

'And you,' he said, indicating me.

'Same,' I replied, unable to remember the address my brother had said.

'Don't say 'same', tell me the address.'

'We all live together,' said my brother, quickly repeating the address.' Then a voice called out.

'That's not where we live.' It was Raymond.

'Giving a false address is a serious offence,' said the policeman. 'Now where do you really live?' Raymond told him the correct address.

'Right, I'll be speaking to your parents later.'

As soon as we were outside, Frankie grabbed Raymond and pinned him against the wall.

'Listen you, we are all in this together. You were in the shop, so you are just as much to blame as we are. You say anything, and it will be the worse for you. Right?'

'But what about the policeman. What are we going to say when he tells them we stole cakes?' said Raymond.

'We just deny it. We say it was not us, and the lady in the shop was mistaken. No matter what your mum or gran say, stick to the story. We were not in the cake shop, do you understand?'

I didn't believe for one moment that Raymond would be able to lie to his Mum, never mind Ma or Pop. I could see us all getting a leathering with the razor strop. Not Raymond of course. Raymond was the apple of Pop's eye. Not only that, Ma would never allow it.

We entered the living room, and as Raymond walked past Ma she pulled him in close to her and kissed him on the cheek.

'So, what have you been up to today?' she asked.

'Nothing much Gran. We just played in the park all day,' he replied.

Suddenly, there was a knock on the front door. Moments later, Ma returned, followed by a policeman.

'What's happened?' asked Aunt Gladys, a look of concern on her face.

'It appears this lot have been stealing,' said Ma, clearly exasperated.

'Oh thank goodness. I thought it was something serious,' said Aunt Gladys. She was always worried that the knock on the door could bring bad news about her husband, who was away fighting in the war.

The policeman explained what had happened, pointing out that the shopkeeper would not press charges if the cakes were paid for.

Ma looked at the sea of faces, all trying to look innocent.

'Did you steal from the cake shop?' she asked, of no one in particular. My brother took it on himself to speak for all of us. He said.

'No Ma, we were nowhere near the shop.'

'Raymond, you were with them, is that right?'

All eyes focussed on Raymond. My heart was thumping so loudly I was sure Ma would hear it. Finally, Raymond answered.

'Yes Gran.'

We finished our tea and went outside to the back alley. A few minutes later Raymond was called in, and we immediately knew Ma was going to question him on his own. Shortly after, we were all called in and told to sit on the floor.

'I'm only going to ask this once and I want the truth. Did you steal cakes from the cake shop today?' asked Pop. No one answered.

'Frankie, you're the oldest. Did you steal cakes today?'

'No Pop,' he replied. Pop turned and slowly took the razor strop from the hook on the wall.

'Are you sure?'

'Yes Pop.'

'That's not what Raymond says.'

'We weren't even near the shop,' he reiterated.

'So, Raymond's lying is he?'

'I dunno. All I know is we weren't near the shop today, were we?'

We all mumbled, 'no.'

'I don't care what you say, you are all in this together. Raymond said it was your idea.' Pop advanced towards Frankie, the razor strop swinging in his hand.

'You're not hitting me with that,' my brother yelled, jumping to his feet.

'Don't you dare talk to me like that; you'll get what's coming to you. When I'm finished with you, you won't steal again.' In a flash, my brother crossed the floor and ran out the door.

'Come back here,' shouted Pop. Instinctively, we all stood up, feeling too vulnerable sitting on the floor, and headed for the safety of the upstairs bedroom. As I went through the door, the strop caught me on the back. I let out a yell, and took the stairs three at a time, diving into one of the beds with two other boys, hoping there was safety in numbers.

We were all expecting Pop to follow us. Several minutes passed and nothing happened. Sneaking onto the landing, I was joined by John and Kevin.

We sat on the top step quietly staring into space, too scared to venture down the stairs. We knew we would have to go down sooner or later, as all three of us slept in the Morrison shelter in the living room. Finally, desperate to hear what they were saying about my brother, I crept downstairs.

Their conversation through the closed door, suggested they were going to the authorities to try and get some of us moved to another home.

'I hope I'm one of them. I really hate it here. I would love to move somewhere else,' said John.

Suddenly, the living room door opened, sending us scampering into the bedrooms and jumping into whatever bed we could. Moments later, we were called downstairs.

We all kept well away from Pop, who was sitting in his chair by the fireside. He deliberately avoided looking at us, as we undressed and crawled into bed. With my brother being away, I enjoyed the extra space.

I had just dozed off, when I felt my arm being pulled. It was Pop. I instinctively pulled away, and moved to the far side of the bed, thinking he was going to hit me.

'It's all right,' he said, trying to reassure me. I kept my distance. 'Do you know where Frankie will have gone?' he asked.

He was obviously shaken by my brother running away. Nobody had ever done that before. I told him I had no idea, which for once was the truth.

The next morning, as soon as I had eaten my breakfast, Ma told me to see if I could find him. I found him in Phear Park sitting in the pavilion. He told me he had spent the night there.

I told him how Pop had chased us all to bed, and I got caught on the back with the razor strop. I also told him what Pop had said about wanting to get rid of a couple of the boys.

'Hope it's us,' he said.

Soon, the other boys joined us, Frankie in his element as he told them where he had slept. It was decided that I should go home and tell Ma.

'Well, did you find him?' she asked, as I walked in.

'Yes, but he will only come home if Pop doesn't hit him with the strop.'

'I'll speak to Pop when he comes home. Go and tell him to come home.'

I ran back to the park and told him. When we returned, Pop was seated in the living room. Ignoring my brother, he reached out and grabbed my wrist as I passed, pulling me close. My brother paused, ready to make a dash for it.

'I know you stole the cakes,' he said, looking me squarely in the eye. 'I know you are all to blame. It's not just the cakes, but you involved Raymond. When you all go home at the end of the war, he still has to live here.' He paused, glancing in my brother's direction.

'I'm going to give you one shilling and sixpence. You can tell the others you will all work it off until I say it is paid, understand?' I nodded, as he slowly released my wrist.

Frankie and I left the house, with me clutching the one shilling and sixpence. Outside, we met the rest of the boys and told them what had happened.

I was not happy Pop had selected me to take the money to the cake shop, and tried to get one of the others to do it. They all shied away, leaving me to face the shopkeeper.

I entered the shop as discreetly as possible, as if not drawing attention to myself would somehow alleviate the task at hand. The bell rang just as loudly. Closing the door behind me, I stood just inside the shop.

'Yes, can I help you?' said the 'cake shop lady' as if she had never seen me before.

'I've brought your money,' I murmured.

She came from behind the counter. I thought she was going to hit me, and cringed away. Instead, she just looked me up and down. She knew who I was, but had no intention of making it easy.

'What money would that be?' she asked.

'The money for the cakes.'

'What cakes?'

'The cakes we took yesterday,' I said, avoiding her gaze by looking at the floor.

'You mean the cakes you stole yesterday?'

I remained silent. I just wanted her to take the money so I could get out. She on the other hand was happy to prolong my agony. I held out the shilling, keeping the sixpence in my other hand. *Never know,* I thought, *she might be happy with just taking the shilling.* Old habits die hard. She made no attempt to take the money.

'So, why did you steal the cakes?' she asked.

'Because we were hungry.'

'Don't you get fed at home?'

'We don't get cakes.'

'Still no excuse for stealing. Right, where's the money then?'

I placed the shilling, now quite warm in my hand, on the counter and backed towards the door.

'Just a minute,' she said.

Bugger, she wants the other sixpence I thought, sheepishly placing it next to the shilling.

To my surprise, she handed me a bag of cakes, after making me promise I wouldn't steal again. For a bag of cakes, I would have promised anything.

'Did she take the money?' my brother asked, as I shared out the cakes.

'Of course she did,' I replied.

'Just checking.'

I wondered what gave him the idea I would try to keep the money for myself!

Chapter Twenty-Three

There is always a lot of rivalry between boys when climbing trees, as to who can climb the highest. Phear Park in Exmouth had an abundance of trees, which we all loved to climb. Often, I would sit amongst the branches and observe the people passing below, many unaware of my presence.

One day, my brother and another boy were taunting each other as to who could climb the highest. They both reached the top, with both of them claiming victory. They then began to descend at which point the watching kids below turned and wandered off. I was sat on the grass under the tree, when suddenly there was a crack, followed by a thump. I turned, to see my brother lying on the grass alongside me. I thought he had jumped from the tree to impress the other boy, never thinking the cracking noise I had heard was the noise of the branch he was standing on snapping. He looked alright, but when he tried to walk, he fell to the ground screaming in pain.

Several of us tried helping him to his feet, but as soon as he put any weight on them, he screamed in pain.

'Don't touch me,' he shouted, dragging himself on all fours into the pavilion. He was obviously in a lot of pain, with none of us knowing what to do.

'Should I go home and tell Ma and Pop?' I suggested.

'No, I don't want them to know I've been climbing trees.'

He was hoping the pain would go away before it was time to go home. But by mid-afternoon, it was no better. In the end, the pain became so bad, he finally consented.

'Okay, but don't tell them I fell from a tree,' he said.

I ran home, taking all the shortcuts. Bursting into the house, I breathlessly explained that Frankie had hurt his ankles and couldn't walk. If I was expecting a show of concern, I was disappointed.

'Take him to the hospital,' said Pop.

'How am I going to get him there? He's broken both his ankles.'

'Take the wheelbarrow,' said Ma.

'Can't I take the pram?'

'No. Aunt Gladys wants to keep it nice, and you'll only scratch it.'

Ma didn't want me using the pram, and Pop was none too happy with me taking his precious wheel barrow. He had made it himself from a crate and a couple of pram wheels, and was very proud of it. He didn't have a car or a bicycle, so it was the only wheeled vehicle he possessed. Normally, he only allowed us to use it to bring the beer home on a Saturday.

Dashing into the yard, I removed the canvas cover only to discover the barrow was full of maggots. After cleaning it out, I went into the scullery to wash my hands.

'You still here? I thought you would have gone by now if he is in such pain,' Ma called out.

I told her the barrow was full of maggots, hoping she would tell me to take the pram. When that didn't work, I asked her for a pillow and a blanket to put in the barrow.

'The only pillows I've got are those on the beds, and you're not taking them,' she said.

'Well, he's got to have something. He can't lie in an empty barrow.'

'Take the mat from the scullery floor.'

It was better than nothing, so I threw it into the barrow and headed back to the park. When I got there, my brother was lying on the bench moaning about the pain he was in.

'You took your time, where have you been? I'm in agony,' he whinged. I told him the barrow had been full of maggots.

'The barrow! What did you bring that for? Why didn't you bring the pram? You can't do anything right. I should have known better than to ask you.' I felt like telling him to get stuffed, the ungrateful sod, but instead said.

'I know, but Ma wouldn't let me take the pram, so it was this or nothing. And, I have to take you to the hospital not home.'

'How are you going to get me to hospital in a wheelbarrow?' The hospital was located at the top of a very steep hill.

'I'll help,' offered George.

After much manoeuvring and laughter on our part, with loads of yelling from my brother, we finally got him into the barrow. His head was at an uncomfortable angle, and his legs were sticking up in the air. I placed the scullery mat under his knees to give him some comfort. I told him we looked like a tank and his legs were our guns. He was in too much pain to appreciate my humour.

We set off for the hospital. It was harder than we thought, not helped by my brother crying out and accusing us of deliberately going over every bump. By the time we arrived at the foot of the hill, we were already feeling the strain.

'I'll need to take a rest, I'm worn out,' I said, sitting down on the kerb.

'Never mind about that, just get me to the hospital, you can rest later,' shouted Frankie, ungrateful as ever for our efforts. After a short rest, we started up the hill.

George and I took a handle each. Walking backwards, we slowly pulled the barrow up the hill. It was heavy going, with my brother moaning and groaning as the barrow slewed from side to side shaking his legs. Our progress was slow. Before long, our arms tired, so we changed things around. George took the handles and pulled, whilst I pushed from behind.

Suddenly, there was a loud crack, and the barrow slewed into the kerb, tipping Frankie onto the pavement. The sight of him writhing in agony on the ground, whilst moaning and calling us names, was too much for George and me. The two of us burst into uncontrollable laugher.

'Shut up you two, it's not funny' he shouted, between fits of moaning and groaning.

My laughter was suddenly cut short when I sighted the barrow. To my horror, one of the handles had broken off.

'Oh no, look at the barrow. The handles broken. How am I going to tell Pop I've broken his barrow?' I moaned.

'Bugger Pop's barrow, get me to the hospital,' whined Frankie.

'Yeah, it's alright for you, but Pop will leather me for breaking his barrow,' I pointed out.

'Alright for me,' he shouted. 'I'm in agony here. Now get me to the hospital.'

Between his crying and my moaning we manoeuvred him back into the barrow and reached the hospital without further incident.

'Can I help you?' said the nurse at reception.

'My brother fell out of a tree and has broken his ankles. I was told to bring him here,' I said.

'Really, where is he now?'

'Outside in the barrow.'

She looked a little doubtful, but followed us outside anyway. Within minutes, she had organised a trolley. George and I tried to follow, but were told to wait in reception.

Now my brother was safely in the hands of the hospital, I began worrying how I would tell Pop I'd broken his wheelbarrow. He'd never believe it was an accident. I was sure a walloping was coming my way.

George said he was leaving. I said I would wait to see if my brother was alright. I told George not to mention the barrow to Pop. I would tell him when I got home.

The nurse finally took me to see Frankie. He was tucked up in bed with both ankles heavily strapped.

'You lucky thing,' I said, envious of his clean bed and fresh hospital pyjamas. Not for him the worry of a broken wheelbarrow and an irate Pop. He asked me what I was going to tell Pop. I said I would just tell him what happened and hope for the best.

I was about to leave, when his evening meal was served, the food putting a smile on his face, despite his pain.

Ignoring my hungry look, the nurse said I should go. My brother was not about to offer me anything from his meal, so I left. I had seen enough of his smirking face as he tucked in.

I found the barrow where I had left it and headed for home. My mind was rambling, as I desperately tried to come up with a plausible story to tell Pop.

What if I hide the barrow and told him someone had stolen it from the front of the hospital whilst I was inside with Frankie. Then I wouldn't have to tell him I had broken the handle. But, wouldn't he be even more angry because I had lost his precious barrow. At least if it was only broken, he could fix it. But, what if I hid it, and a after a couple of days I told Pop I'd found it, but the handle was broken. He would be so happy to get his barrow back he wouldn't worry about the broken handle. That would get me out of trouble.

By the time I reached the house, I had discarded those thoughts, and decided I would tell Pop exactly what happened as soon as I walked in, and get it over with.

I leaned the barrow against the wall and replaced the canvas cover. Taking a deep breath, I entered the house. Pop had already finished his tea and was sitting in his armchair. Gathering my nerve, I prepared myself to speak. Before I could utter a word, Ma cut me off by asking how Frankie was.

I was annoyed by her interruption, but told her both of his ankles were broken. In fact they were only sprained. She made no mention of going to visit him.

I now had to wait for a lull in the conversation before I could again speak to Pop. Battling to find the right words, I steeled myself to speak. Again, I was cut off, when Ma told me to get my tea. She'd set my plate at the farthest away end of the Morrison shelter, which meant I would have to shout to talk to Pop. I didn't dare move to another seat, so sat nibbling my food as I waited for a lull in the conversation.

I knew it was not going to be easy. Being scared of Pop didn't help, as it hampered my ability to find the right words. Also, I knew not to interrupt when grown-ups were speaking, and not to talk with my mouth full. With so many things jumping around in my mind, before I got around to saying anything, Pop had left the room and gone to work. I'd missed my chance. *Now*, I thought, *it will be worse for me, as he'll think I deliberately didn't tell him.*

I finished my tea, went out to the yard, and examined the barrow again, as if by some miracle it would be fixed. Picking up the broken handle, I pushed it onto the broken stump on the barrow. At first sight it didn't look broken. Now, if only it would stay like that, I'd be off the hook. But a quick knock, and the handle fell to the ground. Then, for some inexplicable reason, I decided to tie the handle in place by wrapping an old bootlace around it. Gently placing the barrow against the wall, I covered it with the canvas.

The following day, with all that was going on in my young life, the barrow was the last thing on my mind. That is, until I entered the backyard when I arrived home from school. There, for all to see, was the barrow, uncovered, with the broken handle lying alongside it. After the initial jolt of reality, I was somewhat relieved. Now I wouldn't have to go through the agony of telling Pop. I nervously entered the house. I'd hardly stepped into the living room when Pop said.

'So, what happened to the barrow?' I nervously blurted out what had happened.

'Why didn't you tell me when you came in, and I could have fixed it.' I told him I had tried, but because I was afraid of him didn't know what to say.

'I had a job to do today, but couldn't do it because the barrow was broken.' Grabbing me by the arm he dragged me out into the backyard.

'And you tried to fix it with a bootlace. Did you think I wouldn't notice it?

'No Pop.'

'Do you think I'm an idiot?'

'No Pop.'

'No Pop, no Pop,' he said, mimicking me. 'If anyone is an idiot it's you. What are you?'

'An idiot,' I replied.

'At last, a truthful answer.'

Over all the years I lived with Pop, I never actually had a conversation with him. My relationship consisted of being told what to do, being called names, or just being ignored. He picked up the broken handle, and I immediately withdrew, thinking he was going to hit me with it. He threw it across the yard.

'Get out of my sight before I do something I might regret,' he said. I retreated through the back gate into the safety of the alley, relieved to get away.

The next day, I visited my brother in hospital. He asked me if I had told Pop about the barrow.

'No, not yet.' I lied. I wanted to keep him guessing, just to see how he reacted.

'Why not?'

'I don't know what to say. You know what he is like.'

'Just tell him what happened. He'll find out anyway.' He appeared to be enjoying my predicament.

'Well, when I do, he won't let me use the barrow again, so how are you going to get home?' I retaliated.

'Well, the nurse said I can't walk home, so you will have to sort something out.'

Frankie was due out of hospital on the Saturday, but as usual, I was in the queue at the butcher's shop. Aunt Gladys relieved me, and told me I had to take the empties back to the hotel bar where Pop worked.

'I can't. I have to pick Frankie up from the hospital.'

'Right. Well one of the other boys will have to do it,' she replied.

'But I need the barrow to get him home,' I said.

'Take the pram.'

'The pram! Can I use your pram?'

'Don't sound so surprised. Just be careful with it.'

'I will, I'll be ever so careful, I promise.'

The pram. I was actually being allowed to use the pram. I excitedly rushed off home. Bursting breathlessly into the house, I said.

'I'm going to get Frankie, and Aunt Gladys said I can use the pram.' Ma was onto me like a flash.

'The pram! You sure she said you could use the pram?'

'Yes, because the barrow is being used to take the empties back.'

Ma was very defensive of the pram for some unknown reason, but faced with the choice of her 'Mackeson's Stout' or the pram, the stout won.

'Out of the way,' she said, pushing me to one side. 'I'll get it. I don't want you bashing all the walls.'

She manoeuvred the pram from the dining room, where it was always kept, onto the front step. No way the pram was allowed in the back alley. It made a change for me to leave the house by the front door.

'Don't you dare put a mark on that pram. I'll inspect it when you get back. If there is one mark on it, you'll get it from me, do you hear?'

'Yes Ma. I promise I will be ever so careful.'

'You'd better be.'

The pram was much easier to push than the barrow. I started off pushing it really carefully; almost frightened to go too fast in case anything happened to it. But it wasn't long before I broke into a run, getting the pram up to speed and jumping on it for a free ride. I stopped when I nearly ran into a garden wall. I then began imagining I was a spitfire pilot and the pram was my plane. Making the sound of machine guns, I swerved in and out of the lamp posts, pretending I was shooting down the enemy. It was great fun.

I reached the hospital with the pram unscathed. I had hardly noticed the hill that had given me so much trouble when trying to get up it with the barrow.

Parking the pram inside the foyer, I found my brother sitting on the edge of his bed.

'Did you bring the barrow?' he asked.

'No.'

'Don't tell me you haven't told Pop yet. Now how am I going to get home? I can't walk home.'

'Well you'll have to. Because even if the barrow was fixed, I couldn't have got it, because it would have been used to collect the Stout from the pub. And that is more important than you. So you will have to walk as there's nothing else. You sure the nurse said you can't walk home?'

'Of course I'm sure. Think I'd still be sitting here if I could walk home.'

'Knowing you, yes.' I replied.

Wincing in agony, he eased himself off the bed, forever the drama queen. He said goodbye to the nurse, putting on a brave face as he told her he had to walk home.

'I'll never make it. If you couldn't get the barrow, why didn't you bring the pram?'

'The pram. Do you think they would let me take the pram? No way. And anyway, you're walking alright now.'

'Yeah for those few steps, but my ankles are hurting already. I'll never make it all the way home.'

'Look, if you're going to moan all the time, you can walk home on your own.'

'Well, wouldn't you, it's a long walk.'

We reached the entrance foyer, but he was so intent on moaning he didn't spot the pram. I let him walk on.

'So, did I bring this for nothing?' I said, pointing to the pram standing in the foyer.

He turned and slowly walked back, a smile creeping across his face.

'You little bugger.' He was not sure whether to hug me or hit me. I wheeled it outside.

'Well, jump in,' I said.

The pram was too high for him to get his bottom into, and standing on one leg whilst trying to put the other one in the pram was too painful.

'Tip it down so I can crawl in,' he said.

'No, the pram might get scratched and I'll get into trouble.'

'Right, hold the pram steady and I'll lay across it and then roll over into it.'

I grasped the handles whilst he crawled face downwards into the pram. After much grunting and groaning, he was lying face down with his backside and legs hanging out the back. The sight of him trying to manoeuvre himself around was too much for me, and I burst out laughing.

'Stop laughing and give me hand, it's not funny,' he shouted angrily, trying to turn and see where I was.

'Yes it is.'

His anger made me laugh even harder. The more he struggled, the more I laughed. I was so helpless with laughter, I let go of the pram and sat on the hospital steps, my sides in a knot.

Suddenly, noticing that his struggles could tip the pram over and scratch it, I went to his assistance.

'Stop, stop, just stay where you are, or the pram will tip over,' I yelled, grabbing the handles and steadying the pram.

He stopped struggling and lay exhausted. With great difficulty I manoeuvred the pram over to the entrance steps. After a lot of moaning and saying 'how he was going to get me when he was better,' he wriggled his way onto the steps and sat down.

'Right,' I said. 'We'll try once more. I'll hold the handles, and now you are on the steps you can ease your bum into the pram and then sling your legs over.' He was still unable to get into the pram and sat back down.

'You little twit," he shouted. 'You should have brought the barrow.'

'You didn't like the barrow, and anyway it's being used. So, I thought you would like the pram. But there's no pleasing you. Well, if you can't get into the pram you will just have to walk home.' Fed up with his abuse, I grabbed the pram and walked off.

'Where are you going? You can't leave me here,' he called.

'Bugger off, I have had enough of you. I'm going home and you can get home anyway you like,' I said. Just as he had done with Raymond, he immediately calmed down.

'Alright I'm sorry,' he called. Ignoring him I continued walking.

'Billy come back, I'm sorry,' he shouted. I paused. I knew I couldn't leave him. Slowly walking back, I sat down next to him on the steps.

A few minutes later, a man came out of the hospital and stood on the steps smoking a cigarette.

'Mister, could you help me get my brother into this pram?' I asked.

'He's a bit big to be going into a pram isn't he?' he joked.

'Yes, but he's just out of the hospital and it's the only way I can get him home.'

The man lifted Frankie into the pram with one easy move. The man was right, he was a bit big for the pram. His feet hung over the end between the handles.

'Thanks mister,' we both said.

The prospect of the pram running away from me with my brother in it, made me go the long way home and avoid the hill. A number of the kids were playing in the street as we approached, and I knew they would say something as we passed. My brother had his back to them, so hadn't seen them.

'Look at the big baby in his pram. Do you want your dummy?' one of them called. Then two of them began rocking the pram whilst sarcastically singing, 'rock a bye baby on the tree top'.

My brother eased himself onto one elbow, and punched one of them in the face. He let go of the pram and quickly backed off. Worried they would tip the pram over if I let go of the handle, I kicked out at the other boy and caught him on his shin.

They continued to taunt us from a distance, every so often running in and giving me a push as I twisted and turned to see where they were. I was relieved when the front door opened and Aunt Gladys came out.

'What's going on?' she called.

'Nothing aunty, just some boys messing about,' I called. At the sight of an adult figure, they backed away.

Aunt Gladys helped Frankie out of the pram and into the house. I was about to follow, when Ma appeared.

'Just a minute, I want to check to see there's no damage to the pram,' she said, pulling the pram from me.

Fortunately, the pram had come through unscathed. Ma pulled it inside the hall. I was about to follow, when Ma blocked my way.

'Go round the back, you know you don't use this door.' She pushed me away and shut the door in my face.

I stared at the closed door, unable to believe she would do that. The door had been open, and yet Ma still made me go all the way around to the back. It was not as if it was just down the side of the house. We were the end house of a block of nine. The only way to get to the back door was to go to the end of the of the nine houses and up the back alley. I noticed the boys who had been taunting us were still hanging around.

Discretion being the better part of valour, I decided to wait until the coast was clear, and sat on the front step. By luck, one of the Raymond brothers from next door looked out the living room window, and I managed to catch his eye. Climbing over the dividing wall, I indicated to him to open the door.

'What do you want?' he asked.

'Can I come in?'

'No, I'm not allowed to let anyone in.'

'I want to go to the toilet.'

'Why can't you use your own?'

'There's no one in.'

The voice of his foster parent asked who it was, and told him to let me in. I dashed upstairs to the bathroom, thankful her husband was not at home. He had been wounded in the war, and had a steel plate in his head. It sometimes gave him great pain, and caused him to behave differently. During those times he often beat his wife and the two evacuees under his care.

'Hello Billy, how are you?' his wife asked, when I entered the living room.

I told her about collecting my brother, and how I had to get a man to lift him into the pram.

'My goodness. You mean to tell me you had to get your brother from the hospital in a pram on your own. That's disgraceful.'

I nodded, ever the martyr. A quick look around the living room confirmed she wouldn't be offering me any little treats to ease my troubles, so I excused myself and left by the back door.

I climbed the dividing wall and dropped into our backyard. Aunt Gladys was hanging out the washing and looked at me in amazement as I landed at her feet.

'Why didn't you use the gate, it's easier?' she asked.

'No reason. Just thought I would come over the wall.'

She gave me a puzzled look as I followed her into the house. My brother was sitting at the end of the Morrison table with his feet up on a chair. He gave me a smug smile, enjoying being the centre of attention.

His moment of glory didn't last long. His ankles soon healed, and within days he was being treated just like the rest of us.

Chapter Twenty-Four

Given the number of people living in our house, the only place to get any privacy where you could truly be alone, was in the lavatory in the back yard. In the winter it was freezing, so I didn't stay long. But in the summer, I would sit until someone else, whose need was greater than mine, knocked the door.

So, one summer evening, I was sitting there with my trousers around my ankles examining a needle valve. I had removed it from one of the many street gas lamps around the town. It was about four inches in length, with a knurled knob on one end, and a point on the other. They were easy to come by. All I had to do was shin up a lamppost to where the pilot flame should have been burning, unscrew the valve, and 'voila', a handy little brass tool. Due to the blackout, the street lamps were not turned on, so the needle valves were never missed. At least not until the war was over and they tried putting the street lighting back on.

After examining it, I looked for something to do with it. The squares of newspaper we used, toilet paper not being available, caught my eye. Ripping one off, I stabbed it full of holes.

That was fun, but I needed something else. The fresh distemper on the toilet walls offered a perfect canvas for my creativity. So, before I knew it, I had scratched a short vertical line. I immediately regretted it. If I had had any sense, I would have left it. But I tried rubbing it off with a wet finger. It made it worse. All I had managed to do was make a dirty mark, my fingers being in their usual grubby state. Even then I should have left it, and hoped it wouldn't be noticed. But I couldn't resist adding two more lines, which formed the letter 'F'. Now, you would have thought I would have stopped there, but I was on a roll. Moments later, I had scratched the letter 'G' alongside it, my brother's initials.

I thought no more of it until the next day when I came home from school. There, in the living room, sat the three adults of the household. Pop, the prosecuting lawyer and judge. Ma, his assistant prosecutor, and Glady's, the clerk of the court. Seated on the living room floor, waiting patiently for me to arrive, the rest of the kids, the accused.

Pop took the floor. Standing in front of the fireplace, he glared at all of us as he outlined the crime.

'I have only just whitewashed the outside toilet,' he said. 'And today, I discovered that someone has scratched their initials on the wall. So, they could only have been put there last night.'

'What initials are they?' someone asked.

'The initials are F.G.'

Everybody thought for a while, before somebody suggested that it must be 'Frankie Green'.

'Yeah, well it was not me' shouted my brother, jumping to his feet and looking threateningly at the seated throng of faces.

'Alright, alright,' said Pop. 'Sit down. Nobody said it was you. In fact it would be rather stupid to scratch your own initials. No, I think this is the hand of someone else.' I didn't like the sound of that, so kept my head down.

Pop then asked if anybody had noticed the initials when they used the toilet. Somebody asked if he meant going to the toilet to do a number one, or a number two.

'One or two, it doesn't matter,' he said, irritably.

Nobody remembered whether the initials were there or not, and before long everybody but me was talking.

'Be quiet,' Pop shouted. 'So, you all deny doing it?'

'Did you expect anything else?' Ma said.

'O K, Ma, we'll do it your way,' said Pop.

Aunt Gladys moved amongst us handing each of us a piece of paper.

'Right,' she said. 'Everybody write the initials 'FG' on one side of the paper, and your name on the other.'

Everybody immediately obliged, except me. I knew I had printed the initials, so tried to write them differently. Problem was, my 'joined up writing' was not that good.

'Is this how you normally write?' asked Aunt Gladys when she collected my piece of paper.

'Yes,' I nodded.

'Are you sure?'

'Let me see,' said my brother, 'I'll soon tell you.' She showed him the paper.

'That's not how you write. You always print.' Before I had time to argue she told me to write the initials again, adding.

'This time do it in your usual print. And, just to make sure I will watch you.'

I looked daggers at my brother as Aunt Gladys took my piece of paper. I was 'hoping against hope' that I had made them sufficiently different from what I had written in the toilet.

When everybody was finished, we watched through the living room window as Pop and Ma compared each piece of paper with the initials on the toilet wall.

'Right, we now know who did it,' said Pop, when they returned. The 'super sleuths' had solved the crime of the century.

'However, before I say who it is, I am going to give that person the chance to own up.'

He slowly surveyed the sea of faces looking up at him, whilst Ma gave the game away by looking at me. To avoid her stare, I looked at the floor.

He doesn't really know it was me I thought. *If he did, he would have come straight out and said. He's trying to scare me into admitting it.* I remained silent.

'Right, you have had your chance to admit it, but as usual you do it hard way... don't you Billy?'

Pop grabbed my arm, dragged me to my feet, hauled me outside, and threw me into the toilet.

'This is your piece of paper, and those are the initials you wrote,' he said, showing me my name on the back of the paper. He then held the piece of paper under the initials on the toilet wall.

'They are exactly the same, so it must have been you… are you still going to tell me that you know nothing about those initials?'

I had printed the initials on the paper exactly as I had on the wall. It was the only way I knew how to write. Faced with the inevitable, I knew I could hold out no longer.

'Yes Pop, it was me, but I'm sorry, really I am. I don't know what made me do it, I promise I won't do it again, really, I promise.' I was terrified, and my voice showed it.

'Shut up you little liar, I have had enough of you being sorry. Ma, bring me the strop. This boy needs to be taught a lesson.' Ma scurried off to get the strop.

'This is not for scratching those initials on the wall, but because you lied,' he said. Ma handed him the strop.

He dragged me out of the toilet and into the yard, so he could get a good swing at me. Bringing the strop down, he caught me on my bare legs. I skipped and struggled as I tried to break from his grasp. The second blow caught me across the back, which was not so painful. He readied himself to deliver the next blow, but I'd managed to get behind him. When he turned, so did I, and it looked like we'd invented a new dance.

'Ma, grab him,' he yelled. She grabbed me just as he brought the strop down, missing me and catching her across the arm.

'Ouch that was me you hit you fool,' she yelled, giving him a push and distracting him long enough for me to break free. Like a whippet, I ran for the back gate, expecting at any moment to feel the strop on my back. Throwing the gate open, I ran across the short space and dived between the car and the wall. The car was parked in the corner of the alley. It was covered with tarpaulin, grease, and barbed wire. It was the focal point for us kids, as it waited for its owner to return from the war.

From the safety of the car, I looked to where Pop was standing at the gate. But instead of coming over like I expected, he just closed the back gate and went inside.

I hung around in the alley until the other kids came out. They told me Pop had gone to work. As I had had nothing to eat, I decided to risk going into the house.

'Don't know what you're looking for, there's nothing for liars in this house,' Ma said.

I left the house and called on a couple of my friends, hoping to mooch something to eat from them. I was still unfed when I went to bed that night and lay awake until I heard Pop come in. I nervously listened to him coming down the passage. He entered the living room, and I moved as far away as I could from the edge of the Morrison table. Only when I heard him go upstairs did I relax and finally fall asleep.

The next morning, I polished off my breakfast porridge and hungrily looked around for more. There was none, so I spent the whole morning thinking about my school dinner. Being hungry certainly distracted you from any learning.

When I got home from school, Pop was waiting. I was ready to make a run for it, when he said,

'Follow me.' I followed him outside, ever wary as he opened the door to the toilet.

'There. Now I want it to stay that way. No more initials. Right.' He had again white-washed the toilet.

Chapter Twenty-Five

When I was eight years old, I was told that I had to make my first Holy Communion. I hadn't a clue what was expected of me, and hoped I could avoid the ordeal as I was no longer going to a Catholic school. No such luck. Ma knew I had to go and made sure I went.

During the lead up to my communion, I was told I would have to make my first confession, and the priest would ask me what sins I had committed. Two or more seemed to be the 'norm'.

I thought about all the things that I classed as a sin, but for the life of me couldn't think of anything; at least not anything I would want to tell the priest. I asked some of the other boys what they were going to say, in the hope I could use one of theirs. I also wondered how recent the sins had to be. If a sin was a few years old, did it still count, or must it be a recent sin.

Come the big day, I dressed in my best clothes. My dad had sent me a three-piece-suit; jacket, waistcoat, and short trousers. Because Raymond was the same size as me, Ma dressed him in it. In fact, he wore it more often than I did. But as it was a special occasion, Ma graciously allowed me to wear it. I didn't have a new shirt or tie, and my shoes and socks were a bit tatty, but I felt I was dressed well enough for the occasion.

There was already a number of children making their first confession when I arrived at the church. I sat at the end of the row, so that I could be the last. There were three cubicles. The priest sat in the middle one, and the 'sinners' took it in turns entering the other two. As I edged closer to the cubicles, I became more and more nervous. I hoped the priest would get called away and I would be spared.

I still was not sure what I was going to say as I entered the confessional. One of the adults told me I was to pray for forgiveness while I waited for the priest to hear my sins. I was not sure how to do that, so just sat there.

Alone in the semi-gloom, I began worrying that if I made something up, God would know and smite me for lying. But I couldn't say I didn't have any sins, as I'd been told everybody had sins. I decided to confess to stealing cakes and scratching my brother's initials in the lavatory. I hoped the priest wouldn't mind me saying lavatory in the confession box.

Suddenly, the flap opened, and I could just make out the outline of the priest. *If I can see him,* I thought, *he can see me,* and I had been told the priest didn't know who he was talking to.

Nervously I tried to remember what I was supposed to say.

'Go ahead,' said the priest.

'Umm... Bless me father for I have sinned. Umm... This is my first confession.'

'Yes my child, what do you want to confess?'

'Umm... I stole cakes from the cake shop...'

'Yes, anything else?'

'Umm... I wrote my brother's initials on the lavatory wall.'

'Yes, anything else?'

'No father.'

He mumbled away for a while before saying. 'Your sins are forgiven.'

He gave me a penance, which I didn't really understand. When I left the confessional, several other children were busy mumbling away, so I knew I was not the only sinner. Had they not been there, I would have walked out, but instead sat down and joined in the mumblings.

It was a very harrowing experience for me, and did nothing to enamour me to the Catholic religion.

Chapter Twenty-Six

By 1944, a lot of parents had taken their children back home, believing the worst was over. Brian and George had already gone, which just left the other six evacuees, plus Raymond and Alan; Aunt Gladys's latest addition. Alan was only a few months old, having been fathered by Walter, her husband, during his leave.

Pop decided it was now safe to move a couple of us out of the Morrison Shelter to the upstairs bedroom. It was nice to have a proper bedroom where I could get out of the way, although I didn't like sharing a single bed with my brother. John and Kevin shared the other single bed in the room.

Now that only two boys were sleeping in the Morrison Shelter, it became a handy storage space for boxes and stuff.

One evening, I finished my tea of bread and margarine. Glancing under the table as I silently waited to be given permission to leave the table, I noticed a cardboard box which I hadn't seen before. I decided to check it out.

Ma and Pop always sat at the head of the table surveying us, so it was not going to be easy. Keeping my hands on the table where they could see them, I drooped my eyelids, so they couldn't see my eyes. Looking down in what little light there was under the table, I manipulated the box closer. Easing the lid off with my feet, I could just make out the words, 'Mars'. I had never heard of Mars, but instinctively knew it had to be chocolate. I couldn't remember the last time, if ever, I had tasted a piece of chocolate.

Stretching out my leg, I nudged my brother under the table and indicated the box with my eyes. He gave it a cursory look, and looked away. Worried the excitement on my face would give me away, I placed my hand over my mouth whilst I pondered how I could steal one. Now I knew they were there, I couldn't rest until I had one.

'All right, you can leave the table,' Ma said.

In the ensuing kerfuffle, I seized my chance. Quickly ducking down, I grabbed a bar, slipped it into my pocket, and replaced the lid on the box. Anxious to get out as quickly as possible, but not wanting to attract attention, I slowly eased myself towards the door. Keeping my hand in my pocket, I clutched the Mars Bar. I always had holes in my pockets and couldn't risk my ill-gotten treat falling to the floor.

'What have you been up to?' Pop suddenly asked, as I passed his chair. My heart skipped a beat and I thought he had seen me.

'Nothing Pop,' I stammered.

'Right, I've got my eye on you, so behave yourself, do you hear?'

'Yes Pop.'

I left the house and headed for the back alley, resisting the temptation to look back. Desperate to enjoy my spoils, I slowly wandered off on my own.

'Hey Billy, where are you going?' someone shouted.

'Nowhere,' I replied, annoyed that he had drawn attention to me.

Joining the rest of the group, I patiently waited as we set up a game. As usual it was a war game between the British and the Germans. Normally, I didn't want to be a German as we always structured the game so the British won. However, on this occasion, I became a German, so I could run away and hide. Grabbing my gun, or at least the piece of wood that served as my gun, from under the car, I ran up the alley, jumped into one of the front gardens, and crouched behind the hedge.

Using my grubby sleeve, I wiped the dribbles from my chin as I fondled the 'Mars' bar. I had never had a whole 'Mars' bar before. In fact, I had never had a whole bar of anything before.

Slowly ripping the wrapper away, I gave the beautifully textured chocolate a tentative lick, allowing the sweet taste to tease my taste buds. Suddenly, a body leapt the low hedge and landed in the garden. I quickly pocketed the bar.

'Where's the Mars bar?' asked my brother.

'Mars bar, what Mars bar?' I replied.

'The one you just put in your pocket. Don't try to kid me, I've been watching you. I knew you couldn't resist taking one, so when I saw you sneaking away I followed.'

Annoyed that I would have to share it with him, or at least give him a bite, I slowly removed the bar from my pocket.

'Give us a bite then,' he said.

'Okay, but promise you won't tell anyone.' Clasping my fingers tightly around the bar, I held it near his mouth.

'Let me hold it,' he said, trying to wrest it from my hand.

'No, you'll take too big a bite.' I also didn't trust him to give me the bar back.

He took as big a bite as he could, almost biting my finger, before I pulled the bar away.

'That's it, that's all you're getting.'

I considered saving some for later. But after taking a bite myself, there was not much left. I decided to finish the bar. I was about to pop the last piece into my mouth, when I spotted the pathetic look on my brother's face. Biting it in two, I reluctantly handed him half.

Now that my little delicacy was gone, so was my brother. Quickly jumping over the hedge, he left me staring at the empty wrapper. Little did I realise just how much trouble my stolen moment of bliss would cause me.

It was almost dark by the time Pop came to tell us to get in. Ma had told us many times, that as soon as it got dark we were to go in. But if Pop was working, we would push our luck, often getting in just minutes before he came home. However, on this particular night, he caught us out by coming home early.

As soon as we spotted him, we moved towards the house. The alley was quite narrow, so we had to pass him. Suddenly, without warning, he lashed out with the razor strop he had hidden behind his back.

'Get inside the lot of you,' he shouted. One of the boys ignored him, so he raised the strop, only stopping when the boy shouted, 'I don't live with you.'

Meanwhile the rest of us scattered, running for the house whilst hoping to get upstairs and into bed before he got back in. But as we entered the house, Ma and Aunt Gladys were waiting.

'Sit down,' Ma ordered, directing us to sit on the floor.

Whenever this happened, we all knew something was up. Suddenly, the memory of the Mars bar came flooding back. I moved to the farthest corner of the room, putting as much space as possible between Pop and me.

When he came in, he asked Ma if that was all of us. He told her that he had nearly rounded up a boy who didn't live with us. 'Well, they all look the same to me,' he said.

He took his usual stance in front of the fireplace, legs spread, hands behind his back, and the razor strop visible between his knees.

'Tonight,' he said, pausing for effect. 'Somebody took something that doesn't belong to them. That person knows who it is and so do I. So, they'd better own up and make it easier for us all.'

He looked menacingly at all the wide eyed faces seated on the floor looking up at him. This was Pop's standard scare tactic. Give the impression that he knows who it is so they will own up. Owning up was supposed to lessen the severity of the punishment. I had never owned up and was sure it made no difference. One thing I did know. Owning up would result in a leathering with the razor strop, and I was in no rush to make its acquaintance again. When it was obvious nobody was going to own up, Ma broke the silence.

'This is not getting us anywhere. You had better tell them what it's all about,' she said.

Pop took down a brown cardboard box from the shelf at the side of the fireplace, and held it up for all to see.

I remained motionless, a blank expression on my face as I looked at the box from which I had stolen a Mars bar a couple of hours earlier.

'This box was under the table and contained several Mars bars.'

He removed the lid and held the box so we could see the remaining bars inside.

'Wow Mars,' someone said. Pop ignored them.

'There were six Mars bars in this box when Aunt Gladys placed it under the table this afternoon.' Aunt Gladys nodded in agreement.

'Now there are only five. Someone knows something about it.' He replaced the box on the shelf and glared at all of us.

'Right Ma, let's do it your way.'

'Right,' ordered Ma. 'All of you go and sit where you were sitting at tea time.' I sat in a different chair.

'That's where I was sitting,' John whined. 'I always sit there.'

It was an unnecessary exercise. Ma knew where we all sat, as we always sat in the same place for each meal.

'Billy, that was not where you were sitting. Move yourself,' she ordered.

I grudgingly moved, knowing there was no point in arguing. Pop ceremoniously handed the box to Aunt Gladys.

'Place the box under the table where it was at tea time,' he directed. All eyes were on her as she placed the box under the table.

'Well it's quite obvious who took it,' said Ma, looking straight at me. Aunt Gladys had placed the box right in front of me.

'But, just to be sure, let's see if anyone else can reach it.' A couple of boys reached out, but were well short of the box.

'Right Billy, your turn.' I stretched out my hand.

'You can reach farther than that,' said Ma.

'No, that's as far as I can reach, unless I duck under the table. And if I had done that you would have seen me.'

'This has gone on long enough,' said Pop. 'It could only have been you. It's getting late, so for the last time, did you take the Mars.'

I was about to say 'yes', when my eye fell on the razor strop dangling from his hand, the memories of my last acquaintance with it still fresh in my mind.

'No Pop, I didn't.'

He returned to his position in front of the fireplace, and I began thinking I might just have got away with it. Keeping my eyes averted for fear of giving myself away, I thought, *Surely, he will send us all to bed and that will be the end of it.* After what seemed an eternity, he finally said.

'Well, we will just have to go to the police.' Ma nodded in agreement.

Those words struck panic in me. There for one moment I thought I had got away with it, and now he was going to the police. It was all I could do to stop from blurting out the truth.

'Billy.' I jumped, as if he could read my thoughts.

'Yes Pop,' I nervously answered.

'You were the only one who could have taken it. Your fingerprints will be on the box. Aunt Gladys will take you to the police station tomorrow when you come in from school. They can check the box for fingerprints, and then we will know. So, for the last time, did you take the Mars?' I had denied it too many times to change my mind now.

'No Pop.' I replied.

'Right, get to bed all of you.' We all quickly scattered up the stairs to our respective beds.

'Why didn't you tell him it was you, now you are going to the police station,' said my brother, as we lay in bed.

'Yeah it's alright for you to say, but I would be the one to get a walloping with the strop. And anyway, you are also to blame, you ate some of it too.'

'Shush,' he said, cutting me off.

Someone was outside the door listening. We both lay there in the dark hardly daring to breathe, our every sense straining for a sound. Just when it seemed he'd been hearing things, the floorboards gently creaked and whoever it was silently retreated down the stairs.

Confident that no one was listening, I told him I didn't really think that they would take me to the police, and had only said they would to scare me into confessing. He agreed. With that thought, I fell asleep.

When I awoke the next morning I had already forgotten about the incident, but was quickly reminded at breakfast by Ma.

'Why don't you own up and be done with it? If the police find your fingerprints on the box you will go to jail,' she said.

Everyone looked in my direction. I left the house without saying anything and headed for school. Within minutes of meeting my friends, I forgot all about Mars bars and police stations.

Only when I approached the back gate that afternoon did I give any thought to the events of the previous evening. I entered the house still hopeful it would have been forgotten. To my dismay, Aunt Gladys was waiting for me.

'Right, let's get this over with,' she said, picking up the shopping bag containing the cardboard box.

Again it was on the tip of my tongue to own up, but I still thought they were bluffing and wouldn't go through with it.

'This is your last chance,' said Ma, eyeing me from her favourite armchair. I remained silent.

'Right, let's go,' said Aunt Gladys.

All the kids from our house were already playing in the street. They stopped what they were doing as we passed. The look on my brother's face left me in no doubt that he was pleading with me not to involve him.

As we walked, Aunt Gladys questioned me about the Mars. I continued denying I had taken it, still convinced it was all a ploy to get me to own up. Finally, we reached the police station and paused before entering.

'This is your last chance,' Aunt Gladys said. 'Once we go in, there will be no turning back. If they find your fingerprints on the box, you could go to jail. Are you absolutely sure you didn't steal the Mars?'

The tone of her voice suggested she felt silly going to the police for such a trivial matter, and was imploring me to admit it. I again denied it, convinced she would turn around and go home.

To my surprise she called my bluff. Opening the door to the police station she entered, beckoning me to follow. Only now did I finally accept that she was going to go through with it. Sighting the policeman behind the desk, I grabbed her arm and pulled her back.

'All right, all right, I took it, it was me.' I blurted.

'Can I help you?' asked the policeman, looking up from behind the desk.

'No, I think we have solved our problem,' said a very relieved Aunt Gladys.

'Why did it take you so long to own up? You could have avoided all this trouble?' she asked, when we were outside.

'I was too scared of what Pop would do,' I mumbled.

She took the cardboard box from the shopping bag and told me to take it home.

As I headed home, I desperately tried to think of something that might justify my actions. But no matter what way my mind worked, I couldn't think of anything. I had stolen the Mars, and that was that. I resigned myself to getting a thrashing with the strop. I remembered what Pop had said when I scratched the initials on the lavatory wall. It was not what I had done, but because I lied.

Entering the backyard, I saw a movement behind the curtain of the living room window and hoped it was not Pop. *Please don't let it be Pop*, I thought. *Ma I can handle, but not Pop.*

I steeled myself before entering the living room. Ma was seated in Pop's armchair facing the scullery door, her arms folded across her ample bosom. I knew if she was in Pop's chair, he was out. I relaxed, and placed the box on the table.

'Well, what happened?' she asked. I told her what happened.

'I knew it. I said all along that it was you.' She made a satisfied noise with her mouth, a look of triumph on her face.

'Why didn't you admit it in the first place and save all this trouble?'

It was at that moment that I suddenly had a flash of inspiration. For the life of me, I have no idea why, I found myself saying.

'Because I didn't take the Mars bar.'

'What do you mean, you didn't take the Mars bar? You have just owned up to it.'

'I know, but that's because I was frightened of the police and didn't want to go to jail.'

'So, now you are saying you didn't take it?'

'Yes.'

'I don't believe you.' she screeched. 'You took it, and you know you did, so stop lying. I am not going through all this again.' She was so livid, she almost choked on her words.

My last statement had thrown her. One minute she was relishing the thought of being right, and now her moment of glory had been shattered.

'Get out, get out. I'll let Pop deal with you when he gets in,' she shouted.

Alone in the alley, I considered the situation. *Pop was at work in the pub and would have been drinking; which didn't bode well for me. Therefore, the longer I can avoid him the better. If I am in bed when he comes home, I can avoid any punishment until morning. He won't want to give me a leathering before I go to school; so with any luck I can avoid him until the evening, by which time he will have had time to cool down.*

I drew comfort from my thoughts, as I joined the others. A couple of hours later, we were called in. For a change, I was the first in. I wanted to be well out of the way by the time Pop arrived home.

I was heading for the safety of the upstairs bedroom, when Aunt Gladys grabbed me.

'What's this I hear about you saying that you didn't take the Mars after all?'

'That's right. I only admitted taking it because I was scared and didn't want to go to jail.'

'Well, we will see what Pop has to say when he comes in.'

Wriggling free, I headed upstairs and jumped into bed. I normally slept on the inside next to the wall. Tonight, I was extra grateful, as my brother would form a buffer if Pop came looking for me. John and Kevin slept in the other single bed, which was behind the door.

As soon as we had settled down, my brother asked me what had happened at the police station. He listened quietly until I had finished.

'You shouldn't have admitted it. They would never have known, they would never have got your fingerprints off that box.'

Below, came the sound of the front door being opened, and I knew Pop had arrived home. I heard him walk slowly down the hall, pause to hang his coat, and enter the living room.

I climbed out of bed and listened at the head of the stairs. The sounds suggested that they were about to enjoy their usual evening drink. Unable to hear exactly what they were saying, I crept down the stairs and listened outside the living room door. Ma was telling Pop about the events leading up to my denial of taking the Mars. Suddenly, Pop raised his voice.

'Right, I am finishing this now, once and for all. I have had enough of this nonsense. When I have finished with him, he will wish he had not been born.'

'Don't be too hard on him Pop, I am sure he is sorry,' Aunt Gladys said.

'Sorry, I'll give him sorry.'

His voice became louder, and I realised he was coming towards the door. I took the stairs two at a time, closed the bedroom door, and jumped into bed.

'What's going on?' asked Frankie.

'Pop's coming, don't let him get me, I'm sure he's got the razor strop,' I frantically yelled, cowering behind him.

Suddenly the bedroom door was flung open crashing against John and Kevin's bed behind the door. I nervously peeped over my brother's shoulder and saw Pop silhouetted in the light from the landing, razor strop swinging in his hand.

There was no light in our room, and Pop had no idea which beds we slept in. He approached the bed behind the door. When John saw him, he yelled.

'He's in that bed over there.'

I ducked beneath the bedclothes, making myself as small as I could.

Pop brought the strop down on what he thought was me, but struck my brother across his back. Frankie yelled and jumped out of bed, dragging the bedclothes with him.

Without the protection of the bedclothes, I was fully exposed. Screaming in terror I pushed myself hard against the wall as I heard the 'swish' of the strop. It caught me on my legs as I tried to curl up smaller. The strop came down again, this time catching me across my back.

'No Pop, no, I'm sorry, I'm sorry, don't hit me again please,' I yelled.

Again the strop came down, this time catching me across my buttock as Pop yelled.

'I'll teach you to lie to me.'

I was pushing myself so hard against the wall, the bed moved, allowing me to wriggle through the gap and roll under the bed.

Pop bent down as best he could, given his fat stomach, lashing out with the strop under the bed. I was able to see the blows coming, and rolled out of the way.

'Come out,' he yelled.

When I remained where I was, he became infuriated and dragged the bed away from the wall. But as he moved the bed, I moved with it.

Grasping the bed with one hand, he tried to turn it on its side. It twisted out of his grip and fell noisily back on the bedroom floor. Furiously throwing the strop down, he grabbed the bed with both hands, turned it onto its side, and hauled me to my feet.

'Hand me the strop,' he shouted to my brother.

'I don't know where it is,' said Frankie. Pop flung me into the corner, trapping me between the bed and the open door.

'Stay there and don't move,' he shouted, looking about him.

'There it is, get it,' he said, spotting the strop under the other bed where my brother had kicked it.

Seeing he was distracted, I made a run for it. I was halfway over the upturned bed, when Pop snatched the strop from my brother and aimed a blow at me. I ducked, lost my balance, and fell to the floor.

I was on my feet in a trice. He aimed another blow at me as I dashed out the door, only to meet Aunt Gladys and Ma coming upstairs. Seconds later, Pop stepped into the light of the landing, his face flushed and livid. I let out a yell, and ducked behind Aunt Gladys.

'Out of the way,' Pop yelled, pushing her to one side.

'That's enough Pop,' said Ma.

'I haven't finished with him yet,' he shouted, making a grab for me.

'I said, that's enough,' repeated Ma.

Ma very rarely questioned Pop, but he knew by her tone she meant it. He stopped and leaned on the banister, the sound of his heavy breathing in rhythm with my sobbing.

Pop's breathing slowly returned to normal, and he glanced at the strop as if seeing it for the first time. Without speaking, he went back into the bedroom, righted the bed, and pushed it against the wall. Hiding behind Aunt Gladys' skirt, I watched him slowly descend the stairs and enter the living room.

Gladys and Ma straightened our room. Back in bed, I faced the wall, the bed clothes aggravating the welts on my legs. My brother empathized with me by saying the blow he had received on his back was also sore.

By morning, my legs had stiffened. I ran the flannel under the cold tap, wiped my face, and gently laid it on my legs. One of the other boys came into the bathroom and watched me. I thought he was going to ask me if my legs were alright, but all he said was. 'Hurry up with the flannel, I want to use it.' I threw the flannel on the floor, and walked out.

Downstairs, I picked up a plate, and took it to the fireplace where Aunt Gladys was serving the porridge. Avoiding eye contact, I held my plate out.

'Thank you,' she said, as I headed for the table. I had not said, 'thank you.'

'Thank you Aunt Gladys,' I replied.

The porridge I received each morning was never enough to fill my empty belly, and I always hoped there may be second helpings. But the sight of Aunt Gladys taking the empty porridge pot to the scullery quickly dispelled any hopes of that.

Leaving the table, I limped towards the scullery to return my empty plate, instinctively veering away from the razor strop hanging at the side of the fireplace. Ma followed my glance.

'I hope you've learned your lesson,' she said. I didn't really want to talk to her, but knew better than to ignore her.

'Yes Ma,' I muttered.

I left the house and headed for school, the cold wind stinging the welts on my bare legs. During the day, one of the teachers asked what happened to my legs. I told her that a boy had accidently hit me with a stick during a game. I don't think she believed me, but she didn't pursue it.

When I got home that afternoon, Pop was standing looking in the mirror above the fire. As he sighted me, he reached for the handle of the razor strop. I stopped dead in my tracks, fearing the worst. Glancing at me in the mirror, he slowly stropped his razor.

Keeping one eye on him, I furtively crossed the room and crept up the stairs to my bedroom. The incident was never mentioned again.

Chapter Twenty-Seven

During the five years my brother and I were evacuated, my dad visited just three times. So, when we were told our parents were visiting, I could hardly contain my excitement as we set off to the station to meet them. I was looking forward to seeing my mum as I had not seen her since she waved goodbye when we were first evacuated. I had no memories of her, and couldn't even remember what she looked like. My brother said not to worry, because he would recognise her.

We were far too early for their train. Despite being dressed in our 'Sunday Best' clothes, we passed the time rummaging around in the nearby rubbish dump.

Most of the passengers had alighted from the train before my brother said, 'There they are.' I recognised my dad, but was unsure about the woman with him.

'Is that my mum?' I asked.

'Of course not, it's nothing like her,' replied my brother, leaving me puzzled as to why my dad was with another woman and not my mum.

They came through the ticket barrier, and we both ran over to greet my dad. Never one to show much affection, he 'uncomfortably' hugged us for a few seconds. The woman remained in the background until he called her over.

'This is your 'new mum',' he said.

She was wearing a hat with a net veil, so it was not possible to see her face properly. Not being sure what I was supposed to do, I just stood there.

'Well, aren't you going to say hello?' asked my dad.

My brother and I mumbled 'hello', followed an awkward silence when we all just looked at each other.

'You must be Frankie,' she finally said, giving my brother a hug and kissing him through her veil.

'And you must be Billy,' she said, putting her arms around me and flattening my face against her stomach. Her perfume smelled lovely, and when she bent to kiss me I was able to see she had beautiful blue eyes.

'Well, that didn't go too well,' she remarked to my dad.

'It's early days yet, they'll get used to you,' he assured her.

On the way home, both Frankie and I vied for my dad's attention. I had so many things I wanted to say to him, becoming annoyed when my brother kept interrupting.

Gladys, our 'new mum', followed some distance behind. When my dad called her to join us, she said it was alright, as we obviously had lots to say to each other.

We arrived at the front door of the house, Ma greeted us, and beckoned to us to enter; a rare privilege for Frankie and me. Both Ma and Pop were surprised when they were introduced to Gladys. They had obviously been expecting to meet my mother.

Ma fussed over them, serving tea in the dining room. I don't think she was too comfortable with us sitting on of her good dining chairs, normally out of bounds to the evacuees. Once we were seated, my 'new mum' lifted her veil, and I was able to see her face clearly for the first time. She was an attractive woman, blonde, with blue eyes. Although I didn't know what it meant at the time, Pop commented that my dad was 'punching above his weight' when he got her.

After tea, my 'new mother' surprised me by saying she had a present for me. Although it was just what I needed, I was disappointed when I saw it was an overcoat. I would have preferred a toy car, or something useful.

I put the coat on, and self-consciously presented myself to her for inspection. She adjusted the coat, before pushing me to arm's length to get a better look.

'I was right. I told your dad it would fit. He thought it would be too small.'

After tea, we posed with our 'new mum' whilst my dad took our photo. Ma remarked that if she had known we would be getting our picture taken, she would have dressed us better. That was for the benefit of my dad, as there was nothing else I could have worn. My only other 'decent' clothes were my three-piece suit; which Raymond was wearing that day.

'Isn't that the suit I sent you?' my dad asked, when he spotted Raymond. I nodded, thinking he might say something to Ma and I would get my suit back. He didn't, so Raymond continued to get more wear out of it than I did.

A few hours later, we walked back to the railway station. Their train to London was already standing at the platform. My 'new mum' kissed us both goodbye and boarded the train, leaving my dad to say his goodbyes. I wanted to go with him to the train, and asked him to get me a platform ticket, which cost a penny.

'What do you want one of those for?' he said. 'We can say our goodbyes here. Anyway, the train will be pulling out soon.'

I foolishly hoped he would give us some pocket money, but he just pecked us briefly on the cheek and said goodbye.

When he had boarded the train, my brother and I left the station and ran as fast as we could to the railway embankment by our house. A few minutes later, the train chugged by, and my dad was leaning out the window. We continued waving until the train was out of sight.

It had been an enjoyable day, but I was disappointed that I hadn't seen my mum. I wondered where she was, but didn't ask my dad. I mean, what the heck, my 'new mum' had brought me a new overcoat! I hoped I would get more wear out of it than my three-piece suit. Unfortunately, that was not to be.

Chapter Twenty-Eight

The railway which ran alongside our house was out of bounds. We ignored the signs, and often crossed the railway lines to Kings Lake. Four steel pipes, about four feet in diameter, ran across the lake to the refinery. When the tide came in, the pipes were under the water, but were high and dry when the tide was out. All us boys, desperate for something sensational in our lives, thought the pipes were there to stop German 'U' boats from landing. We lived in hope that one would appear and we could report it.

Despite the yells to 'get off' from the security man in the refinery, when the tide was low we often walked out onto the pipes. It was like a game of chicken, to see who could stay out there the longest as the tide came in and lapped over them.

One afternoon, my brother and I crossed the railway lines, and were idling around at the water's edge, when we came upon a small rowing boat chained to a stake.

The incoming tide had floated the boat, so we pulled it into the bank. There were no oars, but my brother had his 'Robin Hood' staff with him. Using it to punt the boat, we cast off. We only intended sailing a couple of yards off shore, but before we knew it the incoming tide carried us from the shore towards the steel pipes. Frankie's 'Robin Hood' staff was soon too short to be of any use, and I knew by the look on his face we were in trouble.

One of the security guards spotted us from the shore of the refinery and shouted at us to stay away. He obviously didn't realise we had no way of controlling the boat, and were at the mercy of the tide. The boat was soon travelling quite fast, as it headed for the far shore. The incoming tide had already submerged the pipes, so we just sailed over them. Then, just as quickly, the tide slackened and we were becalmed.

Moments later, the tide began going out, and with it our boat. Soon, we were heading towards the open sea.

Although I expected my brother to come up with a solution, I resisted the temptation to ask him what we were going to now, the look of desperation on his face saying it all. It was beginning to get dark, and the thought of being dragged out to sea in an open rowing boat too grim to contemplate. Kneeling in the front of the boat, I desperately looked every which way for a solution. Suddenly, there was a thump, and the boat came to an abrupt halt, throwing me head first into the bottom of the boat.

'That's a bit of luck,' said my brother. 'We're stuck on the pipes. All we have to do now is wait until the tide has gone out, and we can walk across the pipes.'

'What about the boat?' I asked.

'Stuff the boat, it's not ours.'

As the water slowly receded, the boat settled onto the pipes tilting it at a dangerous angle. I became worried it would slip from the pipes and dump us into the water before the pipes were clear enough for us to walk on. Then, to add to our problems, we heard shouting from the shore line.

'There's a man shouting at us,' I said.

'I know, I know, I can see him,' my brother said irritably.

'Do you think it's his boat?'

'How do I know?'

'I hope not, or we are in trouble,' I aimlessly stated.

The man stopped shouting and set off along the shore, by which time the pipes were nearly clear of the water.

'Let's go before he comes back,' said Frankie.

Slipping our shoes off, we nervously eased our way along the cold, wet, slippery pipe towards the shore. One slip, and it was into the freezing water, and I was not the best of swimmers.

We were making good progress, until a shout let us know the man had returned. He was carrying the oars for his boat. Keeping one eye on the man, and the other on the pipe, was proving tricky, as we tried to quicken our pace.

My brother reached the shore first, and immediately sprinted off. A few seconds later, I stepped ashore, by which time the man was waiting and made a grab for me. I ducked clear of his outstretched hand and took off after my brother, dropping one of my shoes. My brother, who was already at the top of the embankment, turned to see where I was.

'Leave it,' he yelled, seeing me pause to pick it up. Seconds later, I joined him at the top of the embankment and looked back to where the man was. Fortunately, he was more concerned with getting his boat back.

'I'll need to get my shoe,' I said, not wanting to explain to Ma how I had lost it. Not only that, they were the only shoes I had, so I would be housebound until some other shoes were found for me.

I began easing my way down the embankment. I was almost to where my shoe lay, when the man spotted me and immediately moved towards me. It became a race. Could I reach my shoe before he reached me. I was literally seconds in front of him. Picking up my shoe, I ducked clear of his outstretched arm, and took off up the embankment. He reluctantly made a bit of a gesture to give chase, but quickly gave up.

Frankie and I spent the rest of the evening listening for a knock at the door. None came. The next day, curious to find out what had happened to the boat, we cautiously revisited the shore. The boat was nowhere to be seen, so it had either been washed out to sea, or the man recovered it.

Chapter Twenty-Nine

On May 7th 1945, seven days after Hitler committed suicide, Germany formally surrendered to the Allied Forces and the war was over. It was just five days before my ninth birthday, so the full significance of the occasion passed me. What was more significant, was the widespread celebrations.

People took tables and chairs into the streets, and there were Union Jacks everywhere. I had never seen so much food. Many people brought out food they had been hoarding, in the belief that now the war was over rationing would end. It didn't, continuing for another nine years before ceasing in the first week of July 1954. The festivities went on for days. People sang, and danced, and talked about what would happen now the war was over.

There was such a widespread feeling of 'bonhomie', that we kids were able to roam from street to street mooching food and joining in the festivities.

Exmouth celebrated with military bands and servicemen marching through the streets, with a big parade in Phear Park. Hundreds attended, and I joined in by waving my Union Jack and cheering, because I had been told to. Prayers were said for those dearly departed, and the women cried.

Now that the war was finally over, parents from all over the country collected their children and took them home. Within days, the town became much quieter.

Tony's parents brought a suitcase with them when they came for him. I was impressed, as all I had ever seen clothes packed into was a cardboard box.

I didn't get a chance to say goodbye to John and Kevin. I came home one day, and they were gone, just like that, after all those years together.

Within days my friends the Irelands, of 'Daddies Sauce' fame, were also on their way. I went with them to the railway station. Their parents told me they were going to London and asked me where I would be going back to. I told them I didn't know.

Sadly, I waved goodbye to them as their train pulled out of Exmouth station, and that was the last I ever saw or heard of them.

Before long, it seemed my brother and I were the only evacuees left in the street. Our house, normally so full, was now quiet. For the first time in years, I had the luxury of a bed to myself. I could also spend more time in the toilet without someone knocking on the door. Also, bath nights were more enjoyable. Small pleasures, but much appreciated.

Apart from my brother and me, the only children left in the house were Raymond and Alan, who would be staying in Exmouth. With fewer children in the house, Ma and Pop became more tolerant. Even the food was more plentiful.

But going out to play was not the same. The back alley, which for so many years had been full of kids, was now deserted. I knocked on the doors of the houses that I had knocked on for years, only to be told that the kids had returned home to their parents.

The only boy still around was the boy with the three-wheeler bike. His mother didn't mind me riding his bike now, as I was the only one left for him to play with. He was not an evacuee, so was staying in Exmouth.

I longed for the time when the alley was alive with kids running and screaming, whilst playing war games. I suppose, strange as it seems, I was sad the war was over.

One fine sunny day, still not used to seeing the alley deserted, I aimlessly wandered over to the car and idly sat on the running board.

The car, which had stood for all the war years smeared with grease, and covered with a tarpaulin and barbed wire, had been a focal point for us kids, as it waited for its owner to return from the war.

My daydreaming was disturbed by the sound of footsteps. Looking up, I saw it was the woman, who for years had chased us kids off the car. I immediately retreated to a safe distance

She began removing the barbed wire and tarpaulin, or what was left of it after being pulled about by dozens of kids over the years. The grease, which had been smeared on the car to protect it from rusting, was now all but gone, most of it on our clothes.

She creaked open the driver's door. It was the first time I had seen the car without its cover, and I moved closer for a better look. She looked up, and I instinctively paused. To my surprise, she called me over and invited me to sit inside. The car had a musty smell after all the years of being closed up. I slid into the driver's seat, fascinated by all the dials and switches. A few moments later, she closed the car door, and went back into her house. I was sure there were tears in her eyes.

The next day, a tow truck arrived, and I sadly watched them take the car away. I followed it to the end of the alley and watched until the car was out of sight. I told Ma the car had gone, and she said that the man who owned it had been killed in the war, so his wife didn't want it around anymore.

Now that the car was gone, I was surprised at how much extra space there was. Squatting in the corner in the afternoon sunshine, I stared at the empty space, an oil spot and tyre marks the only reminders there had ever been a car there.

Over the years, all of us at some time or other had taken refuge behind it; not least the two Raymond brothers from next door. They were no longer around, having also returned to their parents, no doubt thankful to get away from the man with the steel plate in his head.

Alone with my thoughts, my mind went back to the time the Raymond brothers had come screaming out of their house, absolutely terrified, and dashed behind the car. Seconds later, the man with the steel plate in his head came rushing into the alley.

'Where are they?' he shouted, advancing towards a group of us.

We all backed away.

He had been wounded in the war, and had a steel plate fitted in his head. It sometimes caused him terrible headaches, during which time he would lose control and behave like a madman. Even in his quieter moments he could become difficult. He often wanted to play war games with us kids, but would play for real and hurt someone. On one occasion, he threw me down the railway embankment with such force I bounced a couple of times before hitting the bottom. From then on, I stayed well clear of him.

We all knew if he caught the boys they would be given a severe thrashing, so remained quiet. He gave us all a suspicious look, before slowly walking up the alley. Suddenly a voice called out.

'Behind the ca…ar.'

Quick as a flash, he squeezed himself between the car and the wall where the two boys were crouching. They screamed in terror, and ran down the alley. He soon outran them, and dragged them screaming into the house. The familiar yells of someone being beaten could be clearly heard by all of us. I think the beatings they received were worse than the ones Pop gave us.

Disgusted that anyone would do such a thing, we turned to the perpetrator. It was the Ireland brothers older sister. We all began chanting 'traitor', 'traitor'. She was unrepentant, and told us to shut up. Annoyed by her attitude, a couple of the boys began pushing her, but she was older than most of us and gave as good as she got.

Eventually, outnumbered, several boys grabbed her and wrestled her to the ground. During the scuffle, her light print dress rode up above her waist.

'Pull her knickers down,' someone shouted.

She put up a good struggle, but finally her knickers were pulled off. All the boys laughed and pointed between her legs, and for the first time in my life I saw a vagina.

When all the boys had had a look, she was let go. They then began throwing her knickers to one another. She tried to retrieve them, but the boys had her running in circles, continually lifting her dress and laughing at her nakedness.

One boy arrived late and asked what all the hilarity was about. When he was told, he said he also wanted a look. She was again wrestled to the ground, her legs pulled apart, and I saw a vagina for the second time.

Finally, tired of throwing her knickers around, the boys threw them into one of the back yards. She retrieved them, before stomping off yelling that she was telling. I don't know who she intended telling, but we heard nothing more, so she must have kept the incident to herself.

Now the alley was quiet. So quiet, I had taken to sitting on the front doorstep in the hope of spotting someone I knew.

So, one beautiful sunny Sunday afternoon, bored to distraction, I was sitting on the front doorstep of our house, sad that all my friends had returned home to their parents. The last time I had sat on the doorstep was when my dad visited and took our photo. I had not heard from him since.

Suddenly, there was a knock on the dining room window. Aunt Gladys was indicating to me to come into the house. I went to the front door thinking that now the war was over, she would open it. Moments later, still standing looking at the letter box, I got the message. The war may be over, but I still was not allowed through the front door. With no sense of urgency, I slowly wandered around to the back of the house. My brother was already there.

'What took you so long?' asked Gladys.

'Why, what's the rush?' I said.

'Never mind. Now pay attention. I want the two of you to go to the Italian café in town and get some ice cream. Here take this.' She handed me a pudding basin. I thought it was something to eat, but the bowl was empty.

'What's the bowl for?' I asked.

'To get the ice cream in.'

'Ice cream. What's ice cream?' I said, not being familiar with it.

'You'll find out. Now remember, hurry home, do you hear,' said Ma.

We set off with Frankie carrying the money and me carrying the basin. When we arrived at the shop, he made me stand in the queue, whilst he wandered around.

'Yes sonny,' said the man behind the counter.

'Some ice cream please,' I said, handing him the basin.

Moments later, he handed me back the dish, now covered with a piece of greaseproof paper and secured with an elastic band.

We left the shop, and headed home. I wanted to remove the paper and see what was in the basin, but worried I might not get the paper back on and Ma would know.

Holding the basin out in front of me as we hurried home, my arms soon ached. Calling to my brother, I asked him to take a turn.

'Aunt Gladys gave you the basin and me the money,' he said. 'So, you carry it.'

'It's not fair. I carried it all the way there. Now it's your turn. I'm not carrying it all the way back.' I thrust the basin at him.

He refused, holding his hands behind him and increasing my annoyance. Placing the basin on the pavement, I walked away.

'What are you doing? You can't just leave it there,' said my brother.

'Can for all I care,' I replied.

'You can't just leave it there, go back and get it.'

'No, it's your turn to carry it.' He grabbed hold of me and wrestled me back to the basin.

'Pick it up, go on pick it up,' he yelled.

'No, pick it up yourself,' I replied. Grabbing my hand, he forced it towards the basin.

'Pick it up,' he snarled, becoming angry.

'No, and you can't make me.'

'Yes I can,' he said, punching me in the ribs.

I kicked out at him, pulled my hand free, and ran off down the street. When I was some distance away, I stopped. Frankie, by now seething, picked up the basin and followed after me. When he got near, I ran off again.

'Billy, it's alright, I'll carry it,' he called. I ignored him.

'I'm going to get you for this,' he said, aiming a blow at me when we reached the house.

'What took you so long?' said Aunt Gladys. 'I told you to come straight home.'

'We did,' we lied.

'Oh look, it's completely melted,' she said, holding the basin for Ma to see. I moved into a position so I could see, and looked at something that resembled an off-white milky substance.

'Well it's obvious that they didn't come straight home,' said Ma, an exasperated look on her face.

'You can never do as your told, can you? This was supposed to be a treat for you two, but you've spoiled it again. Now you won't know what ice cream really tastes like and it's your own fault.'

Now I knew why Ma had told us to come straight home. I had not put much stock into her words, as she always said that when she sent us on an errand. Just as well she hadn't seen me leaving the basin on the pavement in the hot sun.

Aunt Gladys dished it out as best she could and handed me a saucer. I took a spoonful, and thought it tasted quite good. But I had never tasted ice cream before, so didn't know what to expect.

Chapter Thirty

September 1945, my school re-opened, and I took my seat in the classroom. I had said my goodbyes in June when the school closed for the summer holidays, expecting to be long gone by now.

A month later, just as I was getting back into my school work, we were told we were going home.

'Is my dad coming to collect us?' I asked.

'No, you and Frankie have to get the train to London yourselves,' Ma said.

We were not given much warning, not that we needed it. What few possessions we had were packed into a cardboard box, and secured with a length of rope.

The next day, I dressed in my best attire. I had outgrown my three-piece suit, so wore the only other clothes I had. Trousers, with a patch of a different material in the backside, a woollen pullover, and a jacket that was a bit on the small side. A pair of sandals, and a pair of well-darned socks, completed my ensemble. Now the winter was closing in, I wished I hadn't lost the overcoat my 'new mum' had brought me.

I hardly had any wear out of it, when I lost it in the park. I'd hung it on a tree so as not to get it torn or dirty. Someone obviously thought their need was greater than mine, and stole it. Despite racing around the park to see if I could see anyone with it, I had no luck. I thought Ma would tell me off, but to my surprise she was quite calm about it. Now that all the other kids had left, her attitude towards us had mellowed.

So, the day we were to leave arrived. I was excited, but given Ma and Pop's changed attitude to us over the last few months, was also a little sad. This had been our home for the last four years.

Finally, it was time to leave. Ma cuddled me into her ample bosom and gave me a kiss. I had seen her do it many times with her own grandson Raymond, but this was a first for me.

'Goodbye Billy, take care, I'll miss you. You're not such a bad lad after all.' She handed me a small brown paper parcel. 'Here, I've made you a sandwich,' she said.

'Thank you,' I replied, somewhat surprised. I was not expecting anything, but it was more than my parents gave me when we were evacuated.

Pop said goodbye and gave me a pat on the head. I glanced for the last time at the razor strop hanging in its usual position. He followed my eyes, a wry grin crossing his face.

Aunt Gladys was taking us to the station. I automatically moved towards the back door. She beckoned us to the front door.

Our train was already standing at the platform when we arrived. Aunt Gladys placed our box on the train, kissed us both on the cheek and stood on the platform. I leaned out the window and she gave me a hug.

'Now look what you've done, you've made me cry,' she said, dabbing her eyes.

Moments later, the train pulled out, and we waved until Aunt Gladys was out of sight. Minutes later we passed the house we had lived in for the last four years. Pop and Ma were in the backyard waving. Despite all the hardships, if I had known what I was going back to, I would have stayed in Exmouth.

Years later, my brother, who by then was in the army, found himself in Exmouth and popped in to visit Ma and Pop. They talked about old times with my brother saying we must have been a handful for them. Ma said for all that, she missed us when we left, and we were just, 'Angels with dirty faces.'

Within minutes of leaving Exmouth, I had eaten the sandwich Ma made me. It was supposed to last me until I reached London.

Passengers for Paddington change at Exeter, called the guard, as he walked through the train.

'Did you hear that?' I said to Frankie.

'Yes, but I already knew, he didn't need to tell me,' he replied, as if he was a seasoned traveller.

The guard gave us a hand to get our box off the train and pointed out the platform we needed.

'Wait here, I'll ask the porter what platform we need,' ordered my brother.

'He said that one over there,' I said, pointing in the direction.

'I want to make sure. You wait with the box,' he called, as he wandered off.

'So, what platform do we need,' I asked, when he came back.

'Grab hold of the box and I'll show you.'

We struggled down a set of stairs, through a tunnel, and up the stairs to the platform the guard had pointed out.

'This is the one the guard told us to go to,' I said.

'I know,' he replied, annoyed with me for pointing it out.

When the train for Paddington arrived, it was packed with sailors from Plymouth. One of them gave us a hand to get our box onto the train and placed it just inside the door, the only space available.

There were no seats, so I sat on the box. Every time the train stopped, I was in the way. No matter where I stood, someone needed to get by. At one station, I stepped onto the platform to get out of the way, and nearly didn't get back on the train. Finally, due to all the kicking the box had taken, it split. With nowhere else to sit, I stood for the rest of the journey.

When the train eventually pulled into Paddington Station, there was a mad scramble to get off and our box disappeared.

'Now what are we going to do?' I asked, certain someone had stolen it.

'Stay here and don't move,' said Frankie, heading off to find the guard. I sat down in the empty carriage whilst I waited for him to come back.

'This is the end of the line son, you'll need to get off,' said one of the cleaners.

'I know, but I've lost my box and my brother's gone to try and find it,' I explained.

'Is that it over there?' he said, pointing to a box on the platform. The box was just about falling to pieces and was only being held together by the length of rope around it. Frankie returned, and between us we lugged it towards the station clock.

'There's supposed to be someone here to meet us. You stay with the box, and don't wander off,' he ordered.

We had arrived during the evening rush hour. Hundreds of people going in all directions and everybody in a hurry. Again, no matter where I stood, I got jostled. I had never seen so many people in all my life.

When Frankie told me someone was supposed to be meeting us, I thought it would be my 'new mum'. As the minutes ticked by and he hadn't returned I began to worry, continually looking about me to see if I could spot him. Suddenly, the public address system caught my attention.

'Will the person meeting Frankie and Billy Green meet them under the clock.'

Gosh, I thought, *how did they know we were here?* A few minutes later, Frankie returned.

'They just said our names, did you hear it?' I excitedly exclaimed.

'Of course I did, it was me who told them to say it,' he proudly replied.

A few minutes later, a young girl approached and told us our 'new mum' was too busy to come to the station herself, so she had been sent to pick us up.

Frankie let her know it was him who had gone to the station master to get the announcement made. She was unimpressed, telling us to follow her as she headed for the taxi rank. I had never been in a taxi before, in fact it was the first 'motor car' I'd ever been in. I wished Pop and Ma could see me.

It was slow going as the taxi picked its way through the bombed buildings, rubble, evening traffic, and poorly-lit streets.

'Come on, this is it,' said the girl, when the taxi stopped.

'Where are we?' asked Frankie.

'This is your mum's restaurant.'

A restaurant. My 'new mum' has a restaurant, I thought. First a ride in a taxi, and now a restaurant. This was more than I expected. The smell of food greeted us as we entered.

On hearing the door open, my 'new mum' came out from the kitchen, gave us both a hug, and told us to sit down. Moments later, she said.

'So, what happened to your coat?' I was taken by surprise, having completely forgotten about the coat. I didn't think she even knew I'd lost it.

'I lost it,' I sheepishly replied.

'Well, don't think you'll get another one. I had to bribe people with food to get the coupons to get that coat.'

I silently stared at a bottle of sauce on the table. I thought about saying it would have been too small for me by now, but thought better of it, worried she might think I was being cheeky and not feed me, and I was starving. She returned to the kitchen.

'Why did you tell her I had lost my coat?' I asked Frankie accusingly.

'It was not me. How could I tell her, I've only just got here?' he replied.

'Then how did she know?'

'Ma and Pop would have told her.'

Before I could say anything more, my 'new mum' returned and placed a plate of food down in front of me. The plate was so full I couldn't believe it was all for me.

'Well, eat up,' she said.

I gingerly reached for the sauce bottle, not sure if I was allowed any. She took it off me, and I gave her a guilty look. Then, to my surprise, she poured some on the side of my plate. *All this food and sauce too,* I thought. *Life really is on the up and up.* Little did I know.

We had just started eating, when my dad arrived. He gave us a quick hug and asked if we had a safe journey. After kissing and hugging my 'new mum', she gave him his evening meal and they discussed the day's events as if we weren't there.

I thought the restaurant was where we were going to live, so was surprised when my dad said.

'Okay. Ready for the rest of the journey.'

A taxi took us from the restaurant to Fenchurch Street railway station, where we caught the train to Benfleet. About an hour later, our train pulled into a station and my dad announced, 'this is it.' He and Frankie lugged our battered cardboard box down a poorly lit road to the bus depot, where we boarded a bus for Canvey Island, the final leg of our journey.

In 1931, the Colvin Bridge which crossed from Canvey to South Benfleet was built. Funded by Canvey Urban District Council, and the Ministry of Transport, it cost £20,000 to complete. This was demolished in 1973 and a replacement bridge, which is still used today, was built alongside. A second road on to the Island was opened in 1972, the A130, which connects the Island at Waterside Farm to Sadler's Farm roundabout and the A13 which includes a bridge across East Haven Creek.

The bus followed the only road to the island. Twenty or so minutes later, we arrived at our stop.

The bus drew away, leaving us on a road lit by a solitary street light. The yellowy glow it cast was just sufficient to see a fish and chip shop, which was closed, on the other side of the road.

My dad picked up our box and led the way along a concrete road. Later on I learned it was called Sea View Road. A few minutes later, he turned off the concrete road into an unmade road, lit only by the moon.

'Stick to the cinder path, or you'll be up to your ankles in mud,' he called, leading the way. For something that was little more than a mud track, its name, Dovercliffe Road, was a bit pretentious.

As my eyes grew accustomed to the dark I could make out the outline of what appeared to be a 'bell tent' in the middle of a block of land.

'Home at last,' my dad announced.

A tent, surely we are not going to live in a tent, I thought. My dad kicked open a small garden gate, and I noticed the tent was our next door neighbour.

My dad led the way through the long wet grass and dropped our box onto the veranda. We all waited while he fumbled to get the key in the lock.

'There,' he said, pushing the door open and lighting the gaslight hanging from the ceiling.

Never missing a trick to wind me up, my brother deliberately paused in the doorway. Anxious to see my new home, I shouted.

'Mind out the way,' and angrily pushed him to one side.

The tiny living room was full of furniture, dominated by a dining table and six chairs, which left just enough space to squeeze by. Two armchairs, placed either side of the fireplace, took up the rest of the space.

'Right you two, you'll be tired after your journey, so off to bed. There's no light in your bedroom, but you should have enough light from the kitchen,' pointed out my dad.

'Where's the toilet?' I asked him.

'Now that's another thing. Follow me.' I followed him through the kitchen, out the back door, and into the garden.

'There,' he said, shining a torch onto what looked like a small shed.

He handed me the torch, and I picked my way through the long-wet grass. I threw the door open, and stepped back. My torch picked out what looked like a dustbin with a toilet seat on it. I'd never seen a toilet like that before. It was certainly nothing like the one I had sat on when I scratched Frankie's initials into the wall.

I didn't like the look of it, and decided to wait until I could check it out in the daylight. Closing the door, I peed in the grass and went back into the house.

Over the weekend, I explored the area, and noticed a junior school nearby. Being as it was near the end of October, I thought I might get away with not having to go to school until after the Christmas holidays. No such luck. First thing Monday morning, my 'new mum' took me to the school and I was placed into a class straight away.

Chapter Thirty-One

It was still dark when I awoke early on Christmas morning 1945. This would be my first Christmas for six years with my parents. My eyes soon adjusted to the gloom, and I was able to make out that 'Father Christmas' had been. As I quietly slipped out of bed, my brother joined me. We excitedly examined each present through the wrapping paper, as we tried to guess what it was, knowing not to open anything until we had been told we could.

The bedroom door suddenly opened and my father stuck his head in, sleepily telling us to get back to bed as it was too early to be up.

We did as we were told, but were too excited to sleep. It seemed an eternity before the first shafts of daylight came through the tatty net curtains and brightened the room. I thought my dad was never going to get up. Finally, he stuck his head in our bedroom and told us we could unwrap our presents.

The lino covered floor was cold through my underwear, but I ignored it, too excited with my presents. Minutes later, the hours of anticipation were over.

We wished my dad and 'new mum' a 'Merry Christmas'. She kissed us on the cheek and told us we could play in the front room, adding. 'Just because it's Christmas, so don't think you're making a habit of it.' We were only ever allowed to play in the bedroom, which was cold. So it was a welcome change to be allowed into the front room near the fire.

After hours of smelling the dinner being cooked, we were finally called into the kitchen. I was looking forward to my dinner, having been told we were having roast chicken. I couldn't remember whether I had ever had roast chicken when we were evacuated, so this could well be a first. My excitement increased when I saw the two bottles of cordial on the table. I nudged Frankie, and whispered that I hoped we would be getting some and that it was not just for the adults. My dad carved the chicken, and my 'new mum' asked if I wanted orange or blackcurrant cordial. I chose blackcurrant, because I knew what orange tasted like. The blackcurrant was delicious, and I wanted to gulp mine down. But my 'new mum' said that we should sip it, as we could only have one glass.

After an enjoyable Christmas dinner, we were allowed back into the front room to continue playing with our presents. Frankie had received a 'kazoo', and had been driving me crazy with it all morning. He kept asking what tune he had just played, but I was not in the least bit interested.

He finished his latest rendition, and expectantly waited for me to identify the tune. I didn't respond, so he leaned over and dug me in the ribs.

'What tune was that?' he asked.

'I don't know,' I said, irritably.

'Guess.'

'I don't want to guess, and anyway I was not listening, so I don't know.'

'Right, I'll play it again, now listen.'

He tootled away on the kazoo for a while looking at me for a response. I was not interested so said the first thing that came into my head.

'Goodbye Cowboy Joe.'

'No. You're not trying. I'll play it one more time, so listen.'

'I don't want to listen.'

'You'll listen if I tell you to, now listen.'

I stuck my fingers in my ears, rolled away to the other side of the small front room, and 'lah, lah lah'd'.

This really annoyed him. Suddenly, he leapt across the room and pulled my fingers out of my ears. I continued to lah, lah, lah. Letting go of my fingers, he placed his hand over my mouth. As soon as he let go of my fingers, I put them back in my ears.

This went on until he lost his cool and told me I was stupid because I couldn't recognise a simple tune. I retaliated by saying he was rubbish at playing and that it didn't sound like any tune I knew.

We were about to trade blows, when my dad came into the room. As soon as he sat down, Frankie said.

'Dad, can you recognise this tune?' He played for a little while, and my dad said.

'She'll be coming round the mountain when she comes.' Frankie's face broke into a smile.

'See,' he said, pointing at me. 'You said you couldn't recognise it.'

'Everyone knows that tune,' said my dad.

'I knew it, I just didn't want to say,' I replied in self-defence. My dad went into his bedroom, and returned with a small mouth organ.

'Right Frankie, you can accompany me on your kazoo.'

The two of them played a tune, and I thought my dad was ever so clever because he could play a mouth organ. When they finished, my dad asked if I would like to join in.

'I haven't got anything to play,' I told him.

He produced a comb and placed a piece of tissue paper around it. Pursing his lips, he blew on it, the sound not unlike a kazoo.

'Here, you try.'

The comb reeked of the Brilliantine he massaged into his scalp every day in the belief it would stop his rapidly receding hairline. Before long, I was able to get a sound out of it and the three of us were soon into full flight. My 'new mum' came in from the kitchen and joined in, clapping and humming. It was the best Christmas ever.

Chapter Thirty-Two

My parents travelled to London each day, so were up at the crack of dawn. My brother and I were not allowed in the house whilst they were at work. So, at six-thirty each morning, we were also dragged out of our beds.

I hated the cold winter mornings. With no heating or insulation in the bungalow, the bedroom was so cold the condensation from our breath froze on the inside of the window.

Each morning, shivering in the grubby underwear I slept in, I would cross the cold linoleum floor in my bare feet, pick up the pile of clothes from the old 'gramophone stand', the only other piece of furniture in the room, and dump them on the bed. We didn't need a wardrobe or set of drawers, as we had nothing to put into them. Clothing and shoes were still rationed, but other people seemed to manage to be better dressed than me.

Most mornings, I put on the same clothes as I had taken off the night before. Short trousers, jumper, socks. My footwear was also straight forward. Wellingtons in the winter, sandals in the summer. Usually, two months into winter, my utility wellingtons developed a hole in the sole, well before winter was over. It was always the right one, whilst the left one remained watertight.

I risked telling my dad I had a hole in my wellington. He was not happy, pointing out that I had not had them long, and did I think money grew on trees. He didn't offer to buy me a new pair. I found a piece of cardboard in the gramophone stand, and stuffed it into the sole of my wellington.

Each morning, I picked my way through the long-wet grass to the chemical toilet. My stream of urine would stir up the stinking mixture of chemicals and human waste, often perilously close to the rim, causing me to turn my head and hold my breath. Sitting on the seat brought any dangly bits perilously close to being scalded by the chemicals.

I was never sure what I was expected to do each morning whilst waiting for my meagre breakfast, so would return to my bedroom. Often, I just stared out the window at the old lady who lived in the 'bell-tent' next door.

She shared her tent with two cats and a dog, and was always up at the crack of dawn. Each morning, she lit her small kerosene lamp and hung it on a hook at the entrance to her tent. The small amount of light it shed provided just enough light for her to light a kerosene stove, and place a small kettle on it. She kept her water in a twenty gallon milk churn next to the tent. I had seen her 'lugging' buckets of water, which she bought from the newsagents, to refill it.

My step-mother, now I was living with her the 'gloss' had worn off, so I no longer saw her as my 'new mum', said she probably stunk, as she never washed herself, except for a 'lick and a promise'. She should talk. We had no bathroom, no running water, no electricity, and an outside chemical toilet. Often, when returning to the kitchen from the toilet, I would see her stripped to the waist washing herself in the sink. Once, fascinated by her breasts, I stood watching her. When she saw me, she said.

'Don't stand gawking at me, do something useful.' Draping a towel over her shoulders, she pushed past me, went into her bedroom and shut the door behind her.

And, I was certainly in no position to cast aspersions, given my own personal hygiene. Dunking a flannel into a pint of lukewarm water in the kitchen sink and giving my exposed parts a quick wipe down, was as much as I ever did. We were not unique. No one on our street had running water, or a bathroom.

I was always very wary of my dad. Like Pop, he was not the easiest person to speak to, especially in the mornings.

So, one morning, I was seated at the breakfast table watching him eat a slice of bread and jam, his usual breakfast. I was savouring every bite along with him, and would have loved a slice of bread and jam myself. But my expectations were cut short, when a bowl was placed in front of me. It contained a slice of bread, cut into cubes, with warm, watered down milk poured over it. At least when we were evacuated, we got porridge. It wasn't the first time I had been given bread and milk for breakfast, but usually I was so hungry I just spooned it down me. But instead of picking up my spoon, I just stared at it.

My father had finished his slice of bread and jam, and was rolling himself a cigarette from his tin of Golden Virginia tobacco.

'What's wrong?' he said.

I was about to say, 'Nothing,' as I knew better than to complain, my father not one to tolerate anybody being ungrateful, as he called it. Then, before I knew it, I blurted out that was not what I wanted and could I have bread and jam. My step-mother, who was standing with her back to the gas stove, the warmest place, eating her breakfast, immediately cut in.

'If you don't eat that, then you'll have to go without as there is nothing else.' Ignoring her, I looked at my dad.

'Why can't I have bread and jam like you had?' I asked him.

Again, my step-mother cut in telling me she only had so much fresh bread and there was not enough to go around; pointing out that as my dad worked and paid the bills he got the fresh bread. My father then pointed out that as I didn't work and didn't contribute to the household, I had to have the stale bread, and the only way to make it edible was to pour milk over it.

Taking a puff from his rollup, he blew the smoke towards the ceiling, sat back in his chair, and fixed me with his dark beady eyes, a look reserved for these occasions.

'You should think yourself lucky. Some people will go to work this morning with nothing in their stomachs,' he said.

He then proceeded to lecture me on how well off I was, and that I should be grateful. As he droned on, I became so frustrated, I was on the point of tears, but held them back. My father would have seen tears as a sign of weakness and given me a whack. Knowing I was not about to get anything else, I gulped down my breakfast, the warm watery milk unable to hide the taste of stale bread. Over time I got used to it; it being the breakfast for people who didn't 'contribute'.

Once breakfast was finished, we got ready to leave. I did all I could to delay leaving, as I was in no rush to go anywhere, bemoaning the fact I had been called so early. Six-thirty was far too early for me to get up, as my school was only a ten-minute walk from the house, and I didn't start until nine o'clock.

Putting on my ill-fitting jacket, I sat on the bed until I heard my dad check the back door was locked, before wandering into the kitchen.

'Come on, get a move on,' he said.

Slowly I moved towards the front door. My step-mother, annoyed by my languid approach, grabbed me by the arm and propelled me onto the veranda.

'Move yourself, you're like death warmed up,' she said.

My dad led the way out of the garden and onto to the cinder pathway, made by the residents over the years when they cleaned out their coal fire places. The ashes soaked up the water, making the road passable, as long as you kept close to the fence.

The road had never been made up, as the bungalows were normally only used as holiday homes in the summer. Now, due to the housing shortage caused by the blitz, all holiday homes were taken over by the council and used as full-time accommodation for the homeless. And that was how we came to be living there.

We scrunched along the path in single file, my dad leading. He was followed by my step-mother, then Frankie, with me bringing up the rear. When we reached the corner of Sea View Road and High Road, we went our separate ways.

Frankie headed up the main road to the secondary school on Long Road. The bus my parents travelled on went past his school, but he was not invited to ride with them. My dad told him 'the walk would do him good.' In truth, my dad was too mean to pay my brother's fare.

I said goodbye and dawdled off in the opposite direction towards my school. Minutes later, my parents bus passed me and pulled up at their stop. I watched them get on board. As soon as the bus was out of sight, I ducked under the railings, crossed the field, jumped the well flooded ditch, and returned home.

The old lady who lived in the tent next door was pottering around outside her tent. When she saw me, she called out. It was always the same greeting. 'Morning Billy, you're up early.'

After returning her greeting on the off chance she might offer me a cup of tea from her meagre rations, I sat on my veranda and watched my friend Peter's house across the road.

It seemed ages before a light went on, and I envied him the extra time in bed. I left it for a few minutes before crossing the road and knocking on his door. Timing was important. Knock too soon, and his mum would tell me it was too early and to come back later. Leave it too long, and I could miss out on the chance of mooching a bit of breakfast.

His mother answered my knock and invited me in, telling me to take a seat at the kitchen table whilst I waited for Peter. When he arrived a few minutes later, he was so clean and polished he made me look like a ragamuffin. We chatted, whilst his mum prepared breakfast.

Some people, not me of course, might have been embarrassed accepting her offer of something to eat each morning. But, a lifetime of scrounging can make one rather 'thick skinned'. Then of course, I didn't want to hurt her feelings by refusing.

The warmth from the kitchen stove and the smell of food, added a homely feel to the house. A stark contrast to my own home. I wished I could live there permanently.

Chapter Thirty-Three

A few mornings after telling my dad about the hole in my wellingtons, which I was still wearing, my step-mother surprised me by saying that as she was not going to work that day, so I could stay in bed a bit later.

Jumping back into bed, I settled down, delighted to have the bed to myself. My brother, on the other hand, was getting ready for school, and made it obvious he was not at all happy that I was getting a lie in. Making as much noise as he could, he continually opened and closed the door to the old gramophone stand in the pretence he was looking for something. When I told him to make less noise, he sighed loudly, sat heavily on the bed, and said it was alright for me. Finally, after ensuring I was well and truly disturbed, he and my dad left, and I quickly fell asleep.

The next thing I knew, I was awakened by my step-mother shouting she had slept in, and be quick, as I was late for school. Jumping out of bed, I quickly dressed, and looked about for some breakfast.

'Don't worry about breakfast; you're late enough as it is,' she said, hurrying me towards the door.

'But I'm hungry.'

My stomach was rumbling, reminding me I had not eaten for the last twelve hours. And, apart from my third of a pint of free milk at ten o'clock, I wouldn't be getting anything until my free school dinner at twelve o'clock.

'Well you haven't got time now, just go before you are any later,' she said.

'But if I'm already late, a few minutes more won't make any difference,' I protested.

'You're so ungrateful. I let you stay home a bit later and this is how you repay me. Well, that's the last time. In future, you can go at your normal time, I'm not having this nonsense again.' She handed me a piece of dry bread.

'Eat it with your milk,' she said.

I grabbed the bread, chomping into it as soon as I was out of sight of the house. It was well finished by the time I arrived at school. Although I was late, my progress through the snow was slow. Due to the hole in my wellington, I was walking on my heel like I had a sore foot. I hoped this would lessen the amount of wet snow coming in. By the time I got to school, everyone was already assembled in the auditorium, which faced the entrance to the school. As I awkwardly limped up the drive, I felt as if the whole school was watching me.

Finally, I turned out of view, and entered the main building by the side entrance. Despite my efforts to keep my foot dry, as I made my way to the auditorium my saturated sock made a slushy sound and left behind a trail of wet footprints.

Entering the auditorium, I was hoping to sneak in and merge with the rest. No such luck. As soon as I opened the door, everyone looked my way, not least the teachers on the stage. Holding my breath, as if my very breathing would draw attention to me, I took my place alongside the nearest student. Minutes later, morning assembly finished, and we were dismissed. Being nearest the door, I was first out. I hoped I could make it to my classroom before any of the teachers could say anything to me.

'Just a minute, Green,' a voice called out.

Stopping dead in my tracks, my heart rate immediately increased. Dreading it was the Headmaster, I slowly turned, relieved to see it was one of my form masters.

'I saw you limping. Have you hurt your foot?' he asked.

'Yes sir,' I replied, too embarrassed to tell him I had a hole in my wellington. He looked puzzled.

'But you weren't limping just now. In fact, you were moving quite well; so is your foot better now?'

'Yes sir.' Looking at my feet, he noticed the wet mark my foot had made on the floor.

'Hold your foot up,' he said.

'No, it's all right sir, really.'

'I said hold your foot up.' I lifted up my good wellington.

'Now the other one.'

I lifted my right foot, exposing the large hole, and what remained of the soggy bit of cardboard I had inserted. I was very uncomfortable at having to display my poor footwear, and quickly put my foot down.

'Is that the only footwear you have?'

'Yes sir.'

He looked as if he was about to say something relevant to my predicament, but, obviously unable to offer a solution, said.

'Right, you can go now, and don't be late again.'

Later that morning, of all mornings, we had an activities session in the auditorium and were told to remove our shoes.

Aware of the hole in my wellington, I tried holding my foot in such a way the hole wouldn't be seen as I removed it. It didn't work, one of the girls immediately noticed it.

'Ooh look, you've got a hole in your shoe,' she said, pointing. Everyone within earshot turned and looked at my foot. Several of the girls giggled, adding to my discomfort. Ignoring them, I placed my wellingtons against the wall as far away in the corner as possible, and took my place in line with the rest of the class. The same girl then called out.

'Look, he's got holes in his socks too.'

All eyes again turned to see my big toe sticking out of the hole in my damp sock. I pulled the sock over my toe and tucked it under my foot, trying to make it less obvious. By now, the whole class were tittering. Seeing my obvious embarrassment, the teacher walked over and quietly said.

'Would you like to take your socks off Billy?'

'No Miss, I'll keep them on,' I answered.

My feet weren't that clean, so the last thing I needed was someone to point to the dirt between my toes.

I was annoyed with the girl who had drawn attention to the hole in my wellingtons. Although she was in my class, I never spoke to her, seeing her as a rich kid. Her clothes and shoes, she obviously had more than one pair, always matched. If that wasn't enough, she also paid for her school dinner. To me, she was a rich, spoilt, snob.

The teacher explained that we were going to learn to dance, and told us to pair off. 'Little Miss Spot the Hole' naturally soon had a partner. I stood back, not wanting to ask anyone in case they said no. Soon the class had paired off, but I was still without a partner.

'Right, Billy needs a partner,' said the teacher. Nobody responded. I looked at the sea of faces, all paired off. Just when it seemed no one wanted to be my partner, a girl's voice said,

'I will.'

A girl, dressed nearly as poorly as me, hurried across the floor, embarrassed at being the centre of attention. I smiled at her as she approached, but she just took her place alongside me without returning my smile. We danced together, but any ideas I had of thinking I had won a heart were soon shattered. When the dancing finished, she left me in no doubt that she had only agreed to be my partner because she didn't have a partner either. She may have been dressed scruffily, not as scruffily as me, but she let me know I had not found an ally. Our relationship was purely one of convenience. I on the other hand, didn't feel that way about her. In fact, I thought she was quite pretty and would have been more than happy to have her as my girlfriend. But to save face, I told her the feeling was mutual. We remained dance partners for the rest of the term, but outside of that, we never spoke.

I was never quite sure how dancing would enhance my education and prepare me for life. But romping around in the auditorium was preferable to maths.

Come the first of May, a 'Maypole' was set up on the sports field, where we could put our dancing skills to use. Each dancer took hold of a long coloured ribbon suspended from the top of the pole. The music started, and we danced around the pole, weaving in and out and forming a pattern of different coloured ribbons around the pole.

Maypole dancing is a form of folk dance from Germany, England, and Sweden. There are two forms. The first and most popular consists of dancers that perform circle dances around a tall, garland-festooned pole. In the second, dancers move in a circle, each holding a coloured ribbon attached to a much smaller pole.

In the spirit of the ceremony, a girl was selected as the 'May Queen'. The lads I hung around with joked that she was chosen because she was the worst dancer. In truth, it appeared to be who your parents were, which was why 'Little Miss Spot the Hole' was chosen. I was delighted when I heard a boy say.

'Ugh she's ugly, how did she become queen?'

I had my own idea who should be queen. There was a little girl called Audrey. I thought she was the most beautiful girl in the world, and would make a wonderful queen. But my feelings for her were not reciprocated. She didn't have the time of day for me, but I was smitten. Whenever she was around, I tried to impress her by doing something silly in the hope it would make her laugh. In most cases it backfired, and ended up with her laughing at me, and not with me. What made it worse, was when I saw her walking hand in hand with another boy. I wondered what I would have to do to make her notice me. Maybe a bath, and some new clothes, would have helped.

Chapter Thirty-Four

Each new term, pupils who were unable to pay for their school dinners were given a slip to be completed by their parents. My dad and mum were both working and well able to pay for my dinner. But because I was so poorly dressed nobody queried it when I handed in my slip, so I ate for free. It did however carry a certain stigma.

Every morning, the school secretary handed out the meal tickets in view of the rest of the class, so it was no secret who was eating for free. When I was evacuated, everyone got a school dinner for free, so I accepted it as normal. As far as I was concerned, I just wanted a dinner, and didn't care who paid for it.

My best friend at school was Paul. When I first met him, I thought he was lucky because he lived on a house boat. It sounded more fun than living in a bungalow, even though it had no mains water, gas, or electricity. At least we had gas.

He was also as poor as a church mouse, which was probably why we got on so well. Many mornings, he would come to school not having had any breakfast. Apart from our one third of a pint of free school milk, he wouldn't have anything until he got his free school dinner. On those mornings, as soon as he got into the classroom, he opened his poetry book. It was always the same page, a poem about a crusty loaf. It gave him immense pleasure to read about the delights of a hot, freshly baked loaf of bread. It was as if just reading about it eased his hunger pangs.

'No breakfast?' I asked, one morning.

'How'd you know?' he replied.

'Cos you're reading your poetry book.'

'What about you?' he asked.

'Bread and milk.'

'Lucky you,' he replied, reminding me of my dad's words; 'You should think yourself lucky, some people will go out in the morning with nothing in their stomachs.'

Whenever I was hungry, which was most of the time, I imagined myself eating mashed potatoes with a soft boiled egg mashed through them. I had never had such a dish, or for that matter, a real egg. But I imagined it would be delicious, and promised myself that when I grew up and had some money, I would buy it. I shared my thoughts with Paul. He agreed it sounded nice, adding, any food would be nice.

One morning, we had done our reminiscing about food, and were eagerly looking forward to our free milk. Finally, the bell rang. Paul and I were first in the queue, just in case there wasn't enough to go around.

We grabbed our milk and returned to our desks. Paul opened his milk, careful not to spill the tiniest drop. Taking a sip, he placed the bottle on the top edge of his desk. Hungry as we both were, we always took our time, savouring every little drop, particularly the cream on top.

'Snide Boy', our name for him, was a boy in our class who Paul and I detested. He was always well dressed, paid for his dinner, had a gang of lackeys hanging around him, and always seemed to have money.

As usual, he was strutting around and showing off. Whether by accident or intent, as he passed Paul's desk he knocked his milk to the floor. Paul was out of his desk in a flash, but could only watch as the bottle spilled it contents on the floor. He picked up the bottle, absolutely distraught at losing the only sustenance he would get until dinner time.

'Sorry, sorry, it was an accident,' mocked Snide Boy, smiling at his mates, while Paul stared helplessly at his empty bottle.

'Go and see if there's any left in the crate,' I suggested. He returned empty-handed, close to tears. Seeing Paul's grief stricken face, Snide Boy condescendingly said.

'It's alright, don't cry, you can have mine. Would you like that?'

Paul, who despite everything, still had faith in human nature, looked at him and meekly replied, 'Yes.'

Picking up his bottle of milk, he held it to Paul. The pained look on Paul's face eased as he reached for the bottle. For a moment, I actually thought Snide Boy had a side to him I had not seen before. But just as Paul reached out for the bottle, he snatched it away.

'Do you really think I would give *you* my milk? *You* of all people. *You* must be joking.'

With that, he tipped the milk down his throat, burped loudly, and returned to his mates.

'Did you see that?' he chortled, 'He thought I was going to give him my milk.' They all laughed.

I gave Paul a sip of my milk, but a third of a pint doesn't go far. During the rest of the lesson, Paul kept whispering how hungry he was, and how he was looking forward to his dinner. It seemed the dinner bell would never ring. When it did, we made a bee line for the dining hall, clutching our free dinner tickets.

Snide Boy followed, making sarcastic remarks about the way we were dressed, and that we were spongers. His entourage of 'hangers on' laughed, including Audrey, the love of my life, who tagged along with him. Another reason I didn't like him.

In later life, when I was eighteen years old, I was on leave from the Royal Navy and visited Canvey Island. I met Brian, the older brother of my friend Christopher. He knew I'd been crazy about Audrey and told me she was married to, of all people, 'Snide Boy'. She lived in a council house about six doors along the road from his parent's house.

'Have you seen her since we left school?' he asked. 'No' I replied. 'Would you like to?' 'Yes, I'd love to.'

He knocked at her door, and what a surprise I got; although it was unfair just to show up on her doorstep. 'Hi Audrey, said Brian. 'This is Billy Green. Remember him from school.' She was heavily pregnant, her hair was tied in a bun, and she was wearing no make-up. I couldn't believe this was the woman I'd have gone over Niagara Falls in a barrel for. But the best part was when she realised just exactly who I was, and her embarrassment at how she looked. There I was, resplendent in my new uniform, Gold badges and all. It was on the tip of my tongue to say, 'See what you could have had,' but instead said. 'Hi Audrey. Lovely to see you after all these years'.

'Don't give them too much, they don't pay,' called out Snide Boy, when we reached the dining hall. The dinner lady told him there was no need for that language, and he should be thankful he had parents who could pay.

After picking up their dinners, Snide Boy and his mates headed for their table. As they passed our table, he said.

'Don't sit there, that's where the scroungers sit.'

He was right. It was easy to spot our table. Nobody took their eyes off their plate until they had finished eating, just in case someone tried to snaffle some of your precious food. But there's always one.

Somebody shouted, 'look at that.' The boy, in all innocence, turned to see what was going on. When he looked back, someone had taken his last potato.

'Who took my potato?' he asked.

'Oh no. You didn't fall for that old trick did you?' someone said.

We all chuckled, knowing exactly what had happened. The boy looked perplexed.

'Don't you know not to take your eyes off your plate until it is empty?' Realising what had happened, he became livid at falling for such an old trick.

'Who took my potato?' he shouted, looking accusingly at everyone.

'It was you wasn't it?' he said, glaring at Smithy. 'I know, because you had finished your dinner and now you're eating.'

Smithy denied it, but his face gave him away. A potato doesn't seem like much, but when you are hungry and not sure where your next meal is coming from, it means a lot. It obviously meant a lot to that boy, so much so, that he picked up his plate and smashed it over Smithy's head.

Smithy's face was a picture, as it turned from smirk, to astonishment. Soon, a small trickle of blood could be seen running down his forehead. Smithy was about to retaliate, but the dinner lady, who was clearing a nearby table, intervened.

I was surprised that anyone could fall for such an old trick. My dad had told me things like that happened during the depression, adding, if you are distracted, always remember to lift your plate.

Smithy came back from the kitchen with a sticking plaster on his head looking for revenge, by which time his assailant had left. We all followed, figuring a fight would help pass the rest of the dinner break. Smithy spotted 'Potato Boy' in the playing field, taking him unawares and bringing him down with a rugby tackle.

They both rolled around on the grass, doing their best to get a punch in. Smithy drew blood from 'Potato Boys' nose.

'Now we're quits,' said Smithy, walking away.

'Potato Boy' took a grubby handkerchief from his pocket, and dabbed his nose. He had been close to tears when Smithy stole a potato from his plate, but now, despite a punch in the nose, there was not a tear in sight. A punch in the nose was obviously less painful than losing a potato from your dinner.

Chapter Thirty-Five

Snide Boy continued with his 'snide' remarks about Paul and me, and anybody else who he thought was a 'free loader'. It didn't seem to bother Paul as much as it did me. I told my brother. He told me to give him a smack, and if I couldn't do it with my fists, then hit him with whatever came handy.

'That's the only way to deal with twats like him,' he said. 'Once you've hurt him, he won't bother you anymore.' I told Paul, and suggested we do something about it.

'Like what?' asked Paul.

I didn't have an answer. Over the next few days, spurred on by my brother continually asking if I had 'sorted out that boy in your class yet', whilst goading me by saying I was scared of him, I gave it some thought.

One afternoon, with nothing much else to do, I jumped the fence between us and the old lady who lived in the 'bell tent'. I asked her if she wanted me to take her dog for a walk. I had walked Rex before, and when I brought him back she always gave me a cup of tea and a biscuit.

During my walk, I met Alan, a boy from my class. He was born and raised on Canvey Island, so lacked the advantages of an 'evacuees education'. He was nice enough, in a funny sort of way, but I could never see myself palling up with him.

He asked me if the dog was mine. I told him I took it for a walk because the lady who owned the dog was 'too old'. He said he ran errands for an old lady and was on his way now to get her some sweets. The mention of 'sweets' pricked up my ears, so I tagged along. *If he's like me* I thought, *he's bound to take one for himself, and maybe give me one.* Whilst I waited outside the shop, a voice I knew so well, called out.

'What are you doing here Greeny?'

'What's it got to do with you?' I replied, spotting Snide Boy. Just then Alan came out of the shop.

'Better watch your sweets,' said Snide Boy, looking at Alan. 'Greeny's on the scrounge again.'

Alan set off and I followed. When it was obvious he was not going to open the bag and take one, never mind offer me one, I raised my concerns.

'You going to have a sweet then?'

'No, they're not mine.'

'Yeah I know, but the old lady will never know.'

'No, that would be stealing.'

'What, a couple of sweets? She'll never miss them.'

'No, they're not mine.'

Never having met anyone with such scruples before, I made a grab for the bag, but he pulled it away and ran off. I gave chase, intent on relieving him of at least one sweet. He ran with a deliberate high leg action, which was intended to keep me at bay. So, all I did was knock one of his legs, which caught his other leg and brought him crashing to the ground. Despite falling over, he still clutched the bag of sweets. Before he had time to get up, I dropped onto him and pinned him to the ground. Rex thought this was great fun, and licked his face. Whilst Alan squirmed to avoid Rex's long wet tongue, I made another grab for the sweets.

'Come on, give me a sweet and stop messing about,' I said, still not convinced he was serious.

'No, you're not getting one,' shouted Alan, desperately clinging to the bag.

Finally, realising he was too good to be true, I let him up. He angrily jumped to his feet, yelled he would never speak to me again, and headed across the field. I sat for a minute, unable to understand that there were people so honest they wouldn't steal a sweet when sent on an errand. I mean, how else would you get a sweet.

I took Rex home. The old lady invited me into her tent, placing the small stool she sat on when cooking in the entrance for me. She made me a cup of tea, and gave me a piece of cake, my reward and reason for walking her dog.

She sat on the only other seat, a chair with a drop down back, which formed a single bed. She told me that was where she slept. No wonder she slept fully clothed. This was the first time I had actually been inside her tent, although I had seen inside it when she had the flap open. It was full, not a bit of space anywhere. How she managed to get around and know exactly where everything was, I'll never know.

She told me about the blitz in London. How she had lived in the underground when the bombs were falling, and how her husband was killed when their house received a direct hit. I was fascinated by her stories, and was never in any rush to leave. When it grew dark, she lit a kerosene lamp and hung it from the centre pole. I knew it was time for me to go.

Apart from the open veranda at the front of our bungalow, which provided little or no cover, the small porch on the back of the house was the only place I could shelter from the weather, unless I sat in the smelly toilet. The porch was no bigger than a telephone box, but I found if I slid down the wall until my knees were around my ears, I could sit. When my knees began to cramp, and my backside became numb, I would work my feet up the wall until I was lying on my back, virtually upside down. If my parents were still not home when that position also became uncomfortable, I would wander off. As a last resort I would call on Peter.

Peter was nice enough, but he was too soft, too proper, and too honest for me. But I was glad he lived across the road from me as I could always use our friendship to mooch something from his mum. Peter was one of the more fortunate children who were not evacuated. He thus avoided being exposed to the rigours and unique education of an evacuee. In all honesty, our friendship, so to speak, suited me for my own ends. He lived just across the road, didn't appear to have any other friends, and I was quite happy to let his mother bribe me with food to be his friend. I had no scruples when it came to food. There was so little of it about, you got it where you could. And anyway, anything was better than lying upside down in a tiny porch.

From Peter's house, I could see when the lights went on in my house. My parents had normally eaten by the time they got home, and often brought me something from the restaurant, rather like a 'doggy bag.' I never queried what food my step-mother brought home, eating it without question whilst always remembering to thank her. I knew any disparaging remarks could result in my little titbit being stopped, or being reminded that I had already had a school dinner.

But Paul and I had still not come up with any ideas about how we were going to get even with Snide Boy. Then, quite by chance, one evening, Paul and I were hanging around outside the sweet shop, the centre of our universe, when he came out carrying a bag of sweets. As soon he saw us, he came over. We knew he was not about to offer us a sweet. On the contrary. Opening the bag, he deliberately placed a sweet in his mouth and went 'umm' in my face. That was the last straw. I was so incensed, I hauled off and punched him fair and square in the face, sending him staggering. Before he had time to recover, I grabbed his sweets, and with Paul close behind, took to my heels.

We reached the field, and I thought he had given up the chase. No such luck. Before I knew it, he was upon me, shouting at the top of his voice for me to give him his sweets back. In seconds, the two of us were rolling around on the ground. Finally, I managed to pin him down, but as I placed my hand over his mouth to shut him up he bit me. Annoyed, I pressed so hard his lip split, drawing blood.

During the scuffle, I'd dropped the bag of sweets, which were now scattered across the ground. Paul picked them up, and I warily got off Snide Boy. He got to his feet, and we all stood facing one another.

'Give me back my sweets,' he said.

'What sweets?' said Paul.

'You know what sweets. Those.'

'Oh, you mean these. Are these yours?'

157

'You know very well they are mine. Now give them back,' he said.

Paul held out the bag, and Snide Boy made a grab. As he did, Paul pulled them away.

'Sorry, sorry,' he said, mimicking him like when he spilt Paul's milk. He proffered them again, and again Snide Boy reached out. This time Paul let them fall to the ground. Snide Boy immediately picked up them noticing some were missing.

'What about the rest of them?' he said, putting the bag in his pocket.

'They're ours to make up for Paul's milk you spilt.' I said.

'I'm telling my mum, and you two are in big trouble,' he said, walking away.

As I popped a sweet into my mouth, I noticed the hand he had bitten had drawn blood. We didn't know much about medicine, but one thing we knew. 'Dock Leaves' were good for cuts, or when stung by stinging nettles. Plucking one from the hundreds around me, I cleaned the wound. Paul and I then went our separate ways. I thought that would be the last of it.

But it wasn't to be. The next day, the school secretary was waiting at the entrance to the school, and greeted me with.

'Green, report to the headmaster's office immediately.'

Paul was already waiting, a worried look on his face, when I got there. I nodded to him, but he looked away. I knew we were in trouble, but had no idea just how much.

'Come in you two,' said the headmaster.

Snide Boy, and a woman who could only be Snide Boy's mother, were already seated. She glared at us as we entered.

'Are these the boys?' asked the headmaster.

'Yes Sir,' replied Snide Boy, the split in his lip still visible.

'What have you got to say for yourselves?' asked the headmaster. We both remained silent.

'You do know why you are here don't you?'

'No sir,' I murmured.

'No sir, what do you mean, no sir?'

'I don't know why we are here, sir.'

'Well I'll tell you. Apparently, last evening, you two hooligans assaulted this boy and robbed him of his sweets. So, what have you got to say about that?"

Memories of Exmouth came flooding back. Don't admit anything.

'Don't know anything about it,' I replied.

'Don't know anything about it? Are you going to stand there and deny that you attacked this boy and stole his sweets?'

'Yes sir.'

'He's lying. He held me down and took my sweets,' shouted Snide Boy.

'Quiet boy,' said the Headmaster. 'Show me your hands Green.'

I held out my grubby hands. The headmaster grabbed them and pulled me across the desk.

'How did you get this?' he asked, indicating the bite on my hand.

'That's where I bit him,' said Snide Boy.

'It's a wonder you weren't poisoned…I mean just look at him, he's just the sort to do something like that,' chipped in Mother Snide, staring contemptuously at Paul and me.

'Yes, yes,' said the headmaster releasing my arm and pushing me away like a discarded rag. 'It's obvious to me that you are lying. I'll deal with you both later. Report back to your class.'

We left his office. I turned to speak to Paul so we could get our story straight, but he suddenly became very reluctant to talk. We took our seats in the classroom. A few minutes later Snide Boy came in looking like 'the cat that got the cream', and took his seat.

Normally, I looked forward to our break, but not today. I knew that would be the time the headmaster would send for us. Knowing this, as soon as the bell rang I grabbed my milk and drank it as quickly as I could. A few minutes later, I spotted the headmaster's secretary coming down the corridor and quickly ducked back into the classroom. Trying to stall the inevitable as long as possible, I crossed to the far side of the classroom and looked out the window. The secretary entered the classroom and called my name. I pretended not to hear her.

Suddenly, I felt a tap on the shoulder. It was Snide Boy indicating the secretary. I followed her to the headmaster's office. Paul was already there. This time he was more talkative. He suggested that we should admit to stealing the sweets and hope the headmaster would go easy on us. I wasn't keen on the idea, saying that we had already lied, so whatever we said now we were onto a caning. The secretary called us in, closed the door, and remained in the office.

'Right you two,' said the headmaster. 'It is quite obvious this was a deliberate attack on a fellow pupil, which I will not tolerate at this school. Have you anything to say for yourselves?'

'No Sir,' we both mumbled.

'For your lies, as well as for attacking a fellow student, you will both receive six strokes of the cane.'

He took the cane from the cupboard and gave it a few practice swishes, the noise sending shivers up my spine.

'Right Green, you first. Bend over the desk.'

I heard the swish of the first stroke seconds before it landed squarely on my rounded backside. My thin trousers, now tightened, provided very little protection. At first, I felt nothing. But as the second stroke made contact, the searing pain cut in. I bit my lip to avoid blurting out. The third and fourth strokes felt as if they had landed in exactly the same place, and were really painful. *Two to go* I thought, *and I have managed not to cry out. Please God, I can last out.* My silence seemed to goad the Headmaster, as it appeared he brought the fifth and sixth strokes down even harder. From the corner of my eye, I could see the secretary, wincing with every stroke. I'm sure she didn't enjoy this part of her duty.

'Right, you can get up now,' he said. As I moved away from the desk, I glimpsed the fear on Paul's face.

'You can return to your class now,' the headmaster ordered.

The secretary ushered me out of the office and closed the door behind me. Paul had watched me take my punishment, but I was not afforded the same opportunity.

I entered the classroom, and waited to be told to sit down. Snide Boy watched my every move as I made my way to my desk. My backside was throbbing, but I refused to give him any satisfaction by showing my pain. Easing myself into my seat, I took out my book, and buried my nose in it.

A few moments later Paul came in, his tear-stained face showing he had not held up too well to the punishment. Snide Boy smirked in satisfaction.

As the morning wore on, the welts on my backside felt like I was sitting on hard strips of wood. No matter which way I sat on the hard-wooden bench, I couldn't ease the pain.

Finally, the lesson was ended by the dinner bell, and I eased out of my desk, painfully stretching to an upright position. My backside felt like it was on fire, but it hadn't curtailed my appetite. Joining Paul as we walked to the dining hall, I said.

'So, how did it go?' He continued walking looking straight ahead without answering. Unperturbed, I continued with.

'I wanted to stay and watch, but he wouldn't let me. It's not fair, you got to see me.' He still didn't answer.

'What's up, you not talking to me?' I asked.

'You think it's funny, don't you? Well I don't. It's all your fault. This would never have happened, but for you,' he finally blurted out.

'My fault!'

'Yes. It was your idea to steal his sweets.'

'You agreed. And you had some too.'

'Just leave me alone,' he said, walking away. For once, we ate at different tables.

Before returning to my classroom, I went into the toilets and checked my welts. Wetting my hands, I gingerly laid them on my bare backside, the cold water providing some comfort.

Back in the classroom, Paul was still not speaking to me. *Bugger him,* I thought, *if he is not going to talk to me, he can get stuffed.*

Chapter Thirty-Six

I arrived home, and tried easing myself onto the floor of the porch, but the pain in my backside was too severe. Checking next door, I saw the old lady was up and about. Instead of jumping the fence like I normally did, I walked around to the gate. As soon Rex saw me, he ran over, his long tail wagging. I wasn't up to taking him for a walk. Fortunately, it looked like rain, so I had an excuse.

'Are you alright?' asked the old lady, noticing the stiff way I was moving.

'Yes, I'm fine,' I replied.

'You don't look too good.'

I thought about confiding in her, but decided against it in case it got back to my parents. I made a mental note that I would have to be careful when I went home. If the old lady had noticed I was moving awkwardly, I was sure my step-mother's 'eagle eye' wouldn't miss it.

The rain eased off. I said goodbye, and returned to my own house. Checking my reflection in the glass door, I was pleased to see none of the marks were visible below my trouser line. That night, I placed a wet flannel on my backside before going to bed. My parents were none the wiser.

The following morning, when I arrived at school, Paul was already hanging around by the gates. As soon as he saw me, he came over and said he was sorry. He said he had been on his way round to see me the previous evening, but was put off by the rain. I pretended to be unfazed, but was glad we were speaking again.

But in life, there is always something else. We'd played the 'opening gambit' by stealing the sweets. This was followed by the 'middle game', the caning. Now it was time for the 'end game'.

We were again told to report to the headmaster's office. To our dismay, the secretary informed us the headmaster had written to our parents.

'What are you going to say to your parents?' Paul asked, as we walked back to the classroom.

'Dunno,' I replied. 'What you going to say?'

'No idea, I just know my mum will kill me when she finds out.'

On the way home that afternoon, I thought about telling my dad what had happened before he got the letter. *That way,* I thought, *I can explain my side of the story before he reads the headmaster's letter.* But the more I thought about it, the more I decided it was not a good idea. Far better if he knew nothing at all about it.

What, I thought, *if I can get the letter before my parents get home.* The idea appealed to be. Now all I needed to do was find out what time the post arrived. Peter's mum was in her garden, so I asked her.

'Usually around ten o'clock. Are you expecting something important in the post?' she asked.

'Yes, sort of,' I replied.

That's no good, I thought. *By then I will be in school. Maybe I can tell my teacher I was not feeling well and get sent home before the post is delivered. I could wait on the veranda and get it from the postman. Or, maybe I could tell my parents I was sick and hope they would let me stay in the house. But, I wouldn't get any dinner if I didn't go to school.* I decided against that plan.

Somehow, I had to get into the house. I walked around the house checking the doors and windows, but everywhere was secure. Dropping to my knees, I peered in the letterbox flap cut into the bottom of the front door. There was a letter lying on the floor. *That,* I thought, *is where my letter will land.*

Breaking off a piece of wire from the fence, I bent it into a hook, and inserted it into the letter box. I was just able to reach the letter, and raked it closer to the door. I thrust my hand into the letter box, but my fingers were too short to grab it. I tried shoving my arm into the letter box and nearly trapped it, but the letter still remained out of reach.

Rolling onto my back, I chuckled to myself at the thought of my parents arriving home and finding me with my arm stuck in the letter box. From my prone position, I noticed the door had quite a largish space between it and the floor. With my face flat on the boards of the veranda, I could see the letter under the door. Inserting my piece of wire, I was able to ease the letter under the door. I then posted it back through the letter box, and raked it out again, just to prove I could do it.

Delighted that I had found a way to retrieve the letter, I headed for the creek to share my news with Paul. I asked him how he would get his letter without his mum finding out. He told me that it was not possible to deliver to each boat individually, so they collected their letters from the office. His older sister usually collected the letters. All he had to do, was beat her to it.

'Right, but how are we going to know what the letter looks like? Do you think it will have the school name on it?' I asked.

'No, but it will have the 'Essex Coat of Arms'. I noticed the secretary's envelopes when we were in the office,' he replied.

'That was clever of you,' I said. He smiled, enjoying the compliment.

The next afternoon we both raced home, convinced the letters would be there. I checked through the letter slot and saw a number of letters lying on the floor. I raked each one out, reposting all but the letter with the 'Essex Coat of Arms' on it.

Clutching the letter, I ran as fast as I could to Paul's houseboat on the creek. Within seconds, he greeted me, clutching his letter. We retreated behind the sea wall where we wouldn't be seen, especially by his sister.

'Everything go all right?' I asked.

'Yeah, I got there first before my sister.'

'Right, you go first,' I said.

He tore the envelope open and pulled out the letter. I looked over his shoulder. It was a pretty much what the headmaster had said to us in his office. Then, 'The best laid plans of mice and men often go awry.' There, at the bottom of the page, was something we couldn't have foreseen.

'Please sign and return to the school acknowledging receipt of this letter.'

'Bugger. Now what are we going to do?' I said.

'Dunno,' replied Paul. Seeing my letter still sealed in my hand, he said.

'You going to open yours then?' I looked at my letter.

'Not much point really. It will only say the same as yours.'

'I know. But I've opened mine, now open yours.'

'I will, I will. But it's not going to solve anything, is it? Unless.'

'Unless what?'

'Unless we just threw them away. Then, if the headmaster asks us if our parents have spoken to us about the letter, we say yes. I mean, I doubt if my dad would even answer it even if he did receive it.'

'OK. Now open your letter.'

I put him out of his misery and opened my letter, before ripping it into little bits and scattering them onto the incoming tide.

The weeks came and went with no mention from the headmaster. Paul and I figured he must have given up any hope of getting a reply. Finally, the term ended, and it was the summer holidays.

Chapter Thirty-Seven

I loved the summer holidays. Six glorious weeks to do my own thing. My parents, on the other hand, hated it, as they never knew what I was up to. Just as well. If they had known, it would only have added to their anxiety.

Most days, with nothing but time on my hands, I would mooch around in the hope of finding something to catch my interest. Not far from my house, located at Small Gains Corner, was an ex-War Department (WD) warehouse.

The store was full of stuff left over from the war, all of it of immense interest to a boy of my age. Shelves of empty ammunition boxes, military clothing, soldiers and sailors winter underwear, topcoats, and berets. Due to clothing being rationed, many people, especially workmen, bought their clothing there because you didn't need clothing coupons. Building sites or road works often looked like they were full of servicemen.

As I aimlessly wandered around, mesmerised by all the stuff a young boy like me would have liked, I came upon a huge pile of ex-Royal Navy inflatable lifebelts. After examining one in detail, I decided it was just what I needed to float around in the creek or beach on a long summer's afternoon. I thought about asking the lady behind the counter how much they were. But as I had no money, it wouldn't matter what they cost. Also, I figured, if she knew I was interested in them she would keep a close eye on me.

After much deliberation, I came to the conclusion that being without money should not prevent me having one. After all, the warehouse had dozens of them. I was sure they would not miss just one.

I left the warehouse. To my amazement, I found a lifejacket had somehow got stuck up my jumper. A pang of guilt suddenly shot through my body, but fortunately it soon passed, leaving me none the worse for wear.

When I got home, I gave my lungs a workout inflating the life belt and checking it for leaks, before heading for the creek to meet Paul. He was impressed with my lifebelt, and wondered if he could get the same deal.

Paul and I always swam in the nude, neither of us having the benefit of a costume. There was nobody around to see us, except his sister, and she had seen us naked so many times she took no notice. Although Paul wasn't happy when one hot afternoon she jumped in naked, and he saw me looking a little too interestedly at her. This must have prompted his mother to get them swimming costumes. I was quite envious, as well as a little self-conscious, being the only one who was naked.

This prompted me to nervously ask my dad if I could get a swimming costume. I hoped he would see the benefits of me swimming, rather than mooching the streets. But as always, when it came to money, it was like getting blood from a stone. And there was always the third degree. When he asked if I could swim I said no, adding that if I had a costume I could learn, and nearly blurting out that I had a lifebelt. But when he asked if I thought money grew on trees, I knew it was a lost cause. For once, my step-mother came to the rescue, and gave me an old pair of his navy-blue underpants. I thanked her, even though they were far too big, but I knew I would get nothing else.

The next day, armed with my lifebelt and my dad's underpants, I went to the creek. I launched myself into the water and was busy swimming around, when Paul burst out laughing and pointed to my bum. Air, trapped in the too-large pants, had formed a bubble, which looked like I had a balloon stuck to my bum. No matter how often I deflated it, it still came back. Paul said that between my navy-blue life jacket, and inflated navy-blue pants, I looked like a sea monster.

Now I had a lifebelt, I was able to stay in the water longer, sometimes just floating around for hours. But I had to watch when the high tide changed that I didn't get swept out to sea. There was also another hazard waiting to snare the unwary creek swimmer. Houseboats waited until the tide came in to flush their toilets.

Sea water, which was not available at low tide, was pumped into the pan by a hand pump alongside the pan. This was then flushed into the creek; the debris being carried away on the outgoing tide. I often had to do some nifty manoeuvring to avoid colliding with the contents of a recently flushed toilet. Despite raw sewage being pumped into the creek where we swam, I was never sick.

When I tired of floating around, I would clamber up the bank, wipe off as much water as I could with the underpants, lay naked in the long grass, and let the sun dry me. Having underpants to swim in was a start. But I still didn't have a towel. I hadn't got around to asking my parents for a towel yet and didn't want to push my luck.

But of all the things I looked forward to the most each day during the holiday period, was my school dinner. The Secondary School continued to provide dinners during the school holidays. This was a government initiative, to allow parents to go to work. The country was devasted after the war, and needed every pair of hands to get it back on its feet. Without my free midday meal, I would have spent some long hungry days.

Paul and I were usually the first into the dining hall and the last to leave, the dinner lady even knowing our names. We always hung around to the last, just in case there was any seconds.

After dinner, if Paul's mother had left him chores to do, he would wander off home. On the other hand, I, not being allowed into my house, could freely roam the bazaars, so to speak.

One such bazaar, which always attracted me, was the Casino Ballroom and Amusements on Shell Beach. The music, and the sheer buzz of an amusement park, attracting loads of holiday makers during the summer months. I spent a lot of time mooching around, wishing I had some money. The slot machines always interested me, as I watched people feeding their pennies and half-pennies into the slots.

As soon as someone left a machine, I nipped over in the pretence of playing it, knowing that some people often walked away leaving a coin in the cup. I once found a penny in one, and never forgot it.

Then came my lucky break. One afternoon, whilst aimlessly wandering around checking each machine, a 'coin cup' came away in my hand. I was so surprised, I let it fall to the ground. It made a loud clattering sound. Thinking this would attract the 'change man', who was always wandering around, I quickly moved away with a 'nothing to do with me' look on my face.

After several seconds, and the clatter had not attracted the 'change man', I furtively picked it up. As I went to replace it, I spotted a number of pennies lying in the bottom of the machine. Unsure if I was being watched, I quickly replaced the cup and moved away. For several minutes, I innocently watched the machine from a distance, whilst mulling over my chances of relieving the casino of some of its money.

After several minutes of inactivity in the aisle, I steeled myself for the plunder. To my annoyance, a couple of adults began playing the machines. I aimlessly watched, hoping they wouldn't play my machine in case the cup fell out. Just then, the 'change man' loomed into sight. I immediately wandered over to the dodgem cars.

Finally, the 'change man' left, and I was able to make my move. I was within reaching distance of the machine, when a group of boys noisily entered the casino and began checking the cups for coins in the same way I had. I quickly closed in on my machine. Moments later, the 'change man', attracted by their hilarity, chased them away.

'You too,' he said, indicating me. I wanted to say that I was not with them, but thought better of it, and wandered off. After circling the whole amusement park, I arrived back at the slot machines. To my delight, the area was deserted.

Hurrying over to the machine, I gave the cup a quick pull. It wouldn't move. I tugged harder, but it still wouldn't budge. *Surely the change man hasn't fixed it while I was away,* I thought. I wandered off. This really was becoming a mammoth task. *Why,* I asked myself, *did the cup come out a few minutes ago, and now it wouldn't move?*

I casually returned to the machine. Again, the cup wouldn't move. Then, 'the penny dropped', so to speak. In my excitement to pull off the robbery of the century, I had gone to the wrong machine. Quickly locating the right machine, I pulled on the cup, a smile creasing my face as it came away. In a flash, I raked out as many pennies as I could reach, and replaced the cup. I couldn't reach every penny, as some were tantalisingly just out of reach of my grasping fingers. I made a note to bring my piece of wire the next time.

Over the holidays, I visited 'my bank' several times, my piece of wire allowing me to increase my withdrawals. But like all bank accounts, they eventually run out of money. Arriving one day, I was disappointed to find the machine had been repaired. No doubt the absence of money in that machine a dead giveaway. So, a handy source of pocket money bit the dust.

Often, by late afternoon, especially after a swim, I would be hungry, even after my school dinner. In the absence of any income, I turned my attention to the fresh fruit and vegetables growing in people's gardens. I would help myself to whatever was in season whilst they were at work.

During the winter months, people didn't plant much, so I raided the local farm. There was always plenty beetroots, swede, or parsnip. I was partial to them all, raw. I would clean them by rubbing them in the long-wet grass, spitting out any dirt that I had missed. On one occasion, I popped a lettuce leaf into my mouth along with a friendly caterpillar. I had bitten it in two before I was able to spit it out.

Chapter Thirty-Eight

The summer of 1946 was simply glorious. Warm sunny days, little or no rain, and light until ten 'o' clock at night. I spent hours at the beach floating around in the River Thames on my life belt. I loved it.

But for many householders, like us, who lived on unmade roads with no mains water, it was not so good. Our only source of water was the rain from our roof, which we caught in tanks. We had two tanks. One outside the kitchen window mounted high enough to gravity feed the water tap over the kitchen sink, our only source of water within the house. The other, on the back of the house, which caught the rain from the rest of the roof.

Towards the end of summer, with no rain fall, our water tanks were near empty. My dad was aware of this, but was holding off in the hope it might rain. But when my step-mother complained about the rusty water and sediment coming through the kitchen tap, my dad was forced into doing something.

He thought at first there might be enough in the tank on the back of the house to last until it rained. But after a few buckets it also ran dry. The nearest fresh water was at the newsagents, about three hundred yards away on the corner of Sea View Road and High Road.

'Right, follow me,' he said, one bright, sunny, Sunday morning. I am sure there was a tear in his eye when he realised he would have to pay for something that fell freely from the sky.

The newsagent loaned us some buckets, and my dad reluctantly paid him half a crown. (Two shillings and sixpence, about 12½ p). A two-gallon bucket of water cost a half-penny. So, a half-a-crown would buy sixty buckets of water.

'Hundred and twenty gallons should be more than enough,' said my dad. 'And make sure the buckets are full. And be careful not to spill any, money doesn't grow on trees.'

My dad set off, carrying two buckets, brim full. Frankie and I followed. Two gallons of water was too heavy for me to carry single-handed. The only way I could carry a bucket, was by grasping it with two hands, dangling it between my legs, and walking 'bow legged'. Even so, I needed to stop every few yards for a rest. I was only halfway home with my first bucket, when my dad passed me on his way back. He filled another two buckets and overtook me before I reached home.

'You stay with your mother,' he said, when I eventually arrived home. 'You're no use to me.'

She told me to get up onto the top of the tank outside the kitchen window. The idea was, that my dad would pass me up the buckets, and I would pour them into the tank. But, after passing me the first bucket he told me to get down.

'You're fucking useless. You've spilled more than you've poured into the tank.' I protested that the buckets were too heavy, but all he said was 'bollocks', as he headed off to get another load of water.

Everything seemed to be going well, and the tanks were slowly filling. Then, Frankie's arms tired. Up till then, my dad had been carrying two buckets of water from the shop, and pouring them into the tank. Now Frankie was wearying, he told him to get up on the tank and do the pouring. My dad passed him a bucket, but, Frankie's arms were so tired he let it slip, and dumped the lot over my dad's head.

'You fucking galoot, can't you do anything right?' my dad yelled.

Hearing my dad call Frankie a 'fucking galoot' was too much for me, and I fell about laughing. It was not just what my dad said that had me in convulsions, but his hair. He always combed what little he had to give maximum cover, but now it was plastered down the side of his face.

'What are you laughing at?' he shouted, turning on me. I staggered away, so helpless with laughter, I could hardly walk. As I did, I glanced up to Frankie who was still standing on the tank, empty bucket in hand, and a half smile on his face.

'Get down from there,' yelled my dad, pulling him from the tank.

Fortunately, my step-mother also saw the funny side of it, and laughingly handed my dad a towel. He dried himself off, and it was back to business. After several more buckets, my Dad called us both over.

'Right you two, see if you can do something right for a change. Think you can? because your useless at anything else. We both nodded and mumbled yes. I was still trying to contain my laughter at seeing the water dripping from my dad's nose and ears, and his hair splattered down one side of his head.

'You alright?' said my dad, looking at me.

'Yes,' I replied, as straight faced as possible.

'Right. Pay attention. Take the empty buckets back, and get my deposit. Tell the man I only took forty-eight buckets of water, so he owes me a shilling.'

We picked up the empty buckets, as I anxiously waited for him to tell us to keep a penny for ourselves, so we could get a 'pokey-hat' of sweet crumbs. Crumbs, the broken bits of boiled sweets left behind in the bottom of the jars, were the best value for a penny.

When no offer was forthcoming, we sullenly trudged off to the newspaper shop. To lighten the mood, I optimistically suggested that maybe he would give us a penny when we got home.

'I don't think so,' said Frankie. 'He wouldn't give us the drips from his nose.'

Him mentioning drips from his nose set me off again, and the two of us were soon in stitches, as we relived the sight of water dripping from my dad's ears and nose. Our laugher was overly exaggerated, but was our way of hiding our disappointment at not being given a penny.

'We could tell him he miscounted how much water he had taken, and the man only gave us ten pence,' I suggested.

'No, he knows exactly how many buckets we had, and if we are two pence short, he will go to the paper shop himself,' replied Frankie.

We handed the paper shop man his buckets, and he placed a sixpenny piece on the counter. Frankie said.

'My dad said he only took forty eight buckets of water, so you owe him a shilling.'

'No, he took sixty. My wife counted them.' He indicated the living room window in full view of the tap. We accepted his word, believing his wife was more truthful than my dad.

'Can you give us a thruppenny (three-penny) bit, two pennies and two ha'pennies (half-pennies) instead of the sixpenny bit?' Frankie asked. The shopkeeper obliged.

As we left the shop, Frankie pointed out that my dad would now not be able to say he had no change. After all, a penny is scant reward for a day of humping buckets of water. When we reached the house, Frankie said.

'You give him his change. He's more likely to give you something than me, especially as I spilt the water on him.'

My dad was seated in his armchair and looked up when we entered. Taking my time, I placed each coin into his outstretched hand. First the thruppenny bit, as I knew there was no chance of getting that. Then one of the pennies, all the time watching his face for a flicker of generosity. Slowly rummaging in my pocket, I retrieved the other penny. His hand remained outstretched and motionless until I placed the last of the coins into it.

'Where's the rest of it?' he said.

'That's all the man gave us.' I replied.

'Did you tell him I only took forty-eight buckets?'

'Yes, but he said it was sixty, because his wife counted them.'

'Umm. I'll speak to him about that.'

Wrapping his fist around the six pence change, he placed it into his pocket. I remained standing close to him, but when his hand reappeared it was empty. He went back to reading his newspaper.

I looked towards my brother, willing him to say something, but he just turned and walked out the room.

Unable to bring myself to say, 'can I have a penny please,' I followed him out of the room and into the garden.

'Why didn't you say something?' I asked.

'He would have just said no, and we would have got a lecture about money not growing on trees.' I had to agree with him.

Not long after that, the rain came, so we were spared doing that chore again.

It was also during that same summer, my dad's younger brother Basil visited us. He was on leave from the army. Come the Sunday morning, he was up bright and early ready to go to church. Like his mother and sister, he was a staunch Roman Catholic. His mother was Irish, and regularly visited Rome on religious sabbaticals. To complete the trio, his sister ran a Catholic finishing school for young ladies on the Italian / Swiss border.

Basil asked my dad if he was going to church, but my dad declined. He never quite managed to get his head around religion. Also, with my step-mother being Church of England, he had even more reason not to bother.

Frankie was already up and gone, so my dad volunteered me to go. Basil asked me where the church was, and was not very impressed when I told him I didn't know. He was even less impressed when he discovered how little I knew of the Catholic Church service. He spoke to my dad about it. My dad said he would make sure that in future that I went, but after Basil returned to his barracks, it was all forgotten.

Chapter Thirty-Nine

As the summer months passed, the grass around our bungalow, and there was plenty of it, needed cutting.

My friend Peter's house, across the road, had a beautiful lawn, mowed regularly by his uncle, with a power mower. He was not Peter's real uncle, but his mum's boyfriend, Peter's dad having been killed in the war. My dad half-jokingly suggested that maybe he would cut our lawn. I took the hint, and asked Peter's mum. My dad was surprised when I told him I'd asked, but was not surprised he said no.

'Worth a try I suppose,' he commented.

Our grass was really long, not that it bothered my dad. But the landlord said if he did not cut it, he would get someone in to do it and charge it to my dad. The mention of money coming out of his pocket stirred him into action. A few days later, he arrived home with a pair of grass shears.

'Right you two, cutting the grass is your job. Come with me, and I'll show you how to do it.' Dropping to his knees, he quickly cleared a patch about one square metre in size, and handed Frankie the shears.

Frankie got on his knees. Within minutes, he stopped and stood up.

'You haven't done much, what's up?' asked my dad.

'My arms and back are aching,' he replied.

'You've got to get into a rhythm and keep the shears at the right angle,' said my dad. He picked up the shears and showed him.

'Let me have a go,' I said, thinking it looked quite easy. I picked up the shears, but the grass was so thick I couldn't close the blades.

'Take a smaller cut,' said my dad.

I tried smaller cuts, but in no time my arms were also aching, and I'd made very little impact. My dad was not impressed by my feeble efforts.

'Well, you two will have to do a bit each day until it is all cut.'

'What do we do with the grass?' I asked.

'Rake it up and dump it somewhere, anywhere. Just get rid of it.'

'But we haven't got a rake,' I pointed out.

'Well use your hands. You've got hands, haven't you? You're always complaining.'

Frankie cut a bit more grass, and I used my foot to drag it into a pile. A few minutes later, my dad came back with two pieces of cardboard.

'Here' he said, 'use this.' He demonstrated using them like a pair of big hands. Over the following days, the cardboard fell apart, so I borrowed a grass rake from Peter's mum. I dumped the cuttings on a spare bit of land at the back of our garden. It was so overgrown, nobody noticed.

Each evening, my dad checked on our progress. It took us a week or more to finish, cutting a portion each day until our arms ached. We managed to coerce a couple of our friends into having a go, but they soon gave our house a miss whenever they saw the shears in action.

One evening, just as it was getting dark, my dad grabbed the spade and began digging a hole in the far corner of the garden.

'What you doing dad?' I asked.

'A 'shite job'. Know what a 'shite job' is?' he asked, a smirk crossing his face.

'No.'

He told me he was going to empty the chemical toilet, by burying it in the garden. I asked him why he said 'shite', as I had always known it as 'shit'. He said that's what they called it in Scotland. I couldn't see the relevance, unaware at that time that he was Scottish. Normally he spoke in a very precise manner. It was only when he lost his cool his Scottish accent came to the fore. I thought it was just because he was excited that he 'spoke funny'.

Burying it in the garden appeared pretty disgusting to me, particularly as many people grew their own vegetables in their gardens. I wondered if all the vegetables I had stolen from people's gardens had been grown in 'shite'. I was relieved when I later learned that not everybody buried their human waste in their garden. Apparently, a man in a lorry emptied toilets, but you had to pay. My dad decided he would just bury it in the garden.

He finished digging the hole and called Frankie to give him a hand. Frankie reluctantly joined my dad in the narrow confines of the small toilet.

'Get out of the way,' yelled my dad, pushing him outside after he stood on his foot. My dad carefully lifted the inner container and placed it on the ground.

'Right, take a hold of that side and see if you can do that properly.'

Frankie turned his face away from the rancid mixture, as they slowly edged their way towards the hole. Suddenly, Frankie stumbled, spilling some of the contents onto my dad's trousers and hands.

'You fucking galoot, can't you do anything right?' said my dad. 'Come on grab hold.' Frankie hesitated.

'What now?' asked my dad. Frankie pointed to a piece of paper stuck to the handle.

'That won't hurt you,' said my dad, 'now get hold of it.'

Frankie grasped the handle, but having to touch a soggy piece of newspaper that someone had used to wipe their bum with was more than he could bear. More contents spilled. Frankie looked at his hand as if it was diseased, and quickly wiped it on the grass.

'You useless galoot. What are you?' Frankie didn't respond.

'What are you? A useless fucking galoot. Go on say it,' my dad insisted.

'A useless fucking galoot,' Frankie uttered.

Hearing Frankie say that was more than I could stand. I retreated in stitches, nearly colliding with my step-mother.

'So, now you're teaching him to swear,' she said.

'Swear; he's enough to make a saint swear,' answered my dad.

Finally, the contents were emptied, and Frankie hurried off to wash his hand.

I was still chuckling, when my dad called me over, cutting my merriment short.

'Take that silly grin off your face and wash that pan out and replace it.'

'Wash it. How?' I asked.

'Use your initiative.' He began filling in the hole as I looked to my brother for inspiration.

'Don't look at me…it's your turn now,' he said. 'I've done my bit.'

'I know, but what can I clean it with?'

'You heard him, use your initiative.'

I dragged the pan over to the water tank, but it was too big to fit underneath the tap. Without a hose or cleaning materials, the only thing I could think of was my jam jars.

As I didn't get any pocket money, my only source of income, albeit mere pennies, was collecting jam jars.

Using one of them, I swilled out the pan the best I could and replaced it in the toilet. I was busy pouring in the chemical, when my step-mother came out.

'Have you finished? I need to use that.'

The noise of her peeing into the empty container echoed loudly, so I moved away, not wanting her to think I'd heard her.

'Is it all right?' I asked, when she came out.

'No, you spilt chemical on the seat and I sat in it. I hope it hasn't burnt me.'

Later, when my brother and I were having a chuckle about it, I told him that his and my dad's antics reminded me of 'Laurel and Hardy'. He cut my laughter short when he said it was my turn next to empty the toilet.

Chapter Forty

Arriving home one day, I was surprised to see a car in the garden. My dad proudly told me it was a British Racing Green Wolseley Hornet. I was surprised, because I didn't think my dad had any money, given the way he lectured us about money not growing on trees whenever I asked for something, like new footwear.

Very few people had cars just after the war, with his being the only car in the street. Anyone who owned a car was seen as well off, no matter what model or how old it was.

It attracted the attention of the neighbours, much to the delight of my dad. But not all the neighbours were impressed. Peter's mother remarked he would be better buying his kids some new clothes and feeding them properly, never mind buying a car.

Despite that, I was fascinated by it. My only concern was that no one from my school saw it, or that could be the end of my free school dinners.

My step-mother casually mentioned she thought it was nice. A few weeks later she could have 'eaten her words' when she saw how much time my dad spent sitting in the car without actually going anywhere. Weekends would see him with a screwdriver and spanner checking every nut and bolt. I often joined him, listening intently whilst he explained the pedals, knobs, and dials to me. When I asked how we would all fit into it, as there were four of us and only two seats, he showed me the boot, which opened into a casual seat.

One afternoon, I returned home from the beach just in time to see my dad backing the car out of the garden. Petrol was still rationed, so this was the first time I had actually seen the car move. I wandered behind him, watching in awe, as he slowly manipulated the low-slung car over the bumpy unmade road. When he reached the concrete road, to my delight, he told me to get in.

'Where we going?' I asked excitedly.

'Just up the road. I want to give her a run to charge up the battery.'

Apart from sitting in the car in Exmouth for a few moments at the end of the war, this was my first experience. We travelled the length of Canvey Island, with me watching in awe as he worked his way through the gears. After crossing the bridge onto the mainland, he pulled into the bus depot at Benfleet, looking concerned as he opened the bonnet and peered at the engine.

'Is it broke?' I asked.

'No, but there's an oil leak which is getting into the dynamo and causing it not to charge. I hope I have enough battery to get us home, or we will be pushing it.'

It didn't make much sense to me at the time, but in later life, when I became an apprentice motor mechanic, I understood.

He drove more carefully on the way home, nursing the car along in an attempt to lessen the oil leak. Unfortunately, we were still about half a mile from home when the battery gave up.

'Get into the driver's seat and take the steering wheel while I push,' he said. I couldn't believe it; his misfortune was my good fortune. I was actually getting a chance to steer a car.

Kneeling on the seat so I could see through the windscreen, I tried to follow his instructions. 'Left hand down a bit, not too much. Right hand down a bit. That's it, keep her straight.' I soon got the hang of it, but our progress was painfully slow. Fortunately, a kindly man offered to help, and my dad thankfully accepted. We had nearly reached Sea View Road which would take us off the main road and lead to our unmade road. To my horror, of all the people to come along just then, was Snide Boy. Ducking as low as I could, I hoped he wouldn't see me.

'What an old banger,' he said, laughing out loud. My dad was not amused.

We reached Dovercliffe Road, and after a breather, the two of them pushed the car over the unmade road, my dad continually wresting the steering wheel from my hand and selecting a better route.

Finally, we reached our garden. My Dad thanked the man for his help, but despite my Dad's protests, the man insisted on looking under the bonnet. After much gesticulating and finger pointing, he offered nothing new.

'Everyone's a mechanic,' said my dad, as the man wandered off.

The following Saturday, having obtained a spare part in London, my dad set about fixing the oil leak. It was dark by the time he finished fitting it, so he put off road testing the car until Sunday.

'Where are you going?' I asked, when I saw him pouring petrol into the car, hoping to be invited along. By way of an answer, he handed me the empty can, and said.

'Put that back on the veranda and tomorrow you can get it filled.'

'That'll teach you to ask questions,' said my step-mother, climbing into the passenger seat. My dad inserted the crank handle, and gave the engine several cranks.

'We won't be going anywhere if I don't get it going,' he said, pausing for a breather.

'But if you do get it going, where are you going?' I repeated, hoping he would tell me to jump into the casual seat at the back.

'Never you mind where we're going, you're getting too big for your boots,' said my step-mother, making it obvious she didn't want me along.

The engine finally coughed and spluttered into life. I watched them drive away, before wandering off to the beach. Later, when I returned home, I was surprised to see the car was not in the garden.

Neither was the old lady from next door. But her dog Rex was, and came bounding over when he saw me. I jumped the fence and played with him for a while, before wandering off and climbing a tree. From my vantage point, I was able to see to the end of the road.

It wasn't long before I spotted the car, slowly making its way down Sea View Road. My dad was pushing it with one hand, and steering with the other, whilst my step-mother was pushing at the back. I scampered down from my lofty position, and ran to meet them. As soon as my dad saw me, he told me to steer, and moved to the back of the car.

As soon as he took up his position, my step-mother stopped pushing and walked ahead, obviously not wanting to be associated with such a heap of junk.

'Where are you going?' said my dad. 'I can't push this on my own.'

'I've had it,' she angrily replied. 'I'm not pushing it any further. I'm sick of that car.' He caught her by the arm.

'Come on old girl, it's not much further and we'll be home.'

'No…I've had it,' she said, wrenching her arm away and walking off.

He grabbed her arm again, and again she wrenched it away. He then grabbed her again, becoming a tad angry. This time, he held her so tight she cried out.

'Let go, you're hurting me.' Wrenching her arm free, she pushed him away and strode off.

My dad quickly pursued her, and again grabbed her arm.

'Look,' he said, becoming angrier by the minute. 'I can't push the car on my own, and I can't leave it in the middle of the road, so you will have to help.'

'Have too!' she said. 'There's no have too about it. You bought this heap of junk, you push it. Now leave me alone.' With that, she turned on her heel and walked away.

He watched her disappear around the corner, before dejectedly sitting on the running board. Being a Sunday afternoon, the street was quiet, with not a soul in sight he could coerce into helping him.

'Stay here and watch the car,' he said. 'I'll go and get some help.'

Whilst I waited for him to return, I pretended to drive, making noises and screeching sounds, as I tugged the wheel back and forth. As the minutes ticked by and he hadn't returned, I began wondering if he was ever coming back. I was about to go looking for him, when he came around the corner followed by my step-mother. She was obviously not happy at being shanghaied into pushing the car again.

As the car slowly moved forward, she continued berating him for buying the car in the first place. He replied that if she used as much energy to push the car as she was using to 'mouth off,' we would have the car in the garden in no time. This served to annoy her even more, and she threatened to walk away again.

'Sorry, sorry, I didn't mean it the way it sounded,' he said, changing his tone. She began pushing again, before turning her annoyance towards me.

'It's hard enough to push without you finding all the bumps; steer to the smoothest part of the road,' she shouted.

'I am,' I replied, peering over the bonnet and manoeuvring the car the best I could.

'Don't argue with me, just do as you are told.'

I shut up. I had not had my tea, and didn't want to aggravate her any more in case I didn't get any.

Peter's mum was in her garden, and watched them struggle, without offering to help. But why would she. My step-mother never spoke to her, or for that matter any of the neighbours, thinking herself above them.

Finally, one last shove saw the car thankfully roll into the garden. My step-mother immediately stormed off into the house. I hoped she was not too angry to make something to eat, as I was starving. She later told my dad she was 'mortified' that the neighbours had seen her pushing a car.

The next day, after school, I went for the petrol. It was easy going there with an empty can, but I struggled with a full two-gallon can on my way back. I asked my dad why he didn't take the car directly to the garage. He avoided the question. My brother said it was because he was fiddling the petrol coupons.

For the next week, my step-mother never let up on my dad, taking every opportunity to remind him what a waste of money the car was, as it never worked.

'Why don't you take it to the garage?' she said. 'You've been fiddling with that car every weekend, and it still doesn't work.'

Unable to stand her nagging, he finally took the car to a garage and paid to get it fixed. When he got it back, he suggested they go for a run.

'No thank you,' she said. 'I told you I didn't want to see that car again.'

'Yeah, but it's fixed now.'

'No... now that's final.'

'Right, if you don't want to come... Billy you can come with me.'

I ran out to the garden, removed the wire fence, and jumped into the car. I was desperate to get going in case my step-mother changed her mind. Minutes later my dad slid behind the wheel, looked into the rear-view mirror, carefully adjusted his cap, mandatory for an open top car, and finally started the engine. Taking his time to give my step-mother the chance to change her mind, he let the engine idle, whilst I was willing him to drive away. When it was obvious my step-mother wasn't going to change her mind, he eased the car out of the garden.

We drove to Benfleet and back without the car breaking down, which was something of a milestone. After that, my step-mother slowly warmed towards the car and I was no longer invited.

Chapter Forty-One

Every weekend, my dad pottered about the garden. So it was no surprise when one Saturday afternoon he came home with a load of wood gathered from the bombed houses scattered around the island. He had also acquired a roll of wire netting. My gaze had him telling me he was going to make a chicken run. The following weekend, my step-mother arrived home with a dozen day old chicks.

'I thought we were getting fully grown chickens,' I said.

'No, they'll soon grow, as long as we keep them warm,' she said, placing the box under the gas stove.

The next morning, when I got up, there were two dead chicks lying on the draining board.

'What happened?' I asked.

'It's just one of those things,' she replied. 'The man in the shop told us to expect some of them to die, that's why we bought a dozen.'

I felt a lump in my throat as I stroked the dead chicks. I thought it was so cruel that you had to buy enough chicks to allow for some of them to die, and still have enough left.

'Perhaps you would like to bury them in the garden?' suggested my step-mother.

'I need a box to put them in. I can't just place them in the ground.'

'No, just dig a hole and lay them in it, that will do.'

'No, I can't, I need a box.'

'Well, we haven't got one. And what if tomorrow some of the others die, then you'll need a box for them. I might have known this would happen, nothing is ever simple with you.'

'We could just throw them in the bin,' said my dad.

I couldn't believe he could be so cruel, but caught a sly grin on his face and knew he was joking. I wrapped them in a piece of newspaper and buried them in the garden, well away from where we had emptied the toilet. Several more died, until only five were left to go into the chicken run.

In the meantime, my brother and I lugged a load of cockle shells from the beach, smashed them into small pieces with a hammer, and sprinkled them into their run to give them some grit.

As I was always the first home each day, it fell to me to feed them. My step-mother gave me my orders.

'Right,' she said. 'Pay attention. All you have to do is light the gas under the pot. Always make sure the match is lit before turning on the gas. Once the pot is boiling, turn the gas down and let the potatoes cook for about twenty minutes. Then, being careful not to scald yourself.' She paused, her look suggesting it was inevitable I would. 'Drain the water, add their meal, and mash the whole lot together. That's it. Think you can do that without blowing the place up?' I nodded.

My dad was not keen on me being in the house on my own. But with no other option, he reluctantly agreed to me having a key to the back door.

'And don't take it to school with you. Hide it in the chicken run,' he added.

That afternoon, I rushed home from school, excited at being able to get into the house on my own for the first time. Paul was with me, anxious to see the chickens.

Pretending to check the nesting boxes, I recovered the key. I'd learned not to trust anybody, even friends.

I lit the gas, pointing out to Paul the importance of lighting the match before turning on the gas. He said he already knew that because he had gas on his houseboat, thus thwarting my attempt at one-upmanship.

We went out to the chicken run, and I pointed out each chicken, telling him the names I had given them. He said giving a chicken a name was stupid, as they all looked the same. I told him I could tell the difference. Pointing to one, I said I had named it 'Audrey', after my 'pash' at school. She didn't even know I existed, so the next best thing was to name a chicken after her.

The potatoes smelled good, and Paul said he was so hungry he could eat them himself. I shared his sentiments, but didn't offer him any. He hung around whilst I fed the chickens, but when he saw there was nothing to eat, left for home.

I watched the chickens eat for a while, before going into the house. Only then did it register that for the first time ever, I was in the house on my own. I could 'actually' go anywhere in the house, with no restrictions.

I very rarely went into the front room when my parents were home, limiting my movements to the kitchen and my bedroom. Entering the front room now the house was empty, gave me the same feeling I got when I was trespassing.

Within seconds, I spotted the dish of fruit gums in the middle of the dining room table. I wandered over and stared longingly at them. My step-mother had forbidden me to touch anything. *So,* I thought. *Knowing I would be in the house by myself, why had she left the sweets in full view? Was she testing me? Had she counted them and wanted to see if I would take one.*

I tipped them out, and counted them. Fourteen. If I take one that will leave thirteen, an unlucky number. It could be unlucky for me if I take one and she has counted them.

I counted the sweets back into the dish, and came up with the same number. I lifted a black one, my favourite, and looked at it longingly. I was desperate to eat it, but knew if I did, I would immediately regret it. It would be like the Mars Bar story again. *But,* I thought. *What if she hasn't counted them. I could take just one and she would never know. And, even if she has counted them, I can deny any knowledge of them and she may think she made a mistake.*

I gave the sweet a sniff and placed it on the table. With supreme self-control, I moved away from the dish and turned my attention to the armchairs. I never got the opportunity to sit in them when my parents were at home, as they were always in them. I knew not to push my luck by presuming I was even allowed to. A feeling of guilt came over me as I gently lowered myself onto the front edge of my step-mother's chair. I knew she would 'do her nut' if she knew my scraggy backside had sat on her throne. After a minute or so, I felt confident enough to ease myself back into the chair until my feet were off the ground. The chair smelt of her perfume and that distinct woman smell.

After a few minutes, I moved over to my dad's chair, which smelled of his work clothes and brilliantine. Feeling good about defying my parents by sitting in their chairs, I decided to check out the rest of the room.

The ornaments in the display cabinet caught my eye, but the door was locked.

Again, my eye fell on the sweet in the middle of the table. It was like a magnet drawing me to it. Picking it up, I succumbed to giving it a tentative lick. I was desperate to eat it, but with my mouth drooling, put it back on the table. I still couldn't quite bring myself to putting it back in the dish.

I then turned my attention to the wireless, my dad's pride and joy. I only got to hear it when he was listening to it. But I was well aware it needed an accumulator to power it, because it was my job to get it charged each week. It was also the reason the playing of the wireless was strictly monitored. Each Saturday, I took the accumulator to the electrical shop and swapped it for a re-charged one, which cost sixpence.

I chanced switching the wireless on. Several seconds passed before the dulcet sound of music filtered through. Anxious to see what each of the three knobs on the front of it did, I gave the first one a twirl, delighted as the volume increased. The second one had me losing the music. Worried that my dad would know I'd touched the wireless, I desperately rotated the dial back and forth, panicking when I couldn't find the station. Suddenly, a voice rang out.

'What are you doing?'

I nearly jumped out of my skin, as I turned to see my brother standing in the doorway, grinning.

'You idiot, you nearly frightened me to death.' I shouted. 'Now look what you made me do.'

'What you on about?' he asked.

I told him he had made me lose the music. Pushing me out of the way, he moved the dial.

'There, easy isn't it,' he said.

'You sure that's the right station?'

'Yeah, the 'old man' always listens to the 'Light Programme'.'

'What's that?' I asked.

He explained the different programmes to me and I checked them on the dial. Never know when I might need to know them again.

'You been eating these?' he asked, indicating the wine gums.

'No.'

'So why is this one lying here?'

'Dunno, it must have fell out of the dish.'

'Yeah right. You were going to eat it weren't you?'

'No, as if I would do that. She's bound to have counted them. Anyway, I got into enough trouble with the Mars bar in Exmouth.' He smiled as he recalled the incident.

'Why aren't you at work?' I asked.

'I am. I just delivered a telegram next door. Just as well as it turns out.'

This was also his first time in the house when our parents weren't home. He went into their bedroom and had a look around, before sitting in my step-mother's chair. I followed his initiative and sat in my dad's chair. For a while, we both enjoyed a few moments of forbidden pleasure.

After a while, he stood up, and I followed him out to where his telegram bike was leaning against the fence.

'Can I have a ride on your bike?' I asked.

'No, I haven't got time, I will be late back.' I watched him peddle off, before going back into the house.

After checking the cupboards and drawers normally out of bounds to me, I checked out the pantry. Finding nothing to eat, I wandered back into the lounge for another look at the wine gums. Then I noticed it. The sweet I had left on the table was gone. Quickly emptying the dish, I counted them out. Thirteen. My brother had taken a sweet and my step-mother would think I had taken it. *Well,* I thought. *If I am going to get into trouble, it might as well be for something I had done.*

Taking a sweet, I placed it in my mouth. I'd hardly taken one suck when a pang of fear gripped me. Quickly removing the sweet from my mouth, I carefully checked it for teeth marks, before drying it on the dish towel and placing it at the bottom of the dish. I locked the house and wandered off.

When I returned, my parents were home. Quietly entering through the back door, I was delighted to see my meal was on the kitchen table. *That's a good sign*, I thought. *If I'm getting fed, I have a half decent chance she hasn't spotted there is a wine gum missing.*

I could hear the wireless playing, another good sign. My brother must have put it back to the right station. I slid silently into my chair and began eating. I thought, if all else fails at least I would have a full belly.

After a few minutes, my step-mother entered the kitchen. I pretended not to notice her by focussing on my food, only looking up at the sound of her filling the kettle. She placed it on the gas stove.

'Why didn't you say something when you came in?' she asked.

'I didn't want to disturb you.'

'Since when has that bothered you? Did you feed the chickens?'

'Yes.'

'Everything alright?'

'Yes.'

'You sure? It was your first time in the house by yourself.'

I took a mouthful of food and slowly chewed it. Suddenly, she grabbed my wrist, knocking my fork to the floor.

'Do you think I'm stupid? You fill your mouth full of food; food I have provided, whilst you think up an excuse. I asked if everything was alright.' She looked directly into my eyes as she increased her grip.

'You're hurting me,' I squealed.

191

She slowly released my wrist, moved over to the stove, and made some tea. Now I knew all was not well. I picked up my fork and quickly shovelled the remains of my meal into my mouth. The wireless suddenly went quiet, and my dad entered the kitchen.

'Have you asked him yet?'

'Not yet,' replied my step-mother. 'But he says everything was alright.'

Grabbing my arm, my dad dragged me into the lounge. The sweet dish had been emptied onto the table.

'I asked you if everything was alright and you said it was, but you weren't telling the truth, were you?' said my step-mother. I silently gazed out the window into the darkness, unsure what to say.

'Well...I'm waiting,' she said.

'What?' I mumbled.

'Don't say 'what'. You know fine well what I mean. And look at me when I'm talking to you.' I turned my head as she gestured towards the sweets.

'Do you want me to spell it out? Somebody has been eating the sweets. I know, because I counted them. You were the only person in the house, so it could only have been you, right.'

She paused...

I desperately searched for an answer. I knew my brother had taken the sweet, but if I said anything he might tell them I had touched the wireless. But touching the wireless was not as bad as stealing a sweet; at least I didn't think so.

'I was not,' I finally said.

'Was not what?' she asked.

'Was not the only one in the house,' I mumbled.

'So, you've had your friends in here. What have I told you about bringing people into the house when we aren't here? I told you not to bring anyone into the house, didn't I?' She turned to my dad.

'See, he does nothing he is told. I knew it was a bad idea giving him a key.'

'It was your idea to give him a key, I was the one against it,' my dad pointed out.

'That's right, take his part,' she retorted.

'I'm not taking anyone's part,' he replied.

'Well you should, you should be taking my part. So, who else was in the house?'

'Frankie,' I answered.

'Frankie, how could he? He was supposed to be at work.'

'I know,' I said, desperate to save my own skin. 'But he had a telegram to deliver next door, and came into the house. When he left, the sweet was gone.' Just then the back door opened and closed.

'Frankie, come in here,' my dad called out. When he didn't immediately appear, my dad raised his voice.

'Did you hear me?' A moment later my brother entered the room.

'Did you call me?' he asked, in all innocence.

I looked at his face, and he immediately averted his eyes. I knew he had heard my dad the first time, but had deliberately stalled to give himself time to think up a story.

'What do you know about the sweets?' my dad asked.

'Sweets, what sweets?' he replied, an expression of surprise on his face.

'You know exactly what sweets I am talking about, those sweets.'

'What about them?' he asked, glancing in their direction as if it was the first time he had seen them.

'Billy said you took one. Is that right? Did you take one or not?'

'Me, I mean…when would I have taken one? I was at work, went there straight from school.'

'So, you weren't in the house earlier?'

'No, this is the first I've been in the house since leaving this morning.'

'You're lying.' I shouted. 'He's a liar. He had a telegram to deliver next door and he came into the house after he had delivered it. Ask the people next door, they'll tell you.'

'Oh that. I admit I delivered a telegram next door, but I went straight back to the post office. You can ask the postmaster. I wouldn't have had time to come in here. It's our busiest period.' He was good. He told a bare-faced lie and his face gave nothing away.

'You're lying,' I shouted, my frustration bringing me close to tears.

I looked at my dad. From the look on his face I knew I was losing the argument. I played my last card.

'You're lying and I can prove it, because you were in here and fixed the wireless.'

At the mention of the word 'wireless' my dad's head immediately turned. In one move he crossed over to it.

'What happened to the wireless? he asked, anxiously examining the set.

'No idea,' chipped in my brother.

'Billy?' my dad said. I immediately regretted mentioning the wireless.

'Somebody better tell me what's going on, or there is going to be trouble.' My step-mother eased herself forward in her chair.

'What about the sweets?' she asked.

'Never mind the sweets,' said my dad. 'What about the wireless. Did you break it or what? Tell me what happened?' He moved in my direction.

'Nothing,' I said, backing towards the door.

'So what did you mean, Frankie fixed it?'

I explained what happened. He turned the wireless on listening intently to each station, as if that would detect a fault. Once he was satisfied his precious wireless was alright, he returned to his armchair. My step-mother looked his way.

'So, you going to say something?'

My dad reached for his tobacco, slowly rolled himself a cigarette, and leaned forward. Taking a long drag on his rollup, he blew a plume of smoke towards the ceiling.

'It is obvious you are both lying and that neither of you can be trusted. You no doubt picked up those bad habits whilst you were evacuated. So, I'm going to tell you one…last…time.' He took another drag from his rollup and blew a plume of blue smoke towards the ceiling.

'Whenever you are in this house, nobody, repeat nobody, comes in and you don't touch anything. The only reason you get into the house at all when we are not here is to do a couple of little jobs. Your mum and I are both working, trying to make a home for us all, and all we get is problems.'

'But I didn't do anything,' whinged my brother.

'Yes you did,' I cut in.

'Shut up the pair of you,' shouted my dad. 'One more word and you'll get my hand. Now the two of you, get out of my sight. Go on, go to your room.'

I hurried away glad to be out of it. As soon as the door was closed my brother grabbed me and pinned me to the bed, slapping me around the head.

'You little twit, you could have got me into trouble. Why did you tell them I took the sweet? Now they know I was in the house.'

'Because you did, and I don't see why I should take the blame. And anyway, what difference does it make.'

'Because I don't want the postmaster to know.'

'Who's going to tell him?'

'Never mind. You don't understand.'

The following day, the sweets were gone. I rummaged around and found them at the bottom of my parents' wardrobe.

Some days later, I spotted the dish on the draining board, and wondered who had eaten the sweet I had sucked and put back.

Chapter Forty-Two

The novelty of being allowed into the house soon faded. I had been into every room and rummaged through every drawer and cupboard so there was nothing more to interest me. My main concern was making sure I didn't mention something I could only have known about if I had been poking around somewhere I shouldn't. I had to bite my tongue a couple of times.

With the passing of summer, the evenings became cooler as the winter closed in. Time to start lighting the fire, suggested my stepmother. My dad avoided the suggestion, probably because the longer we went without a fire the less it would cost him for coal. In the past, he had always lit the fire when he came in from work, but decided that as I was in the house anyway, I could light it.

Come the weekend, he and I went to one of the many bombed buildings on Canvey and rummaged for timber. He sawed it into manageable lengths, and I chopped it into sticks. I casually mentioned that the greengrocer's shop sold firewood already chopped and bundled, and why didn't he just buy it and save all the bother.

'Why would you pay for wood that you can get for free,' he smugly replied.

There's a general belief, rightly or wrongly, that the Scots are mean. If anybody helped create this notion, it was my dad.

As soon as we finished chopping the wood, we trudged to the coal yard. My dad bought a 28-pound bag of coal. Coal could be delivered in one hundredweight sacks, but as we lived on an unmade road they wouldn't deliver.

'Do you think you could carry this?' he asked, indicating the bag of coal.

It was far heavier than I thought. If I used two hands, I could dangle the bag between my legs, walk a few yards, take a rest, and so on, like I did with the can of petrol.

'So, if you had to go for a bag of coal, do you think you could get it home on your own?' he asked.

'I suppose so, eventually,' I replied, with little enthusiasm.

'Good, because you just might have too.' Back home he showed me how to lay the fire. After scrunching up a couple of pages of the newspaper, he placed the sticks in a crisscross fashion on top.

'Got to make sure the air can circulate,' he said, placing several pieces of coal on the sticks. He held a match to the newspaper, which immediately flared up, but burnt away before the sticks had caught alight.

'The wood must be damp,' he said, re-laying the fire.

Again, the newspaper burnt away without the wood catching alight. I suggested that it was probably because it was the wrong wood and he should have bought some proper sticks.

'Rubbish,' he snorted, 'Wood is wood.' A few moments later he returned with a can of petrol.

'That should do it,' he said, after dunking several pieces of wood into it. Soon the coal was burning, and we had a roaring fire.

'Right, do you think you can do that without burning the house down?' he asked.

'Yeah, I think so,' I replied.

'But remember, don't touch the petrol. It's too dangerous. Understand?'

I thought about pointing out that if he had not used petrol he would never have got the fire alight, but he was already reading my mind.

'I know I had to use it, but that was because the wood was wet. But you will have dry wood. In fact, let's bring the wood we have

197

already chopped into the house and place it close to the fire so that it dries out. Then, all you have to do is gather some more wood from the bomb sites, chop it up, and leave it on the veranda out of the rain, and so on.'

I left my dad sprawled in his armchair in front of the fire and went off in search of firewood.

Canvey Island, being on the River Thames and adjacent to London, had been hard hit during the war, so there was no shortage of bombed houses. I soon returned home with a couple of roof trusses, the remnants of some unfortunate person's house before the war. When my dad saw them he said.

'That's good timber, too good for burning. Place it under the bungalow, I might be able to use that.' From then on, I only brought home the 'scabby' pieces of wood.

On the Monday, I hurried home from school concerned about lighting the fire. I cleaned out the grate, tipped the ashes on the front path, and laid the fire like my dad had shown me. But, just like when he did it, the paper burnt away and the wood had not caught.

I re-laid the fire. Again, the wood failed to light. I was getting short of newspaper, so if it didn't catch this time, I would have a problem.

Stuff it, I thought, *I'll use some of his precious petrol like he did, he'll never know.* I poured some petrol into one of my jam jars and dunked several sticks in it.

From then on, I became adept at lighting the fire, as long as my dad kept some petrol on the veranda.

Then one evening, I came home and there was no firewood. I dragged one of the pieces from under the bungalow and set about sawing it into lengths. My dad had made it look easy, but when I tried, I had problems. I just wasn't strong enough to hold the wood with one hand, whilst sawing it with the other. Finally, after several attempts, I screamed in frustration and flung the wood across the garden, before running over and kicking it.

Muttering to myself that I didn't care if we had a fire or not, I suddenly remembered I had not fed the chickens. In the kitchen, I found the pot had boiled over and made a mess on the stove.

'Bugger,' I yelled, grabbing the pot and quickly letting it go as it burned my hand. 'Bugger, bugger, shit, bugger,' I screamed, running my hand under the cold-water tap.

'This is what happens when I have too much to do.' I shouted. 'Why can't someone else do something, instead of it all being left to me?'

To make matters worse, by the time I got outside, the hens were already drifting towards the nesting box. I banged the pot with the masher, which normally brought them running, but not tonight.

'Don't go to bed, you haven't been fed,' I shouted.

Opening the nesting box, I chased them out, and stuffed an old sack into the doorway so they couldn't get back in.

I put their food down, willing them to eat it as I didn't want my step-mother knowing I had been late feeding them. After a few minutes, with the food hardly touched, they were attempting to get into the nesting box. Removing the sacking, I picked up the dish and moved it to the back of the run. I hoped the chickens were early risers and would have eaten their food before my step-mother checked on them in the morning.

Back in the lounge, I cleaned out the grate, to make it look like I had at least intended to light the fire. Then I noticed there was no coal.

'Shit. Don't tell me I was supposed to get coal.' I again went into a flat panic as I quickly checked to see if my dad had left any money. My luck was in. No money, no coal, no coal, no fire. Perfect.

Buoyed up now I was off the hook, I made another attempt to saw the wood. I still couldn't cut it, and my short elation quickly evaporated. Throwing the wood onto the grass, completely pissed off, I attacked it with the axe. Minutes later, after taking my frustration out on an innocent piece of wood, I threw it over the fence so my dad wouldn't see it.

My step-mother was hardly in the house, when, despite my attempts to clean the stove, she said.

'Did you let the pot boil over?'

I was about to explain what happened, when my dad asked why there was no fire. I told him we didn't have any coal. He then noticed

199

that we had no wood chopped either, saying that even if there had been coal we still wouldn't of had a fire. I used the opportunity to again ask why we couldn't get firewood from the grocers, pointing out that I had so many things to do when I came in from school that firewood already chopped would make things easier. For my efforts, he gave me a lecture on managing my time more effectively, pointing out that if I chopped some wood each evening, I would always have a store in hand.

After stacking the wood my dad cut, I went to the kitchen to see what there was for eating. My step-mother was standing in front of the oven with her skirt raised warming her backside. My dad remarked on how expensive it was to use the oven in this way.

'Well I'm not standing here freezing; this house is as cold as ice.'

He didn't pursue the issue and joined her. After rolling himself a smoke, he lit it from the gas top, my step-mother laughingly remarking that with his nose he was in danger of singeing it. He just snorted and blew a stream of smoke in her direction.

Without moving from her warm spot in front of the oven, she indicated with a nod of her head the food she had brought home from the restaurant. I began eating.

'Take your time,' she said.

Every time I ate, she mentioned my eating habits. I would momentarily slow down, but I didn't enjoy my food if I didn't stuff my mouth full.

Moments later, she turned off the oven and went into the bedroom. My dad watched her leave the room, looked at the oven, then at me. His expression suggested it didn't matter whether he wanted the oven on or not. She had finished warming herself, so that was that. Had I been in the kitchen by myself, I would have expected it. There was no way she would have left the oven on for my benefit. But as my dad had already commented on it being an expensive way to heat the house, he couldn't really say anything. Stubbing out his cigarette, he followed her into the bedroom and asked if she was going to bed.

'Well there's no fire, nothing on the wireless, and I'm not standing in front of a gas oven all night, so what's the point of staying up.' He closed the bedroom door.

I stared at my empty plate and wished there was more to eat, but there never was, so I silently left the kitchen and went to bed.

The next day, as we were all about to leave the house, my dad pointed out that he had left half a crown in the dish in the front room for me to buy coal. I complained that by the time I fed the chickens, the coal yard would be shut.

'Go for the coal first then,' he said.

'But if I go for the coal first, it will be too late to feed the chickens.'

He grabbed me by the arm and wheeled me into the kitchen. I knew I had pushed my luck too far. He clenched his teeth and put his face close to mine.

'I have had enough of your continual complaining. Every time you are told to do something you have an excuse for not doing it. I am sick of it, and so is your mother.' The nicotine on his breath was rancid in my face, as his big hand squeezed my arm.

'You're hurting me,' I screamed, struggling to get free. He loosened his grip and stepped back,

'Don't be such a baby, I didn't hurt you.'

I rubbed my arm and gazed at him resentfully. He was about to launch into another tirade of words, when my step-mother called out it was time to go.

'I expect to see a fire and the chickens fed when I come in tonight, so don't let me down.'

After school I ran all the way home. No dawdling now. After lighting the gas under the chicken's food, I picked up the half crown and ran to the coal yard, getting there just before they closed.

'Twenty-eight pounds of coal please mister,' I breathlessly blurted out. The man looked at the clock on the wall. For one heart stopping moment I thought he was going to tell me I was too late.

'That'll be half a crown,' he said.

One of the men in the yard tipped the coal into a bag, picked up his shovel and went back to the office.

With the bag dangling between my legs, I left the yard, waddling as fast as I could. I didn't get far before my arms and back were aching. After several more attempts, I didn't feel as if I was making much headway, and worried that I wouldn't be home before the pot boiled over. I wished I had Pop's barrow.

'Do you want a hand with that son, you look as if you're struggling?'

It was the man from the coal yard. He made light work of it, carrying the bag with one hand to the end of my road.

Thankfully the pot had not boiled over and I was able to feed the chickens before they roosted for the night.

When Peter's mother learned I had to go for coal, she loaned me a wheel barrow. Each time I asked her for it she remarked that it was disgraceful that someone my age should be expected to hump coal and light fires.

'After all,' she added. 'Anything could happen, and you in that house alone, the place could burn down.' Little did she know how close to the truth she was.

Chapter Forty-Three

Over the months the chickens grew. Apart from the daily feeding, their run needed continual digging. Also, due to the heavy clay soil on Canvey Island, when the chickens scratched around, small balls of hard mud formed, which had to be broken up. My brother and I spent hours kneeling on a piece of old sacking, whilst breaking them up with a hammer. It was back-breaking work and hard on the knees, but the promise of an egg when they started laying kept me motivated.

I had never actually had an egg to myself, and because we kept chickens our egg ration was cut to two per week, my parents taking them. I did however get to watch my dad eat his. It was a work of art watching him eat a fried egg. He could eat a soft fried egg without spilling a drop of the yolk. As he carefully dipped his bread into the yolk, I would swallow along with him, longing for the day I would get an egg to myself.

Then one evening, I was ecstatic, when I found an egg in one of the nests. As I gently picked it up I noticed it had poo on it. I wondered which chicken had laid it, looking intently at each of them as if there would be some tell-tale sign.

My excitement was too much to keep to myself, so I rushed over to Peter's house.

'Come quick, I have something to show you.' I said, excitedly.

'What is it?' he asked.

'You'll see.'

I hurried him into my garden and around to the back. Opening the door to the hen house I proudly pointed to the egg.

'Look.' I said, standing to one side so he could see it.

'It's an egg,' he said.

'Yeah I know. Isn't it good.'

'Is that it. I thought it was something exciting,' he said, rather disappointedly.

'Well I think it's exciting. It's my first egg, and I reared them from day-old chicks.'

We went back over to his house and his mum asked what was so exciting.

'Just an old egg his chickens have laid,' said Peter. 'Anyone would think it was something great.'

'Well I expect Billy is excited as it's his first egg,' she said, comfortingly.

I left Peter and went back for another look at the egg. I couldn't wait for my parents to come home so I could share the news with them. Finally, I spotted them coming down the road and ran to meet them.

'Guess what?' I excitedly shouted out. 'One of the chickens has laid an egg.' They were not as excited as I thought they might be. Carefully laying the egg on the draining board, I pointed to the poo.

'That's good,' said my step-mother. 'Shows it's fresh.' She washed it under the tap commenting that it was a good size.

'So, what we going to do with the egg?' I asked her.

'We' is going to do nothing with it. But 'I' might bake a cake with it,' she replied.

I was left in no doubt that any eggs the chickens laid, irrespective of any work I did, were not mine, and were for the whole family. The thought of the egg being used to bake a cake seemed such a waste, even though I liked cake.

My step-mother gave me my supper. I thanked her, but would rather have had the egg.

As the weather warmed up, the chickens began laying regularly, sometimes as many as three eggs a day. Then, one Saturday evening, I arrived home and was greeted by my step-mother with.

'Got a treat for you tonight.'

'What is it?' I asked.

'A fried egg for your tea.'

'What, a whole egg to myself?' the surprise obvious in my voice.

'Yes, don't sound so surprised.'

'Well I am surprised. I've never had an egg before.'

The only egg I could remember was powdered egg, which vaguely resembled scrambled eggs.

Now I knew I was getting an egg, it seemed for ever before I was called to the table. Feasting my eyes on my plate I was even more delighted when I saw a couple of fried potatoes. This was the moment I had waited ten years for. I was about to taste my first egg.

Spearing a piece of potato with my fork, I thought about dipping it into the egg yolk, but worried it would spill all over the plate. Frankie on the other hand, pierced his yolk, stuck a piece of potato into it, and shoved it into his mouth.

'That is pure waste,' my father said.

'What is?' he asked.

'That!' My dad pointed to the yolk which had run onto the plate.

'That's alright, I'll rub my spud in it,' said my brother. My dad gave him a scornful look.

'I don't know why I bother to give you an egg,' he said. 'You don't deserve one when you waste it like that. Don't you know how to eat an egg without wasting it?'

Not wanting a similar fate, I watched how my dad ate his egg and followed his moves. After carefully cutting off the white, leaving just the yolk, he carefully broke the pink skin without spilling a drop onto the plate. With a piece of potato on his fork, he carefully scraped some of the yellow liquid onto it, and placed it into his mouth.

Now it was my turn. I nervously prodded the egg yolk with my fork. It wouldn't break. I tried again, hoping it wouldn't burst and run all over the plate. I could feel my dad watching me, which made me even more nervous.

Hands shaking, I pressed the fork a little harder. Finally, the skin broke without the yolk running over the plate.

'You made quite a job of that. I didn't think it was that difficult to eat an egg,' said my dad.

I enjoyed my first egg, but I'm sure it would have tasted much better if my dad's beady eyes hadn't been watching my every move. I hoped the next time I got an egg he was nowhere around.

The following weekend, my step-mother came home carrying a cardboard box. I thought she had bought more chickens.

'Come and see what we've got,' she said. To my delight, lying in the box was a beautiful small brown puppy.

'Oh, he's great. What we going to call him?' I excitedly asked.

'Heinz,' said my dad.

'Heinz. That's a strange name. Why would we call him that? That's the name of the baked beans.' I replied.

'Heinz don't just make baked beans. They make other things as well.'

'I thought that was the name of the beans in the tin. Heinz.'

'No, Heinz is the manufacturer. The beans in the tin are Navy Beans. Heinz just cooks them and puts them in the tin. Heinz makes lots of other things too. 57 of them. That's what Heinz 57 means. They make 57 varieties of food, so any dog that's made up of more than one breed is called a Heinz variety.'

'Wow, I never knew that. I've only ever seen the beans.'

'He's not a mongrel. He's a fox terrier,' said my step-mother in defence, as if there was no way she would have a mongrel. We took him into the garden and I showed him the chickens.

'We'll have to watch him when he gets bigger or he'll have those chickens for his dinner,' said my dad.

'I don't think so,' said my step-mother. 'If he grows up with them he'll be used to them.' It was decided we would call him Gyp.

Whilst we were all out on the Monday, we left him in the house. As soon as school was finished, I rushed home, anxious to see my new friend. As I opened the door he scampered over to me tail wagging. I noticed he had messed on the floor, spilt his water, and the kitchen stank. Cleaning up after him was a rotten job, but because I loved the little 'fella', I didn't mind.

Not wanting my step-mother to know the mess he had made, in case she decided to get rid of him, I played it down and said it wasn't too bad.

After a few weeks, Gyp had grown big enough to leave out during the day. My dad placed a wooden box with an old blanket in it under the bungalow. He loved it.

The first day we left him outside, I couldn't get home from school quick enough. I was worried he might have wandered off, relieved when I saw him in the garden. Rex came to the fence. I hadn't walked Rex since we got the chickens, and hoped he wasn't too jealous of the new puppy. But I still hopped over the fence to visit the old lady in her bell tent. She was always good for a cup of tea and a chat, plus the occasional biscuit.

Chapter Forty-Four

One afternoon, I was hanging around in the garden when I spotted my brother sneaking into the bedroom. I sensed he had something he didn't want my parents to see, and quickly followed him.

'Shut the door. What do you want?' he said.

'Nothing,' I replied.

Turning his back to me, he took something out of his shirt and tucked it under the bed.

'What's that?' I asked.

'Never you mind. And don't go looking at it when I'm not here. I'll know if it's been touched.'

'What is it?'

'Nothing. I knew you would be like this, that's why I didn't want you to know anything. Now just forget it.' I made as if to reach under the bed.

'I'm warning you, you touch it and you will get it from me.' He waved a fist in my face and pushed me onto the bed.

'Tell me what it is. I promise I won't say anything.' The door suddenly opened. It was my step-mother.

'What are you two up to in here?' she asked.

'Nothing mum,' we both said. She looked suspiciously around the room and closed the door.

That evening my brother left the house with the package tucked into his shirt. I quickly followed him.

'What do you want?' he asked.

'I want to see what you've got.'

'Nothing to do with you, now bugger off.' I continued to follow.

'Don't follow me. Go on bugger off.'

'I'm not following you, I can go this way if I want to,' I replied.

The farther we went, the more curious I became. Finally, he said.

'Alright, if I show you what it is, you've got to promise you won't tell anybody.'

'I promise,' I automatically replied.

Removing the package from his shirt, he slowly opened the cloth, delighted when he saw my reaction.

'Wow, a gun, where did you get it?'

'You've got to promise you won't tell anyone about it.'

'I won't say a word, I promise. Can I hold it.' He handed me the gun, which was heavier than I expected. I pointed it at a tree.

'Pieu, pieu,' I said, pretending to shoot.

'Where do you put the bullets in?' I asked, anxious to shoot at something.

'It doesn't fire bullets, it fires slugs.' He took the gun and loaded it.

'Can I have a shot then?' I said.

'Wait, I'll show you how to shoot,' he said.

'I know how to shoot.'

'No you don't, you've never had a gun,' he snorted.

'I've seen them in the pictures.' I said, remembering all the cowboy films I'd seen.

He pulled the trigger. The gun made a short hissing sound and the slug cracked into the tree. I ran over to the tree and found the slug squashed into the bark. I pulled a nail from my pocket, and prised it out.

He reloaded the gun and handed it to me. Pointing it at the tree, I pulled the trigger and the slug whizzed out and powerfully struck the tree. *Wow*, I thought, *I've got to have one of these.*

'Can I have another go?' I asked.

'No, that's all the slugs I've got.'

I suspected he had more, but wanted to save them for another time. I handed him the gun back. He carefully wrapped it and put it in his shirt.

When we went in, I was to distract my parents whilst he hid the gun under the bed. The plan worked well. Each evening I would go in first and greet my parents, whilst Frankie hid the gun under the bed. Normally, that would have been a safe place, as my step-mother very rarely came into our room. But as luck would have it, the following day, Saturday, my step-mother decided to change the sheet on our bed. We were in the garden when we spotted her going into our bedroom.

'We've got to get the gun out of there before she finds it,' said my brother, a note of panic in his voice. 'Sneak in and get it without her seeing you.'

'Me. It's your gun, you'll have to move it. What if I'm caught, what do I tell her,' I replied.

'You won't get caught. Now get in there quick before she finds it.' He grabbed my arm and propelled me towards the house.

'No, it's your gun, you go and get it,' I said, pulling my arm free.

'If she finds it, you'll be in trouble too. Don't forget you had a go of it too.'

When I didn't move, he grabbed hold of me and dragged me towards the back door. The more I resisted, the more anxious he became.

'Stop messing about. Just go into the room and pass it out to me through the window.'

I slunk into the kitchen where I could see my step-mother busy in her own bedroom. Nipping into our bedroom, which was directly off the kitchen, I quietly closed the door and headed for the window. Pulling the tatty net curtains to one side, I could see my brother anxiously waiting in the garden below. Then, something we had not allowed for. The window wouldn't budge. I don't think we had ever opened it. No matter what I did, the window wouldn't move.

'Push it harder,' my brother mouthed from the garden, annoyed it was taking so long.

I decided to leave the window and chance sneaking out with the gun under my jumper. But just as I opened the door, my step-mother came out of her bedroom into the kitchen. Quickly retreating, I put the gun back under the bed. I made a final lunge for the window, pushing it so hard I was worried the glass would break. Finally, it creaked open on its rusty hinges, the creaking not missed by my step-mother.

'What are you up to in there?' she called, opening the door.

'Nothing.' I replied, dropping the gun to my brother. He immediately ran off.

'Why did you open the window?' she asked, pushing me to one side and looking out.

'I wanted some fresh air.'

'Fresh air, since when have you been interested in fresh air? You would sleep in a sewer and it wouldn't bother you,' she sarcastically remarked. I eased myself out the room and went in search of my brother.

'Didn't see anything did she?' he asked.

'No. So, where have you hidden it?'

'In the chicken run under one of the nests.'

That afternoon I checked the hens to see if they had laid any eggs, and found the gun. I couldn't resist checking it out. Suddenly, the door opened, and my brother's face loomed over me.

'I knew you would be in here. What if it had been the old man? I told you not to touch it. Now put it back.'

He punched me in the ribs, and ducked out. I was just about to say something, when I heard my father's voice and Frankie reply.

'Nothing Dad, Billy's just checking to see if there are any eggs.'

Hearing this, I slowly backed out. I sensed my dad was standing there but turned as if surprised.

'Hi dad. Didn't see you there. Look an egg.' He took it from me and wandered into the house.

A few days later, when I noticed the gun was no longer in the nesting box, I looked under the bed. But it was gone. My brother told me he put it back where he found it. He said he couldn't just hand it back to the boy who had lost it, as it would look suspicious. So, he placed it in the field where he found it. Then, on his way home with the boy whose gun it was, he pretended to find it. The boy was so happy to get his gun back he didn't bother to ask how, despite numerous searches, it had not been spotted before.

Chapter Forty-Five

Returning home from the beach one afternoon, I noticed my friend Peter impressing his mother on how well he could ride a two-wheeler bike. *That's got to be a new bike* I thought. I homed in on him.

'Hi Peter,' I said. 'I was looking for you earlier on. Wanted to ask if you were coming to the beach today.'

'I was in all day, why didn't you tell me you were going?' he replied.

'I would have if I had seen you, but I couldn't find you,' I lied.

In truth, I didn't want him with me because he was a bit of a wimp. But now he had a bike. That was a different story.

'Like my bike?' he asked.

'Yeah, it's alright, I suppose.' I was really quite envious of him, but didn't want him to think I was too concerned.

'Is it new?' I asked.

'Not brand new,' said his mother. 'It's very difficult to get new bikes, but my 'friend' has done it up so it's as good as new.' Peter turned the bike around and rode off down the road.

'Have you got a bike Billy?' his mother asked, knowing fine well I didn't.

'No,' I replied.

'Well I'm sure Peter will give you a go on his bike, after all, that's what friends are for, isn't it?'

The look she gave me suggested that if I wanted a ride on his bike, I would have to spend more time with him. *Oh well*, I thought, *everybody has to make sacrifices. And if it means hanging out with Peter to get a ride on his bike, then that's the price I'll have to pay.*

'Give Billy a go on your bike Peter,' she said, as he drew up.

'No, I want to play on it.'

'He is your friend after all.'

'No he's not, he goes off and leaves me,' he whined.

Without thinking I said, 'Well I won't in future, if I go anywhere you can come with me.'

The second the words were out of my mouth I could have cut my tongue out. What was I saying? And in front of his mother.

'There,' she said. 'Can't ask fairer than that can you?'

Reluctantly, he climbed from the bike and handed it to me. I slung my leg over the crossbar and launched myself up the unmade road. It never occurred to me that as I had never been on a two-wheeler bike before, a certain amount of skill was required. I fell in a heap, to the amusement of Peter and his mum.

'Haven't you ever been on a bike before?' she asked.

'No,' I replied, picking myself up.

I tried again, but before I could gather any momentum on the unmade road, I fell over. At least it provided a soft landing.

Peter's 'uncle' suddenly appeared, probably concerned the bike might not last the treatment it was getting.

'Right, sit on the saddle and put your feet on the pedals,' he said.

He held the bike as I climbed on and began pedalling. It was a shaky start, with me wobbling all over the road. At the end of the road I stopped, turned the bike around, and headed back. Without my knowledge, he took his hand away from the saddle, and before long I had it mastered. I was so thrilled to be riding on my own I rode straight past Peter and his mum. Peter ran after me, grabbed the saddle, and pulled me to a stop.

'Why didn't you stop?' he shouted.

'Sorry, I didn't know how to.'

'Pull the brakes on like this,' he said, demonstrating. I had several more go's, so by the time he was called into the house, I was quite confident.

Now I could ride a two-wheeler bike I just had to have one. Ever the optimist, I wondered how I could bring a bike into a conversation with my dad.

Later that evening, I snuck onto the front veranda and peered through the window. Both my dad and my step-mother were reading their newspapers. I saw the dial on the wireless was not lit, so knew they were not listening to their serial. *This is as good a time as ever* I thought. Running around the back, I silently entered the kitchen. After a couple of minutes of listening at the door, I steeled myself and eased into the room. I took up a position behind my step-mother's chair. My dad momentarily looked up, before returning to his paper. I waited for him to say something. After a moment or two and he still hadn't asked what I wanted, I quietly said.

'Dad.' He continued reading his newspaper.

'Dad,' I repeated, a little more loudly. From behind his newspaper he said, 'What is it?'

'Peter's got a bike.' I waited for his response. Nothing.

'His uncle got it for him,' I continued. Again nothing.

My step-mother lowered her paper and half turned in her chair. She looked at me for several seconds, her eyes going from my dirty face and unkempt hair, to my grubby shoes. Without speaking she turned back and continued reading her newspaper. My dad had still not looked up. Undeterred, I carried on.

'Peter let me have a go on it…and guess what?… I can ride a two-wheeler bike.' Still no reaction.

Throughout, he had not put his newspaper down, so I was unable to see his face. I patiently waited, nervously shuffling from one foot to the other. Still no response. Finally, I steeled myself.

'Can I get a bike, do you think?' I asked.

The room was so silent you could have heard a pin drop. Finally, my father lowered his newspaper, carefully folded it, and placed it on the small table at the side of his chair.

Reaching for his tin of Golden Virginia tobacco, he slowly rolled himself a cigarette, lit it, and blew a plume of smoke towards the ceiling.

'Do you know how much bikes cost?' he finally asked.

'No,' I answered.

'No, of course you don't, because it doesn't concern you. Where do you think I would get money to buy you a bike?'

'I don't know, but Peter got one, so why can't I?' He blew a plume of smoke in my direction. My step-mother lowered her paper.

'Just because someone else gets something it doesn't mean you have to get it also,' she said.

'What does that mean?' I asked, dejectedly. Without looking at me she said.

'It means... no... you... can't... get... a... bike. Right. Now that's it.'

It was inevitable she would support my dad; now relieved that the task of actually saying no to me had been made for him. He went back to his paper. This made my step-mother the villain of the piece, and he could content himself knowing that it was not him who had actually refused.

I didn't move, hoping that something, anything, would happen to make them change their minds. My dad kept his face buried in his paper, holding it in front of his face to avoid looking at me. When I made no effort to move, my step-mother looked over her shoulder in my direction.

'You still here?' she sarcastically asked.

Choking back my tears, I stomped out the room, knowing any display of emotion would only result in more sarcastic comments. I left the house and took a shortcut to the main road. On the way, I used my stick like a sword, slashing the thick stinging nettle bushes to shreds. It eased my anger. Gyp thought it was a game and ran in and out of the nettles, no doubt hoping I might scare a mouse out. The nettles didn't seem to worry him, and his antics made me feel better. I dropped to one knee, pulled him in close and gave him a big cuddle. I just loved that dog to bits.

Chapter Forty-Six

Having taken my anger out on the nettles, I made my way to the creek to see what Paul was up to. His mum stuck her head up through the hatch when I called out.

'Oh, it's you Billy, come on down,' she said.

'What about Gyppie boy?' I asked.

'Yeah, bring him too.'

Paul came to the bottom of the steps, and I passed Gyp down to him. As soon as Paul put him down, he disappeared into the boat, sniffing all the nooks and crannies. Paul said he had seen a rat onboard and hoped Gyp might find it. Paul was very fond of Gyp, and always asked where he was if ever I came without him.

'Guess what?' Paul said, as we sat down.

'What?' I replied, thinking he had found a source of free food.

'I'm joining the Sea Scouts.'

'Sea Scouts, what are they?'

He told me what little he knew of them, and explained that they had a large hut at the end of the creek.

'They meet a couple of times a week and go out in boats, and you learn how to tie knots and all sorts.' he excitedly continued.

'When are you going?' I asked.

'Tomorrow; got to be there by six.'

'Okay, I'll join too,' I said.

I knew my parents wouldn't be home at that time, and decided not to mention it to them until I knew more.

The next evening, I ran home, did my chores, and ran to Paul's with the ever-faithful Gyp by my side.

I waited impatiently for Paul, anxious to get going. Finally, he emerged from the boat.

'My mum left me a load of work to do, got to earn my pocket money somehow. Not only that, if we have to pay for the Sea Scouts that'll be more money as well.' I suddenly stopped dead in my tracks.

'What do you mean, pay? I can't pay. I haven't got any money. I thought it was free. If we have to pay, that's me out.'

We set off at a steady jog along the sea wall, with Gyp running everywhere. He loved to let me get twenty or so yards ahead, then come running like mad and race ahead of me. But the thought that we might have to pay had dampened my enthusiasm. As we approached the hut, we saw several boys in their Sea Scout uniforms and followed them, standing uncomfortably by the door. Soon, the scout master spotted us.

'Yes boys, are you interested in joining the Sea Scouts?'

'Don't know, what do you do here?' I asked.

He briefly told us what they did and invited us to stay and watch. After about an hour or so they had a break, and we were invited to join them for a cup of tea and a bun. I commented to Paul it would be worth coming each week just to get the tea and bun. He agreed, as he hungrily stuffed his bun into his mouth.

I called Gyp, who had been sniffing around in the hut, and gave him a piece of my bun. Paul grudgingly followed.

'In future, don't bring your dog,' the Scout master told me.

Most of the scouts were wearing a sailor's round hat with a cap tally that read 'Sea Scouts', a seaman's jersey, and a green scarf held in place with a woggle. They also wore short grey trousers, with green chevrons in the top of their grey socks. I thought they all looked very smart and could see myself in such a uniform.

At the end of the evening, the scout master asked us what we thought and if we would like to join.

'How much is it?' we both asked.

'You don't have to pay to come here as the council funds us. But you will have to buy your uniform.'

'How much is that?' I asked.

'Well you don't have to buy it all at once. You can buy a little bit at a time. I expect you already have trousers, socks, and shoes, so all you will need is the seaman's jersey, scarf, woggle, and hat.'

It was obvious he had not seen my wardrobe. I had none of those things. My clothing consisted of what I was wearing, and by the look the scout master gave me he obviously thought I had something better to wear.

'Don't let the uniform put you off, you are still welcome to join,' he added.

On the way home, we discussed whether we should join or not. I was keen as I liked the idea of the free tea and bun, and was sure I could learn to tie a few knots and do other nautical things.

When I got home my parents were sitting in the front room with their noses stuck in their newspapers. I stuck my head around the corner to let them know I was in.

'Your tea is on the table,' said my step-mother without raising her head from her paper.

Whilst I ate, I pondered how I could tell my dad about the Sea Scouts in such a way that he would buy me a uniform. I hoped it would go better than when I asked him to buy me a bike. But a bike was expensive and could cost as much as a pound, whereas a uniform was much cheaper. That thought gave me hope.

When I finished my tea, I casually entered the front room, taking up my usual position behind my step-mother's chair. I never ventured far into the room when they were in it; I felt like I was trespassing. My dad, true to form, momentarily looked up without speaking, before going back to his newspaper. Taking a deep breath, I said.

'Dad, I've been to the Sea Scouts.'

I waited for him to respond, but again, true to form, he said nothing. Undeterred, I proceeded to tell him all about it. When I finished I said,

'I would like to join.'

'How much is it?' he asked, from behind his newspaper.

'Nothing, the council pays, and you get a free cup of tea and a bun.'

I thought this would go down well as he was always impressed with something for nothing.

'Well it seems like a good thing, so it should be alright.' I breathed a little easier as I left the room.

That was the first hurdle over. I decided not to mention the uniform until I had officially joined. I would then say that I didn't know anything about it costing money, pointing out that he had agreed to let me join, therefore he should buy my uniform.

The following week, Paul and I joined. During the tea break, the scout master asked if we would be buying any uniform parts, as he wanted us to start looking like sea scouts. He suggested we get the seaman's jersey first, as we could then sew any badges we earned onto it. He said he would give each of us a hat for nothing, as he had some spare ones that had been handed in when people left the Sea Scouts.

'Can I have it now?' I asked, anxious to start looking like a sea scout.

'No, you can't just wear a hat, you need at least to have the seaman's jersey, otherwise you'll look silly. Bring your money next week, and I'll get one for you.'

'How much is it?' I asked.

'Complete uniform is five shillings. That includes jersey, scarf, woggle and chevrons.'

When I got home, I told my dad I had joined and detailed all the things we had done that evening. As soon as he showed a flicker of interest, I casually mentioned the uniform, pointing out that the Scout Master wanted us to look like Sea Scouts. His interest immediately waned as he sensed it was going to cost him money.

'It's only five shillings,' I tentatively said.

Reaching out for his tin of Golden Virginia tobacco, his crutch when he needed to stall, he deliberately rolled a cigarette, taking his time to light it. After inhaling deeply, he blew a thick plume of smoke in my general direction. I knew what was coming. Five minutes later, when he finished lecturing me on how much things cost, and did I think money grew on trees, I said.

'I wouldn't have joined if I knew this was going to happen. All the other boys have got uniforms. I'm always the one with nothing.'

He sprang out of his chair, grabbed me by the scruff of the neck, and propelled me into the garden. Giving me a clip around the head, he said.

'You ungrateful little sod. Your mum and I work all week to feed and clothe you, and all I ever get from you is this. Money, money, money. Well, if you want money, get a job, and earn some like your brother. He's got a job, you do the same. Now get out of my sight.'

'I could use the money I get from my jam jars, then it wouldn't cost you so much,' I offered, stepping back and preparing to run.

'Jam jars, that's just about your limit. Get something more tangible, instead of wasting your time collecting jam jars.'

It was easy for him to say get a job. He knew I was too young, but always raised the issue just to get rid of his annoyance at me for asking him for money.

I wandered off, but unlike the last time he had rejected my plea for money, I was surprisingly calm. Probably because I hadn't really expected him to say yes. I sat on the front step of the veranda and realised that if I wanted to be in the Sea Scouts and go to the cinema on a Saturday afternoon, I had to get more money.

Lacking any other ideas of how to earn money, I knew I needed to collect more jam jars. But with my other chores, it was a problem. It was not just the time it took to go from door to door to collect them, but often I would have to wash them. When I was given jars that needed washing, I humped them home and washed them in my back garden using my dad's precious water. Just as well he didn't know about it, otherwise he would have wanted a cut of the few coppers I made. Sometimes, depending on the tides, I washed them in the creek. The man in the newsagents, who I sold them to, always washed and sterilised them before filling them with cockles. But he wouldn't take them unless the jam had been rinsed out. He paid me a penny for a 2 pound jar, and a halfpenny for a 1 pound jar. On a good week, I hoped to sell him enough jars to get me the ninepence entry into the pictures, with a penny or two left over to buy some 'liquorice-root' to chew during the film.

Liquorice root. It was like chewing a small branch of wood. After a while your teeth frayed it and as it became saturated in saliva it tasted like liquorice. It was extremely popular during the War. Children used to chew it both for the liquorice taste and also because the root helped to clean their teeth.

The following evening, I rushed home, fed the chickens, grabbed my step-mother's shopping basket, and accompanied by my ever-faithful friend Gyp, set off on my round. I had already exhausted all my usual calls, and needed to go further afield, to houses and streets I didn't usually venture down. I had only knocked on a few doors when I heard someone up ahead shout.

'Hey Greeny, what do you want? You don't live here.'

It was Delaney, a boy from my school. He was standing looking menacing with several other boys. It didn't bode too well for me. I didn't like him and had little to do with him at school. My feelings were reciprocated.

Ignoring him, I continued down the road, hoping to get past him without too much hassle. But it was not to be.

'You deaf or something? What are you doing on my street?' he repeated.

Flanked by his mates, he stood directly in front of me. I tried to walk around him, but as I moved, so did he.

'What's the shopping basket for. Going shopping for your mum?'

Realising the odds were against me, I thought tact was my best policy. Again, I tried to walk around him, and again he moved in front of me. I cursed my luck for choosing this street.

The sound of dogs fighting suddenly caused a distraction, and I knew immediately it was Gyp; he would fight any dog no matter what its size. Seconds later, he came running out of one of the gardens, chased by a woman wielding a broom.

'Whose dog is this?' she shouted.

The disturbance gave me the opportunity to edge my way around Delaney. I positioned myself to run. I knew Gyp would follow as soon as he saw me running. I just hoped I could outrun them.

'It's his dog,' Delaney said, pointing at me.

She pushed him to one side and stepped in front of me, completely blocking my escape route.

'You should have him on a lead, not letting him run in people's gardens causing trouble… What's your name anyway?' Before I could answer, she continued, 'Do you live around here?'

'No.' I said, easing myself around her. She moved also.

'Well, if you don't live here, what are you doing here?'

'Nothing, I was just on my way home.'

'Where do you live?'

'Over there.' I pointed in the general direction of my house.

'I don't like strange boys hanging around up to no good. So clear off, and take your dog with you.'

'Yes Miss,' I muttered.

Delaney had other ideas, and made a lunge for the handle of my basket. I snatched it out of his grasp, knowing if he got hold of it I would never get it back. They would throw it amongst themselves, with me running around like a fool between them. If I was lucky, I may get it back before one of them jumped on it. One thing for sure, it would not be in the same condition it was in now. My step-mother didn't know I had her basket.

Using the basket as a weapon, I whirled it around my head, attacking the weakest looking boy. He immediately retreated, allowing me the space to make a run for it.

'Come on,' I heard Delaney shout. 'Let's get him.'

Spurred on by the chance of some serious bodily harm, I took off like a scalded cat, outrunning the chasing pack. Reaching the end of the road, I felt safe enough to check if Gyp was still following me. I spotted him sniffing something of interest, and was surprised to see that Delaney was on his own. It seemed his cohorts had lost interest.

'Gyp, here boy,' I called.

Hearing my voice, he came running. But as he passed Delaney, he aimed a kick at him. Fortunately for Gyp, he missed.

Letting out a yell, I rushed at Delaney swinging the basket above my head. There was no way anyone was going to kick my dog and get away with it. I expected Delaney to run, but he stood his ground.

Now I'd committed myself, I had to follow through, and swung the basket at his head. The rough wickerwork caught his face, drawing blood. He looked like he was going to retaliate; so I hit him again with the basket.

'I'll get you for this,' he said, retreating.

Now the interruption to my jam jar collecting was over, I set my mind to the task at hand. I decided to move away from the holiday bungalows, and headed for the more established houses. The holiday bungalows were occupied by family's like my own, people with nowhere to live. Whereas the occupants of the established homes tended to be older, and more settled. As a result, there was generally fewer kids on those streets, so the chances of getting jam jars was greater. Also, because they had mains water, they washed their jars before giving them to me.

Chapter Forty-Seven

I collected enough jam jars to afford a second-hand scarf and a woggle. They had been donated by some rich kids who had bought new ones. But I could never get enough money to buy the seaman's jersey.

Each scout night, I wore my scarf, held in place with my woggle, even though it was the only Sea Scout paraphernalia I had. I thought I looked 'a bit' like a Sea Scout, but the Scout Master had other ideas.

He told me that if I was not going to get the rest of the uniform, he didn't want me just wearing the scarf, as it brought the uniform into disrepute. I told him my mum was buying me my seaman's jersey for my birthday, and asked him if I could get my sailors hat. He agreed. Now I had a hat, I really felt like a Sea Scout.

One evening, we focussed on tying knots. By the time we left, I was confident I could tie a clove hitch, a reef knot, and a sheepshank. The scout master told us to take our lengths of cord home and practice. I ran all the way home, desperate to show my dad what I had learned. I also wanted him to see me in my sailor's hat.

When I entered the living room, he was leaning back in his armchair with his eyes closed. I thought he was sleeping, and just stood staring at him. After a while, he must have sensed I was there and opened his eyes. Reaching for his tin of tobacco, he said.

'Where did you get the hat?' Smiling, I slowly turned like a mannequin.

'The scout master gave it to me.'

'Gave it to you,' my step-mother said, as she entered the room.

'Yes, gave it to me…honest, didn't cost me nothing.'

My dad finished rolling his cigarette, lit it, and blew a plume of smoke in my general direction.

'You look silly in it without the rest of the uniform.'

'Well I can't help that can I. If I wait till I get the rest of the uniform I'll never wear it. Anyway, I've got a scarf and a woggle, so you can tell I'm a Sea Scout, it's not just a hat on its own.'

I wanted to make my point, but didn't want to sound too 'lippy', as my dad called it.

He remained quiet, obviously not wanting to be drawn into a conversation that might cost him some money. After a few moments silence, I pulled the length of cord from my pocket.

'Do you want to see what we learned tonight?' I asked.

I hoped by keeping the conversation alive I could steer it around to the uniform issue again. My step-mother let out a sigh, and sat down in her chair. I could see she was not interested.

I waited for my dad to say something. After a few moments, I moved towards the door to leave.

'Yes, show me what you learned,' he said. His voice had a conciliatory note to it and I sensed he was not really interested.

'No it's alright, it doesn't matter, it was not much anyway.' I continued toward the door.

'Come here and show me what you learned,' he repeated.

'No…it was nothing, it doesn't matter,' I muttered as I left the room.

'Come back here this minute,' he shouted. His voice had taken on a serious note, so I returned to the room.

'What's up with you? I said I wanted to see what you had learned, so show me. And don't you ever walk out on me when I am talking to you. Now show me what you learned.'

His attitude put me on the back foot, diminishing my initial excitement. My heart was no longer in it. I just wanted to get out of there and wished I hadn't said anything in the first place.

Taking out my piece of cord, I went through the motions, deliberately getting it wrong so I could get out of there. Screwing up my piece of cord, I stuck it in my pocket, and said.

'I've forgotten how to do it.'

'Well you didn't learn much did you,' he said.

'I could tie a knot when I was in the scout hut, but now I've forgotten.'

'Is that it then? A whole evening to learn how to tie knots and by the time you get home you have forgotten. Give me the cord, I'll show you.' He held out his hand.

I wanted to say no, but thought better of it.

'Now pay attention.'

I disinterestedly looked in his direction, before casually looking out the window.

'There, how difficult is that,' he said. Catching me looking out the window, he struck me on the leg.

'Pay attention. No wonder you never learn anything. Now, I'll show you again; and this time, watch what I am doing.'

I really did not want him showing me how to tie knots. I knew how to tie knots. It always ended like this. I was supposed to be showing him what I could do, but instead it finished up with him showing me how clever he was.

'Right, now you do it,' he said, handing me the cord.

'No, it's alright, I'll do it later,' I said, moving towards the door.

'You'll do it now, and I want to see you.'

I could feel my emotions rising. Holding back my anger, I quickly tied a sheepshank.

'There,' I said, holding it in front of him. He reached out, gave the cord a tug, and the knot came undone.

'What sort of knot is that, useless. I wouldn't want to depend on you tying a knot for me. Call yourself a Sea Scout. Just because you've got a sailor's hat on doesn't make you a sailor.' He threw the piece of cord in my direction. 'And you wanted a uniform. You can't even tie a simple knot.'

I left the room. A few minutes earlier I had entered the room, excitedly hoping to impress him with my knot tying skills, but instead, ended up being humiliated. Still raging, I went out to the back garden, took off my hat, and threw it. Gyp thought it was a game, and gave chase.

I sat in the chemical toilet. Minutes later, calmed down, I came out to find Gyp chewing my hat. I raced over and took it from him, but it was too late. The hat was full of teeth marks, and a piece of the material had been ripped away completely. I wanted to get angry with Gyp, but knew it was my own fault. My main concern was to conceal it from my dad. I could just hear him calling me a 'fucking galoot', or saying a pity my head was not in the hat when it was chewed.

Leaving the garden, I headed for the large dustbins at the back of the shops. After a quick look around, I stuffed the hat under a pile of rubbish and headed back home.

A couple of days later, I went to the Sea Scouts, hoping the scoutmaster wouldn't notice I didn't have my hat, scarf, or woggle on. Some hope. Within minutes, he came over to me.

'Where's your hat and the rest of your uniform?' I looked him in the eye and innocently said.

'My mum said I couldn't wear it on its own as it looked silly without the full uniform.'

'And when do you think that's likely to happen?'

'I think she's getting me it for my birthday,' I lied.

'And when is your birthday?'

'Next month.' I don't know why I said that. Even if I had a birthday coming up, which I hadn't, there was no chance of me getting a uniform.

For a second or two, I felt guilty about lying to him. The Scout Master paid me very little heed for the rest of the evening. I got the feeling I was not welcome anymore. I thought about leaving, but knew I would miss the free tea and sticky bun.

Then the decision was taken out of my hands. The following Saturday, I went to the cockle man, and he told me he didn't want any more jars.

'Could you not just take these?' I asked.

'Alright, but this is the last. After this I won't be doing cockles anymore.'

He paid me, and I headed for the Rio cinema. There was already a gang of kids waiting to see the latest 'Johnnie Mack Brown' cowboy film.

Within minutes I had forgotten about the Sea Scouts and the cockle man, as I was transported to a world of six shooters, goodies, and baddies. At the end of the film, I galloped home, slapping my bum and shooting at everything with my finger as I relived the cowboy film I had just seen.

A couple of days later I went to the Sea Scouts, but my heart was not in it. I knew I would never have the pleasure of wearing a complete uniform. I knew I would miss the free tea and buns, but as Paul had also left, I never went back.

Chapter Forty-Eight

Having lost my only source of income, I had more time on my hands. One Saturday morning, I was mooching around my garden whilst hoping Peter would appear with his bike, or better still, the chance to mooch some food from his mum. When Peter didn't show, I decided to go to the creek and look for Paul. As I was about to leave, my dad called out to me and told me to get into the car.

'Where are we going?' I asked, delighted to be getting a ride in the car.

'To get the keys.'

'What keys?'

'To the new house.'

'We moving to a new house?' I asked, looking at him in amazement.

This was so typical of my parents. You'd think they were in the secret service. They obviously had known for some time we were moving house, yet kept it to themselves until the last minute. They either thought I didn't warrant being told, or it was part of the secrecy of not letting the neighbours 'know your business'. We collected the keys and drove to the new house.

I followed my dad through the poorly fitting garden gate, noticing it had a rough piece of wood screwed to it with the name 'Swannie' carved into it. The number '13' hung below.

The house was a narrow bungalow, with a corrugated iron roof and a veranda running the length of one side. In the garden in front of the veranda was an 'Anderson Shelter'. Every household had an external shelter made of concrete, and sunk into the ground. It was covered in grass to make it less visible, and to blend in with the garden. I looked forward to checking it out later.

Keen to see where I would be sleeping, I couldn't wait to see inside. I was hoping I might get a room to myself. My dad on the other hand, wanted to look around outside, pointing out where he would put his workshop and the chicken runs. He also pointed out that we had a pear tree, which was already showing the beginning of the coming summer's crop. That immediately got my interest. A ready-made food source in my own garden.

Inside, the house didn't appear to be any bigger than the one we already lived in. It also had only one bedroom, that I could see.

'So, where's my room?' I asked.

'Upstairs.'

'Upstairs, I didn't know there was an upstairs.'

Crossing over to the corner of the living room, he pulled a curtain to one side and pointed to a step ladder.

'There,' he said.

Climbing up a couple of rungs, he pushed open a trapdoor, and climbed into the room. I followed him. It was nothing more than a boarded over loft, covered with lino. The roof joists were visible, with ceiling boards between them to cover the corrugated iron roof. The first time it rained, I couldn't believe the noise. It was so loud, I put my head under the pillow. The chimney from the fireplace in the living room below ran through the highest part of the loft, effectively splitting the room in two. It made movement around the room tricky, but warmed the room in winter. On one of the two outside walls, there was a small window, which looked over the veranda and into the garden of the house next door. In the other, was a door which opened onto an external staircase.

My dad opened it, and I followed him onto the landing. Apparently, the outside steps were at one time the only access into the loft. The landlord, realising the loft was a waste of space when housing was at an all-time premium, boarded it over, and cut a hole in the floor. The problem was, the trap door was right beside the outside door, making it easy to step into the room and fall straight down the open trap door, as I later discovered.

Back in the room, I looked out the small window, and noticed a girl in the garden next door. When she saw me looking in her direction, she waved. I quickly pulled back from the window without returning her wave.

'I think you'll be very comfortable up here don't you?' said my dad.

He had positioned himself in the middle of the room next to the chimney, the only place he was able to stand up.

'Yeah, I suppose so,' I replied.

I followed him down the ladder, missed my footing, and grabbed the curtain in an effort to break my fall. It pulled away from its hooks, and I landed in a heap in the living room with the curtain on top of me. As I scrambled to my feet, I remarked.

'Good job I grabbed the curtain, I could have had a nasty fall.'

Unconcerned about my well-being or whether I was hurt or not, he replied, 'Yeah, now I've got to hang the curtain, as if I haven't got enough to do.'

I left him hanging the curtain and went off to check the rest of the house. To my delight, I was glad to find we had running water and a toilet that flushed. I immediately had a pee in it.

'Well, no more emptying the chemical toilet,' I remarked to my dad.

'As if you would know, you never emptied it,' he pointed out.

'No, but I had to wash it after it had been emptied and put in the chemical.'

We unloaded the car, and placed the stuff in the house. As we made our way towards the front gate, the girl next door re-appeared. I gave her a cursory glance, closed the gate, and got into the car.

'Why didn't you say hello?' my dad asked.

'Who to?'

'Who to…you know who…the girl… she kept looking at you… look she's looking now.'

I ignored him, and was glad when he pulled away. I would get to know her, but not in front of him.

An hour later, we returned with another load. As soon as we drew up, out came the girl from next door. Obviously, we were something of interest in her otherwise boring day. My dad spoke to her, but I pretended to be too occupied with my work. To avoid looking at her, I held what I was carrying in front of me. A little while later, her dad came into the garden wearing a fireman's uniform. He and my dad chatted. Although the girl stood next to her dad during the conversation, I stayed on the veranda. I was still not ready to meet her. We finished unloading, and I followed my dad back to the car. He said.

'No point in you coming. You stay here and keep an eye on the stuff. It'll save me having to lock up. I'll have to bring your mum and Frankie back with me this time, so there will be no room for you.' He started the car, and with a wink said, 'You can get to know the girl next door whilst I am away.'

He drove off chuckling to himself. Deliberately keeping my back to the garden next door, I watched until the car turned the corner. I sensed the girl was watching my every move. Pushing the gate open with my bum, I headed for the veranda, looking anywhere but in the direction of the girl.

'Are you moving in?' she called out.

Bugger, I thought. I was hoping to get into the house without saying anything. But now she had spoken, I couldn't avoid her.

'Yeah of course.' I replied. 'What would I be doing here otherwise?' She was not fazed by my sarcastic reply.

'What's your name?'

'Billy,' I mumbled.

I picked up a box and went into the house. I deliberately took my time, hoping she would go back inside her own house. But as soon as I went outside again, she was back to the fence. She asked.

'Billy what?'

'Green,' I called out over my shoulder. I thought about asking her name, but didn't. I carried the rest of the stuff into the house.

Now that my dad was away, I checked out my parent's bedroom. It was nothing special, but was much more roomy than the loft. With nothing else to do, I sat on the toilet. It was sheer luxury after the chemical toilet. When I had finished, I watched the water swirl around the pan. *Paul will be really envious of me.* I thought. *Maybe I'll invite him to try it out as a treat, after his houseboat toilet.*

Not having spent much time upstairs, I went for another look around the loft; my bedroom. As I passed the window, I noticed the girl next door trying to get my attention. I opened the window, and to my surprise she asked me if I wanted a cup of tea. Now, she had my attention.

Scurrying through the trapdoor, I bounded across the lounge to the open front door, stopping just inside. I didn't want to appear too keen, but at the same time I didn't want to miss out either. Slowly walking over to the fence, I was in time to see a woman carrying a tray come out of the house.

'This is my mum,' said the girl. I nodded and mumbled, 'hello'.

'Pamela says you're moving in,' she said. *Pamela, so that was her name.*

'Yes,' I politely replied, eyeing the cake tin she was carrying.

'Have you just moved to Canvey?'

'No, we live on Dovercliffe Road.'

I was wishing she would hurry up with the tea and not ask so many questions. Any minute now, my dad, my step-mother, and my brother could roll up, and I didn't want them to see me with tea and biscuits.

'I made you a cup of tea. Do you like tea?'

'Yes, thank you,' I replied.

'Do you take sugar?'

'Yes,' I replied.

I was not sure whether I did or not, as I had never been asked before, and usually just drank it as it came. But, true to form, I turned nothing edible down.

'Would you like a piece of cake?'

Cake, not a biscuit, even better. I thought.

'Yes please Mrs...'

'Baker' she replied. Pamela giggled, and her mum told her to behave.

As soon as she had given me my tea, she retreated back into the house, taking the cake tin with her. That dashed any hopes I had of a second piece.

I quickly drank my tea, and had just given Pamela my cup back, when my dad drew up.

'Got to go,' I said, retreating from the fence. But my brother had spotted me talking to her.

'Who's the girl?' he asked.

'Dunno, she just lives next door.'

'Yeah I can see that. What's her name?'

'Pamela, I think.'

'So, you know her name already.'

'Couldn't help it, I heard her mum calling her.'

'Yeah, it looked as though you were talking to her when we drove up.'

'I was not, I just happened to be standing near the fence and so was she.'

'Don't worry, if you want to talk to her you can.'

'I don't. I don't want to talk to her. I mean, why would I?'

'Never mind. Anyway, what's the bedroom like?'

I showed him where it was. After looking out the window, he opened the door to the outside and stepped onto the landing.

'This could be handy,' he said. I looked at him quizzically.

'Don't you see? We can get in and out without going through the house, so we won't have to pass the 'old man'.

'Yeah, that'll be great,' I agreed, although I couldn't actually see what would be great about it. However, the benefits soon became apparent. Crossing over to the window he looked out.

'There's your girlfriend looking for you,' he said.

'She's not my girlfriend, I hardly know her,' I said testily.

He laughed, and lowered himself through the trap door. I was about to follow, when I heard my dad ask him what he was up to and where was Billy. I quickly scooted down the outside stairway, picked up a box, and carried it into the house, meeting my dad on his way out.

'Where were you?' he asked.

'I wasn't nowhere.'

'What do you mean, 'you wasn't nowhere'. You had to be somewhere, it's impossible not to be somewhere.'

'Right,' I muttered, continuing past him into the kitchen. My brother was right. The outside stairway had already proved its worth.

Chapter Forty-Nine

The furniture van arrived, and the men moved our worldly goods into the house. Everything was going well, until it came to getting the double bed up the narrow outside steps into the loft. A couple of times I thought the bed was about to go over the hand rail and land in the garden. Finally, after lots of grunting, they got it into the room. One of the men jokingly remarked that if we moved again, not to bother calling him.

'I think this calls for a cuppa,' said my step-mother.

My brother and I retreated to the veranda as soon as we were given our tea. We were not allowed to sit with the adults, listening to their conversation. Failure to move away drew an icy stare from our step-mother, which was always enough to make us move.

'Where's Gyp?' I asked my brother as we drank our tea.

'Dunno.'

'Didn't you bring him in the car with you?'

'No.'

'Why not?'

'He was nowhere to be seen when we left, and the old man said he couldn't wait any longer.'

'So where is he now?'

'He's probably waiting at the other house.'

'We'll have to get him.' I ran into the house and confronted my dad.

'Dad. Can we go for Gyp?'

'Not now, we have too much to do.'

'We can't just leave him there, he'll be lonely and won't know what's going on. Somebody might take him. Can't we go and get him now?'

'Later, when everything is finished. He'll be alright, he's been on his own before.'

I was not happy, and wondered if they were really going to get him, or just leave him behind.

'And what about the chickens? We need to get them as well.'

'We'll go for them tomorrow. I have to make a run for them first.'

'When you going to do that?'

'When do you think? When I've done the other one hundred and one things I have to do.'

'So who's going to look after them tonight?'

'Nobody, they don't need looking after, they'll be alright for one night.'

'They need to be fed.'

'Yes, that's your job.'

'I know, but how am I going to feed them if they're around there and I'm around here.'

By now he was beginning to lose it. Grabbing me by the arm he pulled me close his face inches from mine.

'Pay attention. We'll go back to the house later, cook the food for the chickens and pick up Gyp, right.' Before I had time to reply my step-mother cut in.

'He's not doing anything useful here, he might as well go back to the house now. He can feed the chickens and bring Gyp back with him. That'll save you going later on.'

'Good idea,' my dad agreed. She went into the house and returned with the key to the other house.

'On the stove you'll see the pot of potatoes. Cook them as usual, feed the chickens, get Gyp, and come home. Right! Do you think you can do that without any mistakes?'

'I know how to feed the chickens, I've been doing it long enough,' I sarcastically replied.

'Less of your lip or you'll get my hand across your face. Now remember. When you leave the house, make sure the cooker is off, and you lock the door properly. Got that?'

'Yes.' Turning to my dad I said.

'Dad, are you going to drive me there?'

He was just about to enter the house. Throwing what he was carrying down to the ground, he turned on me.

'Are you fucking stupid... of course I'm not, you galoot. If I did that I might as well do it myself. I never cease to be amazed at your stupidity.'

He turned to my step-mother for support. Her body language indicated she agreed with him.

Realising I had said the wrong thing I moved towards the gate with him slowly following.

'Walk, you can walk, can't you? You fucking galoot,' he hissed at me.

'Yes, I can walk,' I replied, speedily exiting the garden.

Happy to be out of the way, I ran up road. I had never been to the end of my new road and hoped it was not a dead end, delighted when I discovered that by crossing the field it cut the distance to the old house in half.

Anxious to see if Gyp was alright, I jogged along the gutter. Suddenly, my eye caught sight of a yellow rubber ball about the size of a tennis ball lying there. There were several houses close by, and I guessed it came from one of them. Without breaking stride, I kicked it along the gutter, only stopping to pick it up when I was out of sight of the houses.

As soon as I arrived at the house, I ran around to the back garden delighted to see Gyp lying in his box. I took the ball from my pocket and showed it to him.

'What's this then Gyp.' I said, teasing him with it. He tried to grab the ball from my hand.

'Okay, okay,' I said, throwing the ball. He chased after it, but was loath to give me it back, enjoying the tug of war as much as the chase. We had a great time.

There was very little traffic in them days, so on the way home I kicked the ball along the main road and let Gyp chase it. Half way home I came upon a large building with a high wall and a vacant plot next to it. I threw the ball up the wall. When it rebounded, both Gyp and I raced after it to see who could get it first. He always won. The only way for me to beat him, was to pretend to throw it one way, then throw it in a different direction.

Gyp liked to play games. My brother and I often used him to carry messages. I would tie a note to his collar, and Frankie would go to one end of the field and call him. Then he would write a note, and I would call him. We'd seen the Americans put messages in dog's collars in the war films.

When we reached the house, Gyp was running ahead of me. Not knowing where we lived, he ran past. I stopped at the gate, and said nothing. Suddenly, he realised I was not following him and came running back wagging his tail.

'You didn't know where we lived did you?' I said, laughing.

Before going in I hid the ball under the veranda. I didn't want to explain to my parents how I came by it, and I didn't want my brother to see it either.

When I went in, I found all the stuff had been put into the rooms. My few possessions were in a pile on the bed. I made a beeline for them, and learned my first lesson about living in a loft as a bedroom. I was so intent on getting my stuff, I forgot about the low ceiling. 'Crack'. I walked straight into the main supporting beam with such force I thought I had fractured my skull.

'Ow, bugger,' I yelled, rubbing my head. My brother immediately burst out laughing.

'Shut up, it's not funny,' I yelled.

'You'll have to get used to ducking your head when you go to bed. I'll be alright though.'

He gestured towards his side of the bed. He had chosen the side nearer the middle of the loft in the part it was possible to stand up in.

'Who said you could have that side of the bed anyway?' I whined.

'I did, because I'm the oldest. And anyway, Dad said I could have this side.' Still annoyed at cracking my head, I rushed over to the trap door and flung it open. It banged loudly against the chimney stack.

'Dad, did you say Frankie could have the right side of the bed?' I angrily yelled. The curtain around the steps parted, and my dad looked up.

'Why, what's the problem?' he asked.

'I just banged my head on the beam and he laughed and said you said he could have the best side of the bed.'

'Well, he is the oldest,' he replied.

'It's not fair,' I shouted, slamming the trap door shut.

'See,' said my brother with a satisfied snigger.

He rolled over spreading himself over his side of the bed and sighing. Annoyed, I rushed over, intent on aiming a punch at him. Suddenly the trap door opened, and my dad's head appeared in the room.

'Come here you,' he said, beckoning me with his finger.

'What,' I said, warily advancing towards him. In a flash he grabbed my ankle and dragged me towards him.

'You ever slam that trap door on me again when I am talking to you and I'll give you such a thrashing you won't know what's hit you.'

He emphasised his point by gripping my skinny ankle, causing me to cry out in pain.

'Now get to bed, and don't let me hear another word out of you.'

He released my ankle and disappeared down the ladder, closing the hatch behind him. I limped round to my side of the bed choking back the tears, more from frustration than pain. Throwing myself on the bed, I wriggled under the blankets and turned my back on my brother. I would have left it at that, but my brother couldn't help twisting the knife.

'See, I told you,' he said smugly.

'Shut up.'

'Heh heh heh, not only did you bang your head, you got told off by dad.'

'Shut...up.'

'Is your ankle sore?'

'No…' There was no way I would admit to him I was in pain.

'It looked sore to me; I thought you were going to cry again.'

'Shut up, shut up, shut up,' I shouted, putting my foot into the small of his back and kicking him out of the bed.

He fell loudly onto the floor. Clambering up, he aimed a punch at my head as I retreated to the other side of the bed out of his reach. Climbing over the bed he made a grab for me. Suddenly the trapdoor opened, and my dad climbed into the loft. Jumping off the bed, my brother slid to the floor, letting out a moan as if he was hurt.

'What's going on?' my dad yelled.

'He pushed me out of bed,' whined my brother.

'He laughed at me because I banged my head,' I squealed in self-defence.

'That's it. I have had it with you.'

He made a grab for me. 'Crack'. His head hit the ceiling, the force causing him to reel backwards and stumble over my brother.

'Out of my way,' he yelled. Frankie crawled into the corner giving my dad access to me.

'This is all your fault, you little twat,' said my dad, the blow to his head no doubt adding to his anger. Leaning over the bed, he made another grab for me. I let out a nervous scream and quickly rolled off the bed. Crawling across the bed, he made another grab for me, just as I rolled under the bed.

'Come here you little shite.'

I saw the bed spring move and heard him swear as he hit his head again. Moments later, his feet appeared on the far side of the bed. Getting down on his knees, he looked under the bed at me. I let out another nervous yell, and quickly moved away from his out stretched hand.

'Come here you little twat,' he yelled.

Luckily for me he was too big to get under the bed, so we laid looking at one another. He knew that if he tried to get to me by going on top of the bed I would roll under the bed, and we could be at it all night. He tried a different tactic.

'Come here, I am not going to hurt you,' he said soothingly.

When I didn't move, he looked around the room and spotted my shoes lying on the floor. He picked them up and threw them at me, shouting, 'Come out, or it will be the worse for you.'

Suddenly, my step-mother's voice interrupted things. I could see her bare feet as she entered the loft, noticing her toe nails were painted a bright red. On hearing her voice, my dad sat up and leaned against the bed.

'What on earth is going on?' she asked.

'It's him; he won't come out from under the bed.'

'Do you have to make so much noise, think of the neighbours?'

'Fuck the neighbours, they don't pay my rent,' my dad said.

'Do you have to swear?'

'Swear, he's enough to make a saint swear.'

Getting to his feet, I watched him ease himself through the trap door. Standing on the ladder so his face was level with the floor, he paused. We momentarily exchanged glances, before he disappeared through the hatch.

'Right. Now get into bed and let's have no more nonsense,' said my step-mother as she followed him, silently closing the trap door behind her.

I didn't move from the cramped space under the bed, still not sure it was safe to do so. The bedspring above my head creaked, as my brother climbed into bed. Slowly easing myself from under the bed, I wriggled under the blankets, all the time listening intently to the sounds below. Eventually, I fell asleep.

Despite the fracas of the night before, I slept remarkably well. In the half-light I looked at my brother, who had his eyes closed.

'You awake?' I said.

'No, I'm still sleeping.'

'What do you think Dad will do when we go down?'

'I don't know, it's you that's in trouble, not me.'

'Maybe he will have forgotten by now,' I hopefully suggested. I was worried my antics the night before would result in me not being given any breakfast. And, as usual, I was really hungry.

Gazing at the ceiling, I noticed the watermarks caused by the years of dampness had formed a number of different shapes. Giving my brother a nudge, I said.

'Look at the marks on the ceiling, they look like a face.' Frankie rolled onto his back.

'What you on about?'

'There, see… that looks like an old lady's face.' I pointed to the ceiling.

'I think it's more like an island. See, there's a harbour.'

I said it was more like a face, but when he began pointing out in minute detail how it looked like an island, I reluctantly agreed, otherwise he would have gone on and on until I did.

Hearing movement downstairs, we decided it was safe to get up. I kept my head well down as I worked my way around the bottom of the bed to the area where I could stand up. I was so hungry, I felt weak, and slid to the floor. Even the prospect of stale bread and rancid milk for breakfast seemed appealing.

Believing I was the one in trouble and not my brother, I thought it would be best for him to go down first. But when he finished dressing, he sat on the edge of the bed.

'What you waiting for?' I asked.

'Waiting for you.'

'It's alright, I'm not ready yet, you go on down.'

'You just want me to go down so if there's any trouble I'll get it first.'

'Well, you said it was me that's in trouble, not you.' Opening the trapdoor, he started down the steps.

'Come on,' he hissed.

'I'm coming. I've just got to put my shoes on.'

I made a show of getting my shoes, which were still under the bed where my dad had thrown them.

As soon as he was gone, I quietly descended a couple of steps and listened to the reception he got. The voices appeared to be quite normal. Suddenly, my step-mother's voice rang out.

'Billy, what are you doing?'

'Coming,' I said, making a show of banging the trapdoor and scurrying down the ladder.

Keeping my head down to avoid eye contact, I entered the kitchen. Crossing to the sink, I swilled my face and sat down.

'What are you waiting for?' asked my step-mother.

'Something to eat,' I whispered.

'Do you think you deserve to be fed after last night's performance? Your dad may have forgotten, but I haven't.'

She looked in my dad's direction as she spoke. Adopting his matter of fact attitude, he took a puff of his Golden Virginia roll up, blew a plume of smoke towards the ceiling, and said,

'I hadn't forgotten Glad,' his name when trying to keep in with her. 'I was just waiting for the right moment. Now listen you two, I don't want any more nonsense like we had last night. We are here to stay, so just get used to sleeping in the upstairs room.' With that, he stood up and headed for the door.

'Is that it?' she said.

'It's enough,' he replied, stepping outside.

She looked disbelievingly after him, as she scraped a number of bread cubes onto my plate and poured hot watery milk over them. It was gross, but I was too hungry to care. Anyway, there was nothing else.

I finished eating, and joined my dad and brother in the back garden, the food I had eaten, rancid as it was, giving me a bit of energy, My dad was explaining how they were going to build the chicken run.

'Frankie, you go and find some wood from that bombed house.' He pointed to the house next door.

'Billy, you come with me.'

We jumped in the car and drove back to the other house. After loading the car with the wire netting and nesting boxes, there was no room for me or the chickens.

While he was away, I hopped over the fence and visited the old lady in her bell tent. I hoped she might offer me a cup of tea and a biscuit.

She didn't, but nevertheless was pleased to see me. She asked me about the new house, saying how lucky we were to have water on tap and a flush toilet. She didn't have a toilet, so Peter's mum let her use the outdoor toilet at the bottom of their garden.

Although Peter was no longer my neighbour, when I noticed him in his garden I went over and spoke with him. *Never know*, I thought. *I might need to mooch a meal from his mum. And of course, he still has a bike.*

It was some hours before my dad returned. We rounded up the hens, put them into cardboard boxes, and took them to the new chicken run my dad and my brother had built.

Chapter Fifty

Not long after moving into our new home, it was the school holidays. As usual, we were up early. As soon as my parents left for work, my brother and I were put out of the house, even though we had nowhere to go.

The door was locked, and although I was handed the key, I was told not to go into the house. I was only to go into the house to cook the chicken's food. The rest of time I was to stay outside. She added that she may come home at any time, and if she caught me in the house I was in big trouble. Her lecture was more for my benefit than my brother. He had a part time job, and didn't hang around the house as much as I did.

I wandered out to the road, parked my bum on the kerb, and watched my parents until they reached the end of the road. I gave them a quick wave, but they turned out of sight without looking back.

Moments later I saw the bus pass the end of the road and knew they were on their way. Already bored, I wandered onto the veranda and looked through the stained-glass window into the living room. I discovered that if I altered the angle I looked through the glass, I could make the furniture take on a different shape.

I soon became bored with that, and returned to the kerb. Opposite me was a spare piece of land which backed onto the house on the next street. It was separated from them by a low wire fence. I watched as a boy, who looked about the same age as me, climbed over the fence.

When he reached the road, he stopped and spoke. He told me the road he lived on was unmade and became muddy when it had been raining, so he cut across the spare piece of land so he could walk on a concrete road. His name was Christopher, he had an older brother Brian, and a sister called Cecilia, although he called her Cissy. It seemed his whole family used the shortcut. Whilst we spoke, his mum lifted her bike over the fence; wheeled it across the land, spoke to us, before mounting it on the concrete road.

From that first meeting, Christopher and I became friends. Soon after, we built a den in the corner of the spare piece of land. There was loads of wood and bricks from the bombed house next door to us. Whenever his sister saw us playing around the den, she asked if she could join us. But she was such a big lump of a girl, I was concerned her ample backside would knock our flimsy den down. She complained it was not fair, as we let Pamela, my next-door neighbour, in. But I liked Pamela, as she was quite pretty.

But the days were long, and with the best will in the world, you can only play in a den for so long. So, to help pass the time I traipsed the streets, always on the lookout for what I could mooch. Thankfully, the secondary school canteen still provided a free mid-day meal, the highlight of my day, for children whose parents worked full time. Most days I met Paul. After feasting on free school food, we would go back to his house boat, swimming in the creek during the summer months. Christopher didn't come for school dinners during the holidays, as his mum always fed him.

Other times, I just hung around my own house. This pleased Pamela, as she was not allowed the same freedom as me, and spent a lot of time hanging around in her garden by herself. We became good friends.

One day she brought out a ball and a tennis racquet. I made a bat out of an old piece of wood, and we played tennis, using the wire fence as a net. She hated it when I told her I was going on walkabouts, and always tried to talk me out of it.

Like one Sunday afternoon when my parents had gone out in the car. I was sitting on the veranda step, when Pamela came into her garden. I heard the sound of her kitchen door being locked. When she saw me, she smiled, and came over to the fence. She had a piece of cake in her hand.

'Do you want to play tennis?' she asked.

'No, I'm going for a walk in a minute.'

'No, don't go. Come into my garden.'

'Why? it's no different than mine.'

'I'll give you a piece of my cake.'

I was easily bribed and accepted her offer. Her garden was no different to mine, in fact it was smaller.

Her dad was building a caravan in his garden. I had often heard him banging and sawing, but I had never seen inside.

'Can I see inside the caravan?' I asked.

'No, I am not allowed to go inside. Anyway, it's locked.'

I'd eaten the piece of cake she had given me, the caravan was locked, so there didn't seem any point in hanging around any longer. I told her I was going to see if I could find Christopher, and asked her to come with me. She said she was not allowed to leave her garden.

'Who will know if you go?' I asked.

'My parents.'

'I thought they had gone out!'

'No.'

'So, why is the door locked?'

'Because they've gone to bed.'

'Bed, on a Sunday afternoon?' I asked, quizzically.

She explained they always went for a lie down on a Sunday afternoon, and she was put into the garden, and the door locked. I headed towards the fence.

'Please don't go, let's play tennis,' she pleaded.

'No, I don't want to.' I climbed over the fence, and wandered towards my front gate.

'Wait, I want to show you something,' she said, desperately.

I knew she was just trying to stall me, but waited anyway. She ran around the front of her house. A few seconds later she came back, and beckoned me back over the fence.

'What is it?' I asked, suspecting another delaying tactic.

She put her finger to her lips, leaned close to my ear, and whispered.

'Do you want to see my mum and dad having a do?'

'Having a what?' I asked.

'A 'do', you know.'

She formed a circle with her finger and thumb. Placing the forefinger of her other hand in it, she wiggled it about.

'I don't know what you mean, but show me anyway.'

'You have got to be quiet, promise.'

'Okay.'

I followed her to the front of the house. Sneaking between the bushes and the front bedroom window she positioned herself so that she could see between the window frame and the curtain. I watched her as she looked in the window. Finally, she beckoned to me to take a look. I didn't know what I was going to see, but it came as a surprise. Her mum and dad were both naked on the bed and having sex. Fortunately, her dad had his back to us, and her mum had her eyes closed, or I am sure they would have seen me. I had never seen anyone having sex before. I watched, fascinated, until Pamela pulled me away.

'They do that every Sunday. I always know when they lock the door,' she said, giggling.

I didn't know what to say. Then I remembered hearing the older boys talking about girls and one of them had said, 'Look at the tits on her,' and all the boys looked at this girl who had big breasts. It sounded like a compliment, so unable to think of anything else I said.

'Your mum's got nice tits.'

'Don't say that, it's rude,' she said, immediately changing her tune.

'But it was you who let me see them,' I said, somewhat perplexed.

'Don't ever say that, I wish I had never shown you.'

'Well, what else can I say?'

'Nothing; nothing, you had better go now. Go on, go back to your own garden.' She walked around the other side of her house.

I climbed the fence and headed off up the road, completely confused. My comment was meant as a compliment, but she told me I was rude. *Girls*, I thought, *I'll never understand them.*

A few days later Pamela called out to me across the fence. We chatted as if nothing had happened; although the vision of what I had seen stayed with me for a long time. Out of concern for Pamela, I never told anyone, not even Paul. But from then on, I viewed Pamela's mother differently.

Chapter Fifty-One

Come September, the summer holidays ended, and it was back to school. Gyp, who had virtually accompanied me everywhere during the holiday, followed me. I told him to go home, but he couldn't understand why he couldn't come with me. When I reached the school, he followed me down the drive. I tried to chase him away, but he thought I was playing. When the bell sounded, I nipped inside. Through the windows of the auditorium I could see him sniffing around outside. By the time we got our morning break, he was gone.

I was still having problems with money, or the lack of it, which was more apparent at weekends. Christopher went to the cinema every Saturday. His mum gave him money, and he didn't need to work around the house to earn it either.

Every weekend, he asked me if I was going to the pictures, and every weekend I would reply, 'Yes, if I can get some money.' To which he would say, 'Why don't you ask your mum.' He couldn't understand that my 'mother' was not like his, and that all mothers are not the same.

Fortunately, his mum didn't like him going to the cinema on his own, and often paid for me. My step-mother would ask where I got the money from, looking at me a little suspiciously, unable to comprehend that someone else's mother would actually pay for me to go to the cinema. Not that it made her ever offer to pay.

Despite being paid into the pictures by Christopher's mum, I still wanted money of my own. I hated always being the one who never ever had any money for anything. Even Pamela got paid for doing chores around the house, and would buy me a sweet or ice cream. I decided that one way or another, I had to get a job.

Some of the boys I knew had paper rounds. They seemed to have money, so I decided that might be my best bet. On the corner of Oxford Road and High Street was a newsagent, Burton's. I decided to try them.

I had never had a job before, so was unsure how to go about asking. There were a couple of customers in the shop when I entered, so I waited until they had been served. Mr Burton was behind the counter and thought I was in for cigarettes.

'No cigarettes,' he said.

Cigarettes and tobacco were rationed, so children were sent to get cigarettes for their parents. Often several shops had to visited before managing to secure any, as newsagents and other outlets only sold to their regular customers.

'I don't want fags,' I replied.

'So, what do you want?'

'Got any jobs?'

'No, no jobs.'

'What about a paper round?'

'How old are you, you don't look old enough to have a paper round?'

'I'm twelve,' I lied.

'All the morning paper rounds are gone.'

I remained silent, hoping he would say something else. When he saw I was not moving, he said.

'Sorry, can't help you.'

Desperate not to leave empty handed, I suggested I could maybe clean up around the place.

'No, I have a wife who does that.' I was about to leave, when the curtain parted, and his wife came through to the shop.

'I'm sure we could find him something to do,' she said. 'Just look at him. If anybody needs a job, he does. Come on through.'

Mr Burton gave me a resigned look as I smilingly followed Mrs Burton through to the back. She took me into an outside scullery.

'Do you like ice cream?' she asked.

'Yes, I do.' I replied. If it was edible, I would eat it. The last time I had an ice cream was the watery stuff I had at the end of the war in Exmouth. Pointing to three large tin cans, she said.

'Good. When you have eaten the ice cream, give them a scrub and leave them to drain'.

I was surprised just how much ice cream there was left in each tin. But I hung in there. Would have hated to waste any.

By the time I finished the other jobs she gave me, it was 6pm, closing time. Mr and Mrs Burton were busy clearing up. I hung around, hoping the ice cream she had given me was not to be my only payment.

I watched Mrs Burton take three pennies from the till and place them on the counter. I was delighted, thinking they were for me. I would have liked sixpence, but thought that was probably too much as I had not done much work, and she had let me lick the ice cream tins. But instead of giving them to me, she left them lying. I hoped she wouldn't ask Mr Burton how much to give me, as I thought he was meaner than she was. Fortunately, he left the shop and went upstairs.

'Here,' she said, as soon as he was gone. She handed me a thruppenny bit and three pennies.

'If Mr Burton asks, tell him I gave you thruppence, right. It will be our little secret.'

'Right,' I said, pocketing the money as she opened the door and let me out.

'See you tomorrow then,' she said, locking the door behind me.

I slowly wandered up the road, keeping my hand in my pocket firmly wrapped around my wages. Desperate to look at my newly acquired wealth, I paused under a street lamp. Casually placing my free arm around the lamp post, I gently swung around in a full circle as I checked to see if anyone was around.

Easing my hand out of my pocket, I looked at the coins in my hand. I counted them several times, all four of them. I smiled as it dawned on me that I 'actually' had sixpence all to myself. But the best part was; nobody knew I had it. And that was the way I wanted it to stay.

Taking it home was out of the question. I had seen what had happened to my brother's money. He only earned a shilling, but my dad took sixpence of it as 'boot money'. My dad did his own shoe repairs, and made my brother contribute to the cost of repairs to his boots.

When we lived in Dovercliffe Road, I hid my jam jar money under the bungalow in an old tobacco tin. I still had the tin, but it was a while since any coins had rattled it. I hid it in the bushes at the end of our road.

The following evening, Mrs Burton took me to the ice cream stall outside her shop and showed me how to sell ice cream. When it came time to lock up, I excitedly waited for another sixpence, disappointed when she said.

'I'll pay you at the end of the week.'

By the time Friday came, I'd calculated what I expected to be a big pay day. At sixpence an evening, I figured I would get at least two shillings and sixpence. Mrs Burton handed me one shilling and sixpence. Noticing the look of disappointment on my face, she said.

'I can't pay you sixpence every evening. When I thought you were only going to work for one evening I gave you sixpence, but as you have worked every evening I couldn't possibly pay you that much. However, if you don't think that is enough, perhaps you had better not come back.' I quickly put a smile on my face.

'No, no that's fine.' I said. 'Thank you.'

I left the shop reminding myself not to be so greedy. It had nearly cost me my job.

A few weeks later Mrs Burton paid me my one shilling and sixpence and told me that was my last. The weather was getting colder, and there was no demand for ice cream.

'What about cleaning up around the place then?' I asked.

'Not really enough to do now that we have shut the ice cream stall down.'

'What about a paper round. Don't you need someone to deliver papers?'

'No, we already have paper boys.' I was desperate not to lose my job, but it wasn't to be.

I retrieved my tin, and checked my money. With today's pay I had the monumental sum of two shillings and sixpence. That would get me into the Rio cinema for a couple of Saturdays, but after that it was anyone's guess.

I made a point of seeing more of Christopher, mainly because his mum fed me when I went around for him. It was very self-serving of me, but for a free meal I could tolerate the spoilt Christopher. But I still needed to get some money.

Each evening, I called into the newsagents hoping they might have some work for me, with no success. Then, one evening, I called in and Mrs Burton was behind the counter.

'Hello Billy, I'm glad you dropped in.'

'Why, have you got a job for me?'

'As a matter of fact, I have.' I approached the counter.

'What is it?' I asked.

'You wanted a paper round; well I have one for you.'

A paper round, I thought. *I immediately imagined getting up in the early hours of the morning when it was still dark. I was not the best at getting up in the morning, and had no way of waking up. I would also have to get out without disturbing anybody. Not so bad in the summer, but not nice in the winter months. Also, there was no way I would be able keep it a secret and my dad would know I was earning money.*

'It's an evening round. It's new, so not many customers at the moment. But it will get bigger when more people know about it,' she explained. An evening round sounded much better. I could do it before my parents got home from work.

'So, how many people are there at the moment?' I asked.

'About eighteen. Do you know the area around here?'

'Yes, know every street.'

And I did. I had learned them during my jam jar days and mooching the streets during the holidays.

'Right, you can start tonight.'

She handed me a pile of papers and showed me the address she had written on the top left-hand corner.

'You only need to pop them through the letter box each night.'

'What about the money?' I asked.

'Collect it at the end of the week. That way they may give you a tip.'

She gave me a knowing smile. I left the shop, and within half an hour I was back. Thinking I might get some more work, I hung around the shop. When closing time came, I noticed a number of newspapers lying on the counter.

'What you going to do with those papers?' I asked.

'We return them tomorrow,' said Mr Burton.

'Can I take them?'

'No, I need them for a credit otherwise I will have to pay for them. Anyway, what do you want them for?'

'I was going to try and sell them at the bus stop.' He glanced at Mrs Burton who nodded her approval.

'Well, I suppose it's worth a try. Any you don't sell, put them behind the ice cream stall and I'll get them in the morning.'

'What about the money?'

'I'll get it tomorrow night. Here take this.'

He pulled a bag out from under the counter. I noticed it had the name of a popular newspaper on it, the 'Evening News'. He counted the newspapers into it and handed me the bag. I hurried to the bus stop in front of the cycle shop, the main drop-off point for people returning home from London via Benfleet.

Outside the cycle shop, a group of young men were gathered. They were encouraging a man riding a bicycle on a training machine to go faster.

'Star, News or Standard.' I yelled.

A couple of the men momentarily looked my way. Sensing a sale, I moved closer.

'Give me an 'Evening News,' said one of them handing me a penny. My first sale, and I had only been out a few minutes. I was delighted.

257

Every scruffy newspaper boy I had ever seen at the movies always wore a 'too big' cap, usually worn at a jaunty angle, and accompanied by a cockney accent. I didn't have a cap, but the accent was no problem. With each sale I would say, 'Thank you guvnor', and tip my forehead.

After a while, the cycle shop closed, leaving the street lamp as the only source of light. I still had a few papers left, mostly 'Evening Standards', which for some reason were the least popular paper in my area. I decided to wait for one more bus and then call it a day. As soon as the bus stopped, I called out the names of all the newspapers, although I only had Evening Standards left.

'Give me an Evening News,' a man said.

'Yes Guv,' I replied, rummaging through my bag.

'Sorry Guv, none left. Like a Standard?'

'That all you got?'

'Yeah, sorry the rest have all gone.'

'Go on then.' He handed me a thruppenny bit.

I fumbled in my pocket for his change, but he was already walking away. I separated two pence from the other money and slipped it into my pocket. *Mr Burton doesn't need to know about that,* I thought. I went back to the shop, hid my newspaper bag behind the ice cream stall, and went home.

The house was still in darkness. I had earlier fed the chickens, but as per my parent's instructions had locked the house up. I decided not to risk going into the house, knowing my parents would be home soon. I sat on the kerb under the streetlight, and counted the money.

I had sold fifteen papers. *I'm sure Mr Burton will be pleased with that,* I thought. *He may even give me six pence.* So, counting the bloke who didn't take his two pence change, I could get as much as eight pence.

Happy with my evenings work, I retrieved my Golden Virginia tobacco tin from the bush where I had hidden it, and added my takings. I liked the tobacco tins, as they had a rubber seal which made them water tight; not that I anticipated ever having any paper money.

When I got back home, my brother was sitting outside on the kerb reading a book under the street light. I was glad to see him, as we didn't see much of one another during the day. He looked up from his book and smiled when he saw it was me.

'What you been up to then?' he asked.

'Not much, just mooching around,' I answered.

I sat down next to him on the kerb and noted how cold it was, my thin trousers gave little protection. My brother was seated on a piece of cardboard he had folded to keep out the cold. He couldn't sit on the veranda as there was no light to read his book, and he loved reading.

I thought about telling him I had a paper round, as I knew it wouldn't be long before he found out. I was about to say, 'Guess what... I've got a paper round,' when he turned back to his book. The kerb was too cold for me to sit on, so I sat in the veranda in the dark.

As expected, my brother found out I had a paper round and asked me how much money I was earning. I lied about what I was getting. He jokingly threatened to tell my dad, but never did. As it happened, he didn't need to.

Friday was the best evening of the week. That was when I collected my one and sixpence paper round money, plus any tips. And, with what I got from selling newspapers on the street corner, I was doing quite well. On a good week I made as much as four shillings, about 20p in today's money.

Then, one Friday evening, I was calling out my now well-versed sales pitch. The Star, News, and Standard were flying out of my bag. Then a voice, which I would have recognised had I not been so busy, said. 'I'll take an *Evening News*.'

'Yes Guv,' I replied.

I turned and came face to face with my dad. The paper was practically out of the bag and I was ready to take his money. I let the paper fall back into the bag, as if it would hide the fact that I was working. I then noticed he already had a paper folded up in his hand. He no doubt would have bought it in London to read on the train during the journey home.

'How long have you been selling papers then?' he asked.

Before I had time to perjure myself, I was distracted by someone wanting to buy a paper. It gave me breathing time to conjure up a lie. My step-mother had already wandered off, not wanting anyone to think she was associated with me.

'Well I'll see you at home,' he said, quickly following her. I knew he would ask me how long I had been selling papers. I could see this leading to him finding out about my paper round, and possibly my ice cream job as well.

As I continued selling the rest of my papers, I racked my brains to come up with a story to tell him.

Shall I tell him everything and hope he won't be too hard on me for not telling him I have been working. But, if I do, he's bound to ask me what I've done with the money, which is mostly spent. I could tell him I only started this week, and unless he actually asks Mr Burton, he'll have no way of knowing. But, he goes into Burton's for his tobacco.

I arrived home, by which time my dad was seated in the living room listening to the wireless. I sat down at the kitchen table, and had hardly started eating when he sidled in and sat opposite me.

'So, you've got a job, why didn't you tell me?' I wanted to say, 'because you would have taken most of my money,' but instead said.

'I was going to, but I just didn't get around to it.'

'So, how long have you had the job?'

I filled my mouth and made a big thing of chewing and swallowing before mumbling

'Umm, not long, a few days.'

This was not exactly a lie, as I had not had the job of selling newspapers on the street that long anyway.

'Well, I knew you could do it if you put your mind to it. So, what's old Burton paying you then?'

'Don't know.' I replied.

'Don't know. You are working for someone and you don't know what they are going to pay you. You're a bright spark. That's the first thing you should have found out. He may not give you anything.

Only you would take a job and not know what the pay is. When you working again then?'

'Tomorrow.'

'Ask him what he is going to pay you, unless you want me to.' He smirked, left the room, and I heard him tell my step-mother.

'Well what do you expect?' she replied. 'What does he know about working? Maybe now he'll learn the value of money and how hard it is to earn.'

The next night, I told my dad that I was being paid one shilling and sixpence, which was true. I didn't mention my tips. He told me I had to give in sixpence towards my keep. Come the Friday, I took my time handing my step-mother the money, hoping she might tell me to keep it. She didn't. She took my sixpence without so much as a smile.

A few weeks later, Mr Burton cancelled my evening paper round. It seems there were not enough customers to make it worthwhile.

I still continued selling newspapers on the street, but by the time I handed in sixpence it was just was not worth the time I put in. I stopped going to the newsagents, except to buy tobacco for my dad. I still greeted Mr and Mrs Burton when I saw them, and later heard that they had bought the piece land next door to us. I never did work for them again. Now it's a spice shop.

Chapter Fifty-Two

My brother, being two years older than me, always seemed to have a job and was working at the local greengrocers. I had tried for several jobs, but always seemed to be too young, or too small.

Then, one weekend my brother told me he was packing his job in. I had often seen him with fruit he had been given by the greengrocer, and thought I would like some too.

'Has he got someone else yet?' I asked.

'Why, don't think you could do it, do you?'

'Yes, why not?'

'You're not strong enough, that's why.'

'If you can do it, so can I.'

'Yeah, can you lift a sack of spuds?'

'Course I can.'

'Right, I'll tell him that you will be in on Saturday.'

For the rest of the week all I thought about was the free fruit I was going to get, never mind the money. I gave no thought to what I might be expected to do.

Saturday morning, bright and early, I told the greengrocer who I was.

'You're not very big. I was hoping for someone bigger. Can you ride a bike?' he asked.

'Yeah,' I enthused. This was better than I imagined. Free fruit, money, and I get to ride a bike as well. This was the job for me.

'You sure you are going to be able to deliver the groceries, they can be quite heavy?' he asked, not too convinced.

'I'm sure I can,' I said, worried that he might not give me the job. 'Have you worked for anyone before, or is this your first job.'

'Yeah, I've worked for Burton's the newspaper shop.'

'Delivering newspapers is different to delivering potatoes.' He seemed to take for ever before saying.

'Alright, go out the back, get the bike, and bring it here.'

I found the tray bike, grabbed the handlebars, and kicked it off its stand. Before I knew it, I was wrestling to stop the bike falling to the ground. It was much heavier than I had imagined. Up to now the only bike I had ridden was Peter's, which was much smaller and much lighter. Fortunately, the grocer didn't see me struggling with the bike or my career in the greengrocery business would have been over before it started. I sorted out the bike, and wheeled it to the front of the shop, surprised at how heavy it was. I hoped that once I was rolling, it would be easier to handle.

The grocer placed a box of fruit and vegetables in the tray and handed me the sales slip. I could feel his eyes on me as I mounted the bike. Standing on the pedals I pushed as hard as I could. It seemed the bike was never going to move. *God,* I thought, *I never knew these pedals could be so hard to push.* Slowly, the bike gathered momentum. As soon as the bike was going fast enough, I tried sitting on the saddle, only to discover the seat was too high. I continued standing on the pedals. On my way back, after delivering the groceries, I called into the bike shop.

'Can you lower this saddle for me mister?' I asked the mechanic.

'Is this the greengrocer's bike?' he asked.

'Yeah, I work for him now,' I stated proudly.

'Bit small, aren't you?'

'No, I'll be alright when the saddle's lowered.' I left the shop, the bike handling better now I could sit on the saddle.

My next delivery was a sack of potatoes. The grocer lifted them into the tray whilst I held the bike between my legs.

'Right, off you go, and be careful.'

After a wobbly start, and an equally wobbly ride, I arrived at the address. It was alright riding there, but as soon as I slowed and lost momentum, the bike, with a one hundredweight bag of spuds in the tray, fell over, taking me with it. The sack of potatoes rolled onto the grass verge. Quickly extricating myself from the bike, I looked around to see if I had been spotted. Nobody came to help, so I guessed not.

I righted the bike, and propped it up on its stand. So far, so good. Now all I had to do was get the sack of potatoes from the grass verge into the customers house. I tried lifting them, but was too weak. I then laid the bike on its side and rolled the sack into the tray. But as I lifted the bike, the sack rolled out. I didn't know what to do. I couldn't go back to the greengrocer.

I decided to knock on the door of the delivery address in the hope someone in there could lift the potatoes in. The door was opened by a middle-aged woman, who was probably no stronger than me. I explained the situation. She was unimpressed, telling me that she couldn't lift a sack of potatoes, and that was why she had them delivered.

'Wait here.' she said, angrily stomping off. A few minutes later she returned with the man from next door. He lifted the potatoes into her house and the woman reluctantly paid me. I returned to the shop, and the grocer asked me if the delivery had gone alright.

'Yes. No problems,' I said. After sweeping up the shop he gave me two shillings, and I left.

The following Saturday, when I reported for work, the grocer said he didn't need me anymore as he had taken on a bigger boy. I think the lady must have complained. I watched the new boy mount the bike and ride off, with not as much as a glance in my direction. So ended my short career in the greengrocery business.

Chapter Fifty-Three

Before long, the winter months were upon us, and my chances of getting a job became even more limited. One thing though. I was glad I didn't have to stand in the street selling newspapers.

Then, as if we weren't crowded enough, I arrived home to find that my step-mother's brother, Bill, had just been demobbed from the army, and was moving in with us. I wondered where he was going to sleep. I soon found out. A single bed and small cupboard were placed in the roomiest part of our crowded bedroom, taking up most of what little floor space there was left.

My step-mother was glad to see him, being her only living relative. My dad, on the other hand, was not too impressed. They didn't seem to have much in common with each other.

It wasn't long before Uncle Bill, as we had been told to call him, or Nunky Bill as my brother and I named him, got a job as a lorry driver for the Shell Oil Company. He also met his new girlfriend Vi, who he went on to marry.

It soon became obvious that Nunky Bill sleeping in our room was not a good idea, especially at weekends. He liked to lie in after being out on the Saturday night, so I had been told not to make a noise.

One Sunday, a typical cold wintery day, I was in no rush to go anywhere. I was wide awake, so slipped out of bed and passed the time playing with my Fort, being careful not to drop any of the lead soldiers and make a noise. Becoming bored, I looked for something else to pass the time. Sneaking over to Nunky's bed, I silently watched him snooze. I had it in my mind that if I stared at him long enough, he would wake up and go downstairs. He was sleeping peacefully, his bottom lip gently flapping as it made a 'poot poot' sound like water dripping.

When my staring didn't work, I looked for something more positive. Spotting his socks tucked into his shoes under the bed, I picked one up and brushed his nose with it, giggling as he brushed it away with his hand. Suddenly, a noise caught my attention and I thought it was someone coming into the loft. Dropping the sock, I jumped back into bed. After a few minutes and nobody appeared, I crept back. Picking up the sock, I approached his bed.

'What are you up to?' he said, catching me completely off guard.

'Nothing.' I said, dropping the sock as I noticed his eyes were open. Raising himself on one elbow he looked to where I had dropped his sock.

'What were you doing with my sock?'

'Nothing.' I replied.

'I don't trust you, there's something weird about you.'

He slowly climbed out of bed, pulled on his trousers and shirt, lifted his socks, and went downstairs.

I waited a few seconds before lifting the trap door. I could hear him telling his sister about the sock. She murmured in agreement, obviously also thinking I was weird.

Quietly closing the trapdoor, I made my bed, whilst concocting a story should my step-mother question me about the socks. Now he was out of the room, I decided to check his cupboard to see if he had anything of interest. But like most of the soldiers who returned from the war, he had few possessions. Army underwear, socks, a couple of shirts, and his 'demob suit'. A civilian suit was given to all service personnel when discharged. Not much to show for six years serving your country at war.

Now that the cold nights had arrived, I was back to lighting the fire when I came home from school. I hated that job as I never had any success at lighting fires. And, just like the last house, the wood was always damp, and there was never enough newspaper. But like the last house, my dad kept a two-gallon can of petrol on the veranda. He had again warned me not to use it, but I knew it was the only way I could get the fire started. However, unlike the last house, I didn't need to go for coal.

Some nights were better than others. There was no rhyme or reason why a fire caught on some nights, and on others it didn't. Then one particularly cold afternoon, I arrived home. It had been sleeting most of the day and the house was freezing. Grumbling away to myself to keep my spirits up, I cleaned out the ashes, laid the fire, and struck a match. The newspaper burnt away without the wood catching alight.

'I hate this job,' I muttered, pulling the wood and coal from the grate and trying again. Still no luck.

Worried I would run out of newspaper before the wood caught alight, I stomped out to the veranda, poured a liberal amount of my dad's precious petrol into an empty tin can, and returned to the fire. I intended dipping each piece of wood into the can of petrol before relaying the fire. Then, I noticed a small glow where one of the sticks had caught. Thinking this would save me relaying the fire, I held the tin-can above the fire and slowly dribbled the petrol onto the flame. Before I knew it, the flame had shot up the dribble of petrol, and I was left holding a can of flames. Jumping to my feet, I scurried to the kitchen, the can now so hot I was in danger of dropping it on the carpet. Just as my finger-tips were about to be seared to the can, I half-dropped, half-threw, the can into the sink, expecting the petrol to run down the drain. To my horror, the whole of the sink became a raging fire. Instead of the petrol running down the drain, it was floating on a basin of greasy water. I reached in to empty the dish, but only managed to singe the hairs on my hand. It was at least a couple of minutes before the flames died away and I was able empty the dish down the sink.

Now the immediate panic was over, I breathed a little easier. I really didn't want my parents knowing about this little set-back and thought I had salvaged the situation quite well. But my elation was short lived. Above the sink hung a pair of under pants and a vest, displaying distinct brown stains. It wasn't in the crutch, so I knew they must have come from the flames. I knew immediately they were Nunky Bills'. The underwear was part of his demob clothing. Clothing was rationed, so apart from what he was wearing, was probably the only other underwear he had.

I pulled the underwear from the line and laid it out on the kitchen table, mortified when I saw they had large scorch marks on them. I tried rubbing them away with a wet finger, but the marks were permanent.

Turning the underwear inside out, I hung it back up, but the singe marks were still clearly visible. Flumping myself down on one of the kitchen chairs, I again examined the underwear, as if it by some miracle I could make the singe marks disappear.

I desperately racked my brains as to what I would tell my parents, but was unable to come up with an answer. I knew the minute it was spotted, I would be given a leathering and sent to bed without any tea. Also, time was not on my side. I had to think of something before my parents got home.

Then came my 'aha' moment. Without further ado, I grabbed the spade, dug a hole in the garden, and buried the underwear.

Congratulating myself on a job well done, I returned to the kitchen, letting out an audible moan of despair as I noticed the wall above the sink. There, as plain as day, was a brown mark where the flames had licked it.

Bugger, I thought. *If these marks don't come off, I'll have to dig the underwear up and tell my parents what happened. And the underwear will be full of mud. This could only happen to me. It's because I have to light that stupid fire. Oh no, the fire.*

In all the excitement I had completely forgotten about the fire. With pulse racing, I dashed back into the front room, dreading what I might find. Fortunately, my luck was in, and I quickly added some coal to the glowing embers.

Returning to the kitchen, I grabbed the 'Vim' and began scrubbing, my heart beat returning to normal as the marks disappeared. When I had finished, I checked from every angle that the last vestiges of my little mishap had been flushed down the drain, never to be seen again.

Satisfied that I had left no evidence, I stood in front of the fire enjoying the heat on the back of my bare legs. I thought about staying in until my parents arrived home, but decided I was in no hurry to face the inevitable confrontation. Checking one more time all was well, I stoked the fire, left the house, and headed off to the high street. I positioned myself where I could see their bus arrive, constantly reminding myself that no matter what my parents said, I would deny all knowledge of the underwear.

Before long, their bus arrived, and I discreetly followed them home, watching from a safe distance until I saw the kitchen light go on. Moments later, Nunky Bill passed without seeing me, and entered the house. Fifteen or twenty minutes later, the kitchen light went out and the living room light came on.

Knowing the rickety old gate would give warning of my arrival, I took a run, leapt the fence, and silently landed in the long grass. Keeping to the shadows like a cat burglar, I worked my way around to the to the side of the house where I could peek around the ill-fitting living room blind. I could just make out my dad reading his newspaper, whilst my step-mother and Nunky Bill were engaged in conversation. From what bits of the conversation I could make out, plus their body language and facial expressions, I was sure they were talking about the missing underwear.

Creeping around to the back of the house, I silently entered the kitchen, noticing there didn't appear to be any supper laid out for me. On tiptoe, and with heightened senses, I crept over to the living room door. Dropping to one knee, I placed my eye over the keyhole. Within seconds, the door was flung open, and there, highlighted by the light from the living room, stood my step-mother towering above me. She must have had ears like a dockyard rat.

'What are you up to, listening at the keyhole?' she said, the vitriol evident in her voice.

'No, I was just doing up my shoe,' I stammered.

'Yeah, and if I believed that I would believe anything. Come in here. Uncle Bill's got a bone to pick with you.'

I entered the living room. My dad momentarily looked up from his newspaper, gave me a cursory glance, reached for his tin of Golden Virginia tobacco, and settled back in his armchair. He was making himself comfortable for the obvious confrontation, whilst looking forward to my defence. Nunky Bill, on the other hand, appeared less happy.

'When I went to work this morning,' he said. 'I hung my underwear above the sink in the kitchen. When I came home, it was gone. Do you know anything about it?'

Pulling a grubby piece of rag from my pocket, I made a show of blowing my nose.

'Never mind blowing your nose whilst you think up an answer,' chipped in my step-mother. She knew all my dodges, but I still resorted to them.

'Sorry, what did you say was gone?' I muttered, holding the piece of rag in front of my mouth.

'Put that away and pay attention,' said my step-mother, taking over the conversation. 'There was underwear on the line when we went to work this morning, now it's gone. You are the only one who has been in the house, so you must know something about it. Now, what have you done with it?' Her voice was like a knife slicing through my very fibre.

'Nothing.' I said. 'I mean… why would I want your underwear?'

'You could have sold it,' ventured Nunky.

'Sold it. Who too?' I asked.

The suggestion that I could have sold the underwear seemed to amuse my father, much to the annoyance of my step-mother. Not that my father's light-hearted approach was any help to me. I still needed to be on my game. Drawing on all the devious skills learned whilst I was evacuated, I continued to deny any knowledge of the underwear.

Finally, they had no other option but to accept my story. But I knew Nunky Bill was anything but convinced.

My step-mother told me to go to my room. I wanted to point out that I had not had any supper, but went to my room thankful to be out of that situation. A few minutes later, the trap door opened, and Nunky Bill appeared. I was sitting on the floor on the far side of the room behind the bed in the semi-darkness. I watched him rummage through his cupboard, occasionally pausing in thought. *You're not going to find your underwear in there,* I thought. He must have forgotten I was in the room, because he suddenly noticed me looking at him and was visibly startled.

'Bloody hell, I didn't see you there - can't you make a noise or something, you could have given me a heart attack.'

'Well, you knew I was here,' I mumbled.

'You are definitely weird,' he said. 'Sitting in the darkness staring at me.'

'That's because we don't have a light in this room.'

'Yeah right. You're still weird.'

He left the room. Moments later I decided it was too early to go to bed. Not only that, I was hungry. Silently opening the outside door, I sneaked down the outside staircase into the garden. As I passed the kitchen window I ducked low, but couldn't help noticing Nunky Bill standing by the sink with a quizzical look on his face. I hoped I had done a good job at cleaning away all the evidence. Swiftly crossing the garden, I leapt the fence and ran over to Christopher's.

Christopher's mum answered my knock and invited me in. The living room was warm and inviting, and the family were playing cards around the dining table. In the corner of the room, Christopher's dad was doing some fretwork on a little table. Quite a contrast to the house I had just left. I joined in the cards, and gratefully accepted the snack Christopher's mother offered me.

An hour or so later, I left and returned home. Entering my room via the outside door, I silently snuck in and slipped into bed. I hoped no one had checked on me, but as they rarely did, I assumed my parents were none the wiser I had been out.

The following night, as soon as Nunky Bill arrived home, he sought me out. Cornering me in the bedroom, he came straight to the point.

'What did you do with my underwear?'

'I never saw your underwear.'

'Liar, you must have seen it, you were the only one who could have taken it. Now what did you do with it?'

'I'm not a liar, I never saw it.' Grabbing my arm in a vice-like grip, he pulled me close to his face.

'Tell me what you did with it, or it will be the worse for you.'

'Let go your hurting me.' I said, wriggling free.

'From now on I'll be keeping my eye on you. I never did trust you, always sneaking around. If I do find out you had anything to do with the disappearance of my clothes you can stand from under, because I'll be on to you like a ton of bricks.' With that he left the room.

I hope no one does any digging for a while, I thought, as I gazed out the window at the spot in the garden where the underwear was buried.

The loss of his underwear must have played on his mind. Some months later, long after he had moved out of our house, he was still looking for answers.

He came around one day to visit his sister. I was digging in the vegetable garden, not too far from where I had buried his underwear. Putting on a big smile, he sidled up to me and put his arm around my shoulders. I was immediately on my guard. In his most condescending voice he said.

'Billy. I know it's all water under the bridge now, but what did you do with my underwear? I mean if you sold it, well that's it. But I would just like to know what happened to it.'

I eased myself away from his patronising arm, stepped back, and looked him squarely in the eye. From the look on his face I'm sure he thought I was going to tell him. Instead, I just smiled and said.

'I have no idea.'

'Damn. You can tell me now,' he said, the frustration obvious in his voice. 'It doesn't matter anymore. I just need to know.'

I never did tell him or anyone else, not even my brother. If I had known I was going to write a book I would have said, 'read the book.'

Chapter Fifty-Four

The following Saturday, I was told to clean out my room, or as my step-mother put it, get that 'glory hole' cleaned up. Nunky Bill was delighted, as he thought he might find his underwear.

When we first moved in, I found an old toy fort along with a load of lead soldiers in the loft. I was delighted, and got a lot of pleasure from it. My step-mother, on the other hand, was not so keen. She immediately grabbed it, and took it into the garden, intent on throwing it out. I complained to my dad, who was also a bit of a hoarder. He agreed I could keep it.

As soon as we finished cleaning the room, I retrieved the Fort. I wanted to get it back into my room as soon as possible, just in case my step-mother, despite what my dad said, threw it out.

It wasn't that heavy, but was quite cumbersome. I was taking it up the outside stairs, and due to its size, I couldn't see where I was going. I got to the top of the stairs, paused for a breather, adjusted my grip, and stepped into the room. At precisely the same instant, Nunky Bill opened the trapdoor, and I planted my foot squarely on his head. As my feet flailed for a foot hold, I lost my balance, tipping dozens of lead soldiers onto Nunky Bill's head. He lost his footing and went crashing to the bottom of the steps, with me close behind.

'Get off me you little twat,' he shouted, throwing me to one side and staggering to his feet. 'Why can't you be more careful you little idiot. I could have been injured. Why is it always you causing trouble?'

'It was not my fault, you opened the trap door. I couldn't see you as I was carrying the fort,' I replied. My brother, who was in the loft, peered down on us, his face sporting a huge grin, before roaring with laughter. Having had my fall broken by landing on Nunky Bill, I was unhurt. Seeing the funny side of it, I joined him.

'Stop laughing you little twit,' shouted Nunky Bill. 'You too,' he yelled, causing Frankie to laugh louder.

'And anyway,' he said, turning back to me. 'Your mum told you to get rid of that fort, it's just a piece of junk.'

'No it's not, and my dad said I could keep it.'

'Your dad, your dad, is that all you can say, you little idiot.'

He stomped off to the kitchen and I heard him telling my step-mother what happened. I retrieved my Fort and joined Frankie in the loft, where we continued chuckling. Although it had given us a moment of fun in our humdrum lives, I knew I would be glad when Nunky Bill moved out.

Some weeks later, my prayers were answered, when my step-mother excitedly announced Bill and Vi were getting married and he was moving out.

Both my dad and I shared in the excitement, but for different reasons. My dad, because he and Nunky Bill were not the greatest of friends. I think my dad was jealous of the relationship between him and his sister. Me, because it would get him out of my room.

A few days later, he moved out, taking his bed, and set of drawers with him. I was thankful for the extra space in our room. There was still no sign of his underwear.

Chapter Fifty-Five

Not long after the underwear saga, I had another slight misfortune with fire. Only this time, I was not so lucky.

During the winter months my step-mother had a habit of brushing her long blonde hair whilst standing in front of the gas stove to keep warm. She would then pull out the hair caught in the brush, and place it in the drip tray under the stove top. A disgusting habit I know, but who was I to say.

One evening, whilst waiting for the pot of potatoes for the chicken's food to boil, I noticed the blonde hair ball. After examining it, I held it in the gas flame. It instantly flared up, catching me by surprise. Instinctively flicking my hand, I sent the burning hair ball straight onto the net curtains in the window alongside the stove. Within seconds, the tatty net curtains were alight. By the time I'd patted them out with the tea towel the curtains were ruined.

It was a complete catastrophe. How was I going to talk my way out of this mess. In my mind, an offence of this magnitude was punishable by death. But as it was against the law, my step-mother would have to settle for slapping me around a little, followed by deprivation of food, followed by being sent to my room to ponder my 'arson' tendencies. The slapping and being sent to my room I could take, it was just routine. It was the 'no dinner' that was the killer.

Fortunately, this time I was not alone in the house. No, we had a cat. We had not had it long and it was not much more than a kitten.

Here was the solution to my problem. Picking up the cat, I held it close to what was left of the nets. In true cat form, he hooked his claws into them, and I let him hang. Within seconds, the frayed and tattered curtains ripped asunder and the cat dropped to the floor. *Perfect,* I thought, as I removed what was left of them and threw them in the dust bin.

Within minutes of arriving home, my step-mother spotted the empty window and asked what happened to the curtains. I said the cat had jumped up and ripped them to pieces.

'So where are the curtains now?' she asked, giving me a long suspicious look.

'I took them down and threw them in the bin.' I replied. I was not altogether convinced she believed me, but left it at that.

The next morning, when I went into the kitchen for my 'sumptuous' breakfast of stale bread and watery milk, my step-mother was waiting. She immediately pulled me over to the window.

'What's this?' she asked, pointing to the glass. Being the 'super sleuth' she was, she had examined the window and discovered small fragments of burnt curtain sticking to the glass. She then showed me the curtains she had retrieved from the bin and asked me how the cat could have scorched them. After slapping me around the head, she told me to get out of her sight, saying, I was not being punished for burning the curtains, but for blaming the cat. She really loved that cat.

That evening, my dad told me that he and my step-mother had decided on some changes. In future, she would cook the chicken's food the night before and leave it on the veranda. All I had to do was mash it, mix in the meal, and serve.

'So, now there is no need for you to be in the house anymore,' he said.

'What about the fire. Who's going to light that?'

'Well, after the last incident, certainly not you. If necessary, I'll light it. Sometimes, by the time we get home it's time for bed, so a fire is just a waste.'

I was relieved, and was why I was not allowed in the house on my own. But even when my step-mother was at home, she didn't like me being in the house.

One winter afternoon, around four o'clock, I returned home from school and was surprised to find my step-mother was already home. Initially, I was delighted, figuring I would get out of the cold, or at least be allowed into my bedroom. She was entertaining visitors; so as soon as I stepped into the kitchen she told me to go out and play. I pointed out that it was snowing, and asked her if I could go to my bedroom in the loft.

'No. I don't want you listening to our conversation through the floor.'

One her guests remarked that it was not a very nice day to be playing outside, but my step-mother cut in with. 'He loves to play in the snow, don't you?' I knew better than to contradict her, so just nodded my head.

She stuck two mint sweets into my hand, whilst giving me a look which left me in no doubt that I had better take them, and not give her a showing up.

I left the house, and headed to the bombed house next door. There was no roof, but at least I could shelter from the wind. Squatting in the corner of one of the rooms, I sucked my peppermints to keep warm. I wondered how long it would be before the guests left and I could get in, and hopefully get fed.

Then, I spotted Nunky Bill coming down the road. He was hunched into his army great coat to keep out the cold. He no longer lived with us and was coming to pick up his wife who was one of my step-mother's house guests. As he passed, I called out to him.

'What are you doing hanging around a bombed building in the snow?' he asked. I told him what my step-mother had said.

'You can't play in this. Come with me,' he said.

I followed him into the house and my step-mother immediately asked what I wanted.

'He can't stay outside in this weather,' he said.

She was annoyed, but not wanting to contradict her brother in front of guests, told me to go to my room. It had no heating, but was warmed by the chimney going through the room. And, it was out of the snow.

On my way to my room, I passed through the living room to get to the steps leading to the loft. There were a few sandwiches left on the plate, but I was not offered one. I climbed the ladder to the loft and leaned against the chimney, enjoying the warmth on my back, whilst I listened to the merriment below.

When I heard the last of the guests leave, I crept downstairs, although I normally waited to be called. My step-mother glared at me as I entered the kitchen. She let me know in no uncertain terms she was not happy that I had used Nunky Bill as an excuse to contradict her.

I nodded, mumbled sorry, and told her I would not do it again, more concerned with keeping in with her so that I could get fed.

She gave me the bits and pieces left over from her little soiree, which filled a hole in my ever-hungry stomach.

Chapter Fifty-Six

～～～

September 1947, the summer school holidays ended, and I started at the same secondary school as my brother. Although we went to the same school, we didn't walk together as he didn't want me around. He was always trying to get off with the girls, and I was in the way.

Come dinner time, I finished my dinner and headed for the sports field. If I had known about the ritual, I would probably have given it a miss. I was immediately pounced on and thrown into the ditch around the sports field, along with all the other newbies. In winter, the ditch was full of icy cold water. Fortunately, it was still dry.

Anyone with any sense would have just stayed in the ditch; but that would have spoiled the fun. All the older boys lined along the top of the ditch using their foot to shove anyone attempting to climb out. I looked up, just in time to see my brother use his foot to shove me back down and roar with laughter. By the time the dinner break was over, I was covered in dead grass and mud. I hoped I would be able to clean up my already tatty clothes before my step-mother saw them.

A few weeks later, as the colder months crept in, I noticed I was the only boy in our class wearing short trousers. Even my friend Paul, who only had a mum, was wearing long trousers. I wondered how I could broach the subject with my parents. My attempts to get a bike or a sea scouts uniform had not gone well. My brother was now in long trousers, but he said he had bought them himself from his earnings.

Within days of the cold weather setting in, my knees became red, and painful to touch. I showed them to my step-mother.

'Look at my knees. They are really sore.' She momentarily glanced at them, but refrained from commenting.

'Could I get long trousers?' I said.

'Ask your dad. I haven't got money for long trousers.' I knew that would be a waste of time.

The next morning, before I left for school, she handed me a jar of Vaseline and an old pair of my dad's socks. She had cut the feet out of them, and sewed them so the wool wouldn't run.

'Rub some Vaseline into your knees, and pull the socks over them,' she said.

I didn't know whether to be glad or sad. They looked ridiculous, and kept falling down. But the Vaseline helped. In the end, I just let the socks hang around my ankles, only pulling them up when I was seated in the class. But I had not counted on the derision from the other boys.

'What's that on your legs Greeny, your Granny's stockings?'

That night I told my step-mother that they kept falling down and that everybody laughed at me. I couldn't bring myself to ask my dad for long trousers, and hoped she would ask. She was either unsuccessful, or didn't bother. The next morning, she gave me two lengths of 'knicker-elastic' sewed into a loop.

'Pull the socks up your leg so your trousers cover the tops, and hold them up with the elastic. Nobody will see it.'

Despite the laughter from my classmates, I continued wearing the feetless socks with the elastic holding them up. The wind was less painful on my knees, but they were hardly a substitute for long trousers. My appearance made sure I spent very little time in the company of girls. Having a bunch of boys laughing at me was one thing; but girls giggling was more than my pride could stand. The only girl who accepted my appearance was Pamela from next door.

Chapter Fifty-Seven

December 1947, and the Christmas holidays were upon us. One of the highlights at the local cinema was the kid's Christmas party. Instead of showing a film on the Saturday afternoon, the Rio cinema threw a party, with games and lots of free food.

So, that Saturday, I was around Christopher's house bright and early. I had fond memories of the previous year, when I won the bun eating contest.

Six children were invited onto the stage where six buns were suspended on strings. We were each placed in front of a bun and told we were not allowed to use our hands. The winner was the person who ate their bun the quickest. After several minutes of chasing the bun around with our mouths and nobody scoring a bite, they allowed us to hold the bun with one hand. On the word 'go', I was like a shark in a feeding frenzy. I devoured my bun in seconds, and gratefully collected my present.

I kept telling Christopher to hurry up or I was going without him, mentioning that once the cinema was full, they locked the doors. But his mum, who was getting him ready, insisted we had plenty of time. Then, just as I predicted, we arrived at the cinema and the doors were locked.

I was furious, and immediately blamed Christopher. But as I calmed down, I thought all is not lost. I told him to follow me. I knew the toilet window would be open. So, if we couldn't get in through the door, the window was the next best thing. With the cinema full of screaming yelling kids, they would never notice a couple of extra faces.

'Right. You go first,' I said, bending over so he could climb on my back and wriggle through the window.

'No, I don't want to,' he said.

'Ok. If you don't want to go first, then make a 'backy' for me.'

'No, I don't want to,' he whinged.

'Why not? You want to go to the party, don't you? Then make a backy for me.'

'No, I don't want to. You'll leave me.'

'No, I won't. As soon as I'm inside I'll pull you in. My brother and me have done this many times before. Now bend over.'

'No, I don't want to.'

'Well, if you don't want to bunk in, I do. So, bend over.'

'No, and you can't make me.'

'Yes I can,' I said, grabbing him. He began crying. I couldn't believe it. I was completely taken aback. Not for one second did I see this coming. I'd never known anyone to cry just because we were 'bunking in' to a cinema. At precisely the same time as he began his whining, a roar of laughter and screaming went up inside the cinema, adding to my frustration. *How on earth did I get stuck with a cry baby like him.* I thought. Grabbing him by the collar, I pushed him up against the wall.

'Stop crying and make a 'backy' for me,' I said, scrambling onto his back and wriggling through the window, the noise of merriment now just the other side of the door. I was on the point of joining in the fun and leaving Christopher outside, when his wailing reached a new high. Despite the noise coming from inside, I was sure someone would hear him. Climbing on the toilet pan, I leaned out the window.

'Give me your arms and I'll pull you in.'

'No, I don't want to,' he cried, refusing to take my outstretched arms.

'Right. Bugger you, I'm leaving you and you can go home on your own.'

I stepped down from the toilet pan, and was on the point of opening the door into the cinema, when his wailing reached a crescendo only reached by banshees and wild dogs. Unable to stand it any longer, I climbed back onto the toilet seat and leaned out the window.

'Shut up. If you're not coming in, go home, you big baby. Somebody will hear you. Now either let me pull you in, or go home, but don't stand there whining.'

'No, I don't want to go home.'

'Then give me your arms and I'll pull you in.'

'No, I don't want to.'

'So, what do you want?'

'I want you come back outside.'

'But I'll miss the party. Come on, give me your arms.'

'No, you come back out.' With that he launched into another torrent of tears and crying.

'God give me strength,' I shouted, climbing back out. Outside I let him have it.

'What is wrong with you? Standing there crying like a big baby. It's your fault we were late anyway. And then because you are such a sissy, you don't want to bunk in. Why didn't you just go home and let me have my party? I've looked forward to this all year. And now because of you, you big cry baby, I've missed it.'

I gave him a shove and walked away. This only served to increase his incessant whining and whinging, as he followed me calling out not to leave him.

'Go away,' I said. 'I've had it with you. Stop following me.' I increased my pace and headed for the field, a short cut to our houses.

Undeterred, he followed, still crying. His crying was really getting through to me. Unable to stand it any longer, I agreed to go home with him, just as long as he shut up. After several more heart-rending sobs and lots of sniffing, he finally stopped. Then, as soon as we neared his house, he began crying again. His mother was in her garden and was out like a flash.

'What happened?' she said, giving me a suspicious look, and wrapping her arms around Christopher. Whilst he continued to sob into her ample bosom, I explained that we were late getting to the cinema and the doors were locked. It completely slipped my mind to mention the bunking in through the cinema's toilet window. When I finished, she said.

'Don't cry, I'll give you your own party. And you can stay too Billy.'

She made us sandwiches and cake, and we played games. It was not as good as the cinema's party, but it was more than I got from my own parents.

'It's your own fault, you should have got there earlier,' said my step-mother, when I told her.

Next year I'll go on my own, I thought.

Chapter Fifty-Eight

Christmas was soon upon us, and I awoke to find 'Father Christmas', in all his wisdom, had left me a toy carpentry set. Why my dad thought I was interested in carpentry, I'll never know. He would have thought twice if he had known what I would do with it.

The first mistake I made was asking my dad what I could make. He thought I was genuinely keen to become a junior carpenter, when in fact I felt obliged to at least show some interest in his wonderful present. I didn't expect the task he gave me. Handing me a length of wood, he explained how to make a couple of brackets, and left me to it.

I was hoping for something more interesting, but never the less, set about cutting the piece of wood. I soon wished I had said nothing, as I realised how difficult it was.

My brother Frankie had received a fretwork set, and was faffing around trying to create the impression he was doing something significant. In fact, he spent more time making sarcastic remarks and sniggering every time my crappy little saw jammed. Finally, I hurled the piece of wood to the floor, kicked it across the veranda, and stormed off to complain to my dad. He was not in the least bit sympathetic, telling me a bad workman always blamed his tools. Marching me back to the veranda, he gave me a few pointers on how to do the job, before telling me to stop whining and get on with it.

I made several more attempts to saw the piece of wood, cursing and swearing every time the saw jammed. The more I cursed and swore, the more Frankie sniggered, which only added to my frustration. Finally, I cut the wood in two. It had taken me about an hour, by which time my crappy little saw was bent in all directions.

I felt a little better, being sure nailing the two pieces together would be easier than sawing. Resting one piece of wood on the doorstep, I held the other piece of wood against it. But before I could hit the nail, the wood fell to the floor. I picked it up and tried again, with the same results. This really tickled my brother, and he made no attempt to hide his mirth.

'Give me a hand instead of laughing,' I shouted, angrily.

'No, you got the carpenter's set. I only got a fretwork set,' he sniggered.

Again my piece of wood fell to the floor, and again he roared with laughter. He was really testing my patience.

'Shut up, shut up,' I yelled, dashing across to where he was sitting on a low stool. Before I knew it, I had hit him on the head with the hammer. His laughing stopped, but his grin remained, at least until the blood began to course down his forehead. The minute he saw the blood, he began screaming.

I said sorry several times, worried his screaming would bring my dad running. But he was having none of it. He pushed me out of the way and ran crying to the back of the house.

I was still standing with the hammer in my hand, when my dad appeared. He grabbed me by the arm and shook me so hard the hammer flew from my grasp. Dragging me from the veranda onto the grass, I could see he was intent on teaching me a lesson. Attracted by all the screaming, my step-mother came to see what all the commotion was about, momentarily causing my dad to relax his grip. Like a whippet, I was off, out the gate and into the road, screaming as loudly as I could in the hope the neighbours would come out and deter my dad.

'Get back in here,' he shouted.

From the safety of the road, I turned and looked at him, all the time keeping a safe distance. He slowly eased himself out of the garden, and took up a position on the kerb facing me. Knowing he was working out how he could catch me, I watched him like a Hawk, ready to flee. Slowly, quite casually, he eased himself from the pavement into the road. As he moved, so did I. Suddenly, he made a dash for me, and I took off down the road screaming at the top of my lungs. I sensed he was gaining on me, and screamed all the louder. He was a good runner, but I was better. Thankfully, all the roll-up cigarettes he had smoked came to my rescue, and he stopped. Breaking into a fit of coughing, I watched him slowly walk back to the house. My step-mother had taken up a position by the gate and called him in. By now, most of the neighbours were out wondering what all the shouting and screaming was about.

I slowly followed from a safe distance and watched him go back inside. I knew I would have to go in sometime, but hoped by then he would have calmed down.

Brian, Christopher's older brother, who was more Frankie's friend than mine, had also been attracted by the ruckus and asked me what was going on. Thinking I had a sympathetic ear, I told him what happened. To my surprise, and my annoyance, he said I deserved all I got. Brothers shouldn't hit one another over the head with a hammer, no matter how frustrating they were. Just as well I wasn't still holding the hammer.

A few minutes later, Frankie came out with sticking plaster on his head and told me I had to go in; adding that he was going to get me for what I had done. I didn't want to go in, but knew if I delayed going in, the worse it would be.

As I passed the front door, I spotted my dad sitting in his armchair in the living room. I nervously approached, but remained in the doorway, keeping as much space as I could between him and me.

'What made you hit Frankie on the head with a hammer?' he asked.

Noticing he had returned to his pragmatic self gave me confidence to explain my side of the story. He remained quiet, puffing on a roll-up, until I had finished. He then explained the benefits of controlling your temper, pointing out that if I didn't keep it under control it could get me into trouble in later life. I heeded his advice, but thought, *having a brother like mine is enough to try the patience of a saint.*

I eventually finished making the brackets. My dad used them to put up a shelf in the veranda. Frankie put some of his fretwork stuff on it. I threw it off.

Chapter Fifty-Nine

One weekend, I was hanging around in the road hoping somebody, or something, might turn up to brighten my day. I then spotted my dad removing the tarpaulin from his car. I nipped over, hoping that if I gave him a hand he would give me a ride. He didn't. He just climbed into the car and drove off, leaving me standing on the pavement.

An hour or so later, several of us were playing football in the road with a small rubber ball, when the sound of an engine sent us scattering to the kerb. I watched as a motorbike and sidecar drew into our house, only then realising it was my dad. I dashed over, excited that he had bought a motorbike.

My step-mother refrained from sharing in his excitement, but it didn't deter him from giving me a lengthy explanation on how we would all fit in. My step-mother would ride in the front seat of the sidecar. I was to ride in the boot, which converted to a seat. Frankie would ride on the pillion.

The following day ,we went on our first run. Frankie complained he was cold, as his clothing was inadequate for riding on a motorbike. My dad, on the other hand, had all the gear. Weather proof overcoat, leather gauntlets, goggles, and hat. My brother had to make do with his Blue Melton overcoat.

'At least you've got a coat,' I pointed out, after one trip when he was having a moan.

'Yeah, but you're alright. You can duck down and get out of the wind.'

In the end, he complained so much my dad stopped inviting him. Frankie told me he was glad he didn't have to go anymore. In fact, when he saw my dad getting the motorbike out, he kept out of the way.

Meanwhile, fed up with looking at my skinny shivering frame, my step-mother acquired a used overcoat from somewhere. It was made of a sort of 'shaggy brown' material. Frankie laughed, and said I looked like a teddy bear in it, but I knew he was just jealous. Once Frankie stopped going with us, my dad stopped asking me along, so my parents went out on their own.

So, I was somewhat surprised, when one Saturday my dad called me over and told me they were going to the pictures. I just stood there wondering why he was telling me, as they normally just rode off leaving me standing in the road looking after them.

'Well, don't just stand there, get in,' he said.

'What, am I going also?' His invitation had taken me completely by surprise. Being told where they were going was one thing, but being invited to the pictures too much to comprehend. With no time for frills, in case they changed their mind, I jumped into the back of the sidecar.

The movie was 'The Paleface', starring Bob Hope and Jane Russell. My dad said he liked Bob Hope, but my step-mother said it was just because the big-busted Jane Russell was in it. Must admit she was well endowed in the 'boob' department. All that aside, I enjoyed the movie getting a lot of laughs from it.

When we came out, my step-mother suggested we all go for a fish and chip supper. I couldn't believe my ears. *Being taken to the pictures was one thing, but a fish and chip supper as well. Whatever next?* I thought. *Just wait until I tell Frankie. He'll be so jealous.*

I took my seat in the café, anxiously looking forward to a plate of fish and chips. I was still wearing my 'Teddy Bear' overcoat buttoned up to the neck. My dad told me to take it off and hang it on the back of my chair whilst I ate my supper.

'No, it's alright, I'll just keep it on,' I said.

'Take it off. You kept it on in the cinema. You look stupid eating a meal with an overcoat on.'

'No, I'm alright.'

'What is wrong with you? Take it off.'

'I can't.'

'Why not?'

'My shirt is dirty.'

'Show me.'

I undid the top button and showed him my filthy, frayed shirt, which hadn't been washed for ages.

'Why didn't you change your shirt?'

'I can't. It's the only shirt I've got.'

'Is that right Glad?'

'What do you think? If it was left to you he wouldn't even have that.'

I kept my coat on, but that set the tone for the rest of the meal, which we ate in silence. That was the first and last time I was ever invited to go with them to the pictures.

Chapter Sixty

I was idly dawdling along on my way home from school one day, when my eye caught something glinting in the sunlight. Lying in the grass outside a small bungalow, was a pair of scissors. Quickly looking about me, I picked them up and continued on my way. When I was well clear of the bungalow, I stopped to examine them. They were large, like a dressmaker would use. By the green on the blades, they were probably being used to trim the hedge.

When I got home, I cleaned them up a bit and offered them to Pamela's mum, thinking she would pay the most. She said she had no need for them, so I offered them to Christopher's mum. She asked me where I had got them from. When I told her I had found them, she said I should put them back. I told her I would, but knew I wouldn't. Instead, as a last resort, I offered them to my step-mother. She looked at me a little suspiciously when I told her I had found them, but took them anyway.

'I must give you something for them,' she said. I thought they must be worth at least sixpence, maybe even more.

Next morning, she handed me a thruppenny bit. 'For the scissors', she remarked, smiling.

I wanted to say that I thought they were worth more, but instead, thanked her and took the money. I was annoyed with myself for not asking for more, but was worried if I did she might not give me anything. And anyway, three pence was better than nothing.

That night, as I went up the steps to bed, I noticed the scissors sticking out of her sewing basket. I quickly lifted them. The following afternoon, on the way home from school, I paused outside the bungalow. There was a lady in the garden, so I called out to her.

'Excuse me lady, are these your scissors? I said, holding them up for her to see.

'Yes, where did you find them?'

'I spotted them under the hedge as I was passing.'

'No wonder I couldn't find them. I've been looking everywhere for them. You are a good boy. Wait there a moment.' She went into her house.

I thought she might give me a piece of cake or something, but to my surprise, she pressed a sixpence into my hand.

I couldn't believe my luck as I happily skipped off down the road. I would have liked to have told my step-mother. It might have taught her not to be so mean.

Some days later, she asked me if I had seen the scissors anywhere.

'No, no idea where they could be,' I replied.

Chapter Sixty-One

Easter 1948, and it was time for school holidays again. My parents were still working in London and not getting home until late, so I was still mooching the streets.

I would have liked a job, but there are not many options when you are still a month off becoming twelve years old. I had kept in contact with the Burtons in case any jobs came up, with no luck.

After the Easter break, I returned to school and was sent for by the headmaster. On the way to his office, I racked my brains for anything I could have done to attract his attention. To my surprise, he told me that my results in the end of term exams qualified me for boarding school, and did I think I would like that.

'Where is the school?' I asked, knowing there was not one on Canvey Island.

He told me it was in Surrey, a four-hour road journey from Canvey Island.

I was immediately interested, the thought of getting away from my parents more than enough incentive. He handed me a letter for them to sign.

I left his office completely amazed by what had just happened. I had never seen myself as a 'swot'.

I watched my father's face as he read the letter, trying to gauge what my chances were of him signing. After reading the letter, he passed it to my step-mother without making a comment. Whilst she read it, he asked me how I felt about going to boarding school.

In truth, I couldn't get there quick enough, but mumbled something like. 'It would be alright, and I suppose it would be good for my education'. My dad looked at me as if to say, 'since when were you interested in education', but agreed it would be good for me to go. His remark buoyed me up, and I was sure he would sign the letter. But that was before he saw the list of clothes and other stuff I needed to take with me. He questioned every item. 'Where do they think I'm going to get the money to buy all this?' he whinged.

Fortunately, my step-mother was keen to see the back of me and pointed out that most of the items were everyday clothing; except for school uniform, toiletries, and sports gear.

'If you don't think we can afford it, say so now and he can stay at home,' she said, 'It's all one to me.'

'No, no Glad. I just need to think about it.' my father replied. As usual, when it came to him spending any money, especially as he couldn't see what he would get out it, he delayed. I thought things were going too well. But at least he had agreed in principle I should go.

The weeks passed, and each week the headmaster asked me if my parents had signed the letter. I told him I thought things were progressing, even though I had no idea how many items I was short. Finally, when he could wait no longer, he issued me with an ultimatum. If my letter was not signed by the end of the week, he would withdraw my name. My dad signed, and the headmaster handed me my letter of acceptance. I was to report to Elmbridge Boarding School, Cranleigh, Surrey, at the end of the Summer Holidays.

My dad said I could use his suitcase, emphasising to my step-mother to be sure to bring it back. The case was not very big, but I was assured that I had everything on the list.

My step-mother and I left Canvey. Four hours, and two coach rides later, we arrived at a large sign which read, 'Elmbridge Boarding School'.

We scrunched up the long drive, and were shown into the Headmaster's office. He gave me a long look, and I sensed he was not that impressed with my appearance. He told me I would be in 'Abbey House'.

When we left his office, he shook my step-mother's hand, holding it longer than necessary. She was an attractive blonde, and had that effect on men.

Mr Raimonds, my housemaster, looked me up and down. I don't think he was very impressed by the way I was dressed either. He introduced himself to my step-mother, trotting out a well-rehearsed speech supposedly for my benefit, although he spent more time looking at my step-mother's legs than at me.

'Competition,' he said, 'is good for the mind and body, and develops a boy's character, don't you think? Mrs Green.' He gave her a smile reserved for parents. She agreed. I remained silent. Then, turning to me, he asked if I could do maths.

'Yes Sir, I think so,' I replied, a little uncertainly.

'Think so, you'd better know so, I'm your maths teacher. I only like bright boys in 'Abbey House'. I later learned that 'Abbey House' tended to be for the more affluent parents' children. I lasted one term, before being moved to 'Roding House'.

Mr Raimonds finished his speech, and asked my step-mother if she had any questions.

'Yes, there is one thing. I haven't packed any towels for William. I completely forgot.' I knew that to be a lie, but remained silent.

'That's a bit of problem. A boy can't expect to survive without towels. If he is not properly equipped, he can be asked to leave. We shower every night, so he'll need them right away. What do you intend doing about it?'

'I'm going to go into town now and buy some. I'll return later with the towels.' She afforded him one of her most seductive smiles. 'Will that be alright?'

'Yes of course Mrs Green. Just drop them off at the secretary's office.' He showed my step-mother and me to my bunk and locker.

'If you want to stay and help him unpack, you may.'

She made no effort to help, saying I would have to get used to looking after myself. My locker had two shelves, so I placed my clothes in such a way it created the illusion I had plenty of stuff.

I walked with her to the end of the driveway and waited until she caught her bus, before going back to my dormitory.

I sat on my bunk and wondered if in my desire to get away from my parents I had made the right choice.

'Boys are not allowed in the dormitory during the day,' said Mr Raimonds'.

'Sir.' I replied, immediately standing up.

'I'll make an exception, being as it's your first day. In the meantime, you can sweep the veranda.' He showed me where the broom was and pointed to the bins.

'Put the dirt in there.'

'Yes sir.'

What else would I do with it. I thought. Later on, his remark made sense, as most of the boys just threw the dirt over the handrail into the grass. A few minutes later, he was back.

'Have you finished?'

'Yes sir.'

'Haven't made a very good job of it have you? I can see I am going to have to knock you into shape if you are going to be any good for 'Abbey House'. We only have the best here. Understand?'

'Yes sir.'

'Go on then, off you go and get your tea.'

He pointed me in the direction of the dining hall, which by the time I got there was full of noisy chattering boys. Standing awkwardly in the entrance, I looked around, unsure what I was supposed to do. One or two boys turned to check me out, but nobody came to help me. Suddenly the noise of scraping chairs filled the dining hall, as everybody got to their feet, followed by complete silence. Moments later, came the command, 'Be seated'. The noise of chairs being scraped across the floor was deafening.

Finally, a Prefect came over and showed me to a table where several other boys were already seated. In front of me was a plate, with two slices of bread spread with margarine, and a dollop of jam on the side. One of the boys at the table joked that it was just as well I sat down when I did, or he would have had my tea. Food, like everywhere I had ever been in my short life, was at a premium. There was just enough to keep body and soul together. *So, what's new,* I thought.

After tea, I checked at the main office to see if my step-mother had dropped off the towels. I needn't have bothered. She had obviously boarded her bus and kept going.

Back in the dormitory, I met Brian Reece, who had the bunk above me. He told me he came from Ilford in Essex. It turned out this was a boarding school funded by the Essex County Council, so all the boys were from Essex. When I told him I was from Canvey Island, he said he had never been there. I said not to worry, as I had never been to Ilford.

He asked me if I had a hobby, as we all had to go to a hobby group in a few minutes.

'I haven't got a hobby,' I said.

'Well you had better pick one, or you might get put into something you don't like.'

'What's your hobby?' I asked.

'Rug making. I don't really like it, but it's better than gardening,' he answered. Faced with the choice of gardening or rug making, I followed him, and got into the rug making class. It was quite interesting. I even made a 'not too shabby' rug.

The boarding school routine was tight, with very little time to ourselves. During the winter months, we played sport in the afternoons, and did our lessons in the evening. Hobbies and sport were encouraged, but not compulsory. However, anyone not participating found themselves weeding flower beds, digging allotments, or cleaning up the school grounds.

Back in our dormitories after supper, the Prefects were in charge. Their badge of office was the rubber sole of a size fourteen plimsoll, which was liberally used to coax the junior students into behaving themselves.

The bathrooms were in a separate block and shared between two 'houses'. Dressing gowns, for those fortunate to have one, were worn whilst waiting to use the bathroom. My wardrobe didn't run to the luxury of a dressing gown, so I wore my teddy bear overcoat, which drew some unappreciative stares and comments. Over the years it had become the worse for wear, and was a tad too small for me. Then, one day, I was given the task of cleaning out the wardrobe at the end of the dormitory. I found a perfectly good raincoat with a name sewn into it of someone I didn't recognise. Not wanting to alert anybody to my find, I discreetly asked about him, and learned he had left the school some months ago. When the opportunity presented itself, I removed the name and hung the coat as far back in the wardrobe as I could. Again, biding my time to see if the coat had been left to anyone, I waited several days. When it was apparent that no one else had laid claim to it, I discreetly sewed my own name into it. Nobody queried it, so I won a perfectly good raincoat to add to my sparse wardrobe.

When it was our turn to use the bathroom, there was a mad dash to claim a washbasin. As there were never enough, some boys went straight into the showers. As I didn't have any towels, I stuck close to Brian, so I could borrow his. He insisted on using it first, so I always got a wet towel. It was a bit of a problem when we both came out of the shower at the same time, as I had to stand shivering until he had finished drying himself. I longed for the pleasure of my own towel.

The showers held eight boys, and the allotted time was about five minutes. When the duty teacher called time, you scurried out as the next group came in. After drying yourself and putting on your pyjamas, you were inspected. A toothy smile showed you had brushed your teeth, before your hands were inspected to check your finger nails were clean.

All the teachers, including the women, took a turn at supervising. The art teacher was a young attractive blonde woman, who all the boys fancied. There was always a buzz of excitement when it was her turn. Some boys deliberately played with their 'Willie' to make it look bigger, whilst pretending to wash it. Then, when she called time, walked as close as possible to her as they reached for their towel.

She seemed unmoved by it all, hardly batting an eyelid, no doubt having seen it all before. Because she was an attractive woman, it was rumoured that she didn't wear panties. This was brought about because she often stood with her hands in her skirt pockets. Any movement of her hands to a bunch of horny teenagers was interpreted as her playing with herself. Several of us discussed finding out if it were true, by looking up her skirt. I don't know if I was set up, but I drew the shortest straw and the task fell to me. I thought I would have no problem. But as the next art lesson loomed ever closer, I began to have second thoughts.

She had a habit of walking up and down the aisles between the rows of desks, often leaning in to check the work of the far away student. This, I was told, would be my opportunity to drop my pencil on the floor and look up her skirt as I bent to pick it up. I was not too happy, and found it quite nerve racking. I had visions of her looking down on me and asking, 'Are you looking up my skirt?' I mean, what would I say? I might even be thrown out of school. I could just imagine my parent's reaction if I told them I had been expelled for looking up a teacher's skirt to see if she was wearing any knickers.

Art was not my strong subject. In fact, I was useless at it. But that morning, my stress level was so high I found it impossible to focus. Several times she walked past my desk, and I could see my mates egging me on. The nearer it got to the end of the lesson, the more I despaired. I had just resigned myself to letting it pass and risk being called a wimp by my mates, when my opportunity came. She came down my aisle and leaned over my desk to check the student next to me. It was the perfect opportunity, and there was no way I could get out of it. I let my pencil roll from my desk, bent down and looked up. I am sure she knew what I was up to, but she remained leaned over. I retrieved my pencil, and sat back up in my seat. Moments later, she straightened up and looked me squarely in the eye. My heart was racing nineteen to the dozen, and I was sure she was going to say something. Instead, she just looked at my 'art work', and walked away.

Outside, my mates crowded around me desperate to know. In truth, she was wearing knickers. But not wanting to destroy the illusion, I told them she was not, and I'd seen everything. This would give them something to think about the next time they were masturbating.

Chapter Sixty-Two

To ensure we were never without a meaningful task, as our masters put it; Saturday mornings were spent cleaning up the school grounds. The only way to avoid this 'meaningful' task was to be involved in an even more meaningful task. The 'Young Farmers Club' fell into that category, as did having an allotment.

I put my name down for an allotment and to join the YFC. Both were keenly sought after, so naturally there was a waiting list.

Then, one morning, we took our seats in class to be told that this morning's lesson was on bee-keeping. *Bee keeping,* I thought, *god give me strength. When in my life will I ever need to know about keeping bees.* To my surprise, it grabbed my interest, and I actually found it all very interesting. Such was my level of enthusiasm, the master asked if I would like to help him with the bees. I really took to the task. When we were later asked to write an essay on a subject of our choice, I chose bee keeping. The master was so impressed, the school entered it into the Surrey County Education Department competition. From all the essays from all the schools in the county, to my never-ending surprise, I won third prize. That was the only time the Headmaster gave me a favourable mention at school assembly.

The honey collected normally sold for two shillings and sixpence a jar. It was too expensive for most of us so was sold to one of the local shops, or brought out on parents visiting day. So, when the Bee Keeper gave me a jar for my efforts, I was obliged to share it with my mates. I didn't mind, as I had precious little else to share with them.

Saturday afternoons we got to ourselves. But there was no sitting around in the dormitories or school halls. You had to be out and doing something. Most of us headed for the football pitch for a kick around. Often there wasn't enough of us to make up two teams, so we went exploring in the woods around the school.

There was a canal which ran the length of the school sports grounds. Over the years, students had built rafts which were passed down to the incoming students. It basically was a first come first served basis. Their construction was quite basic. A wooden platform, made by lashing several branches together, were loosely secured to a number of empty oil drums. The raft was propelled by punting it with a pole. The fun was never knowing when an oil drum would break loose and tilt the occupants into the cold muddy canal.

If a raft wasn't available, there was always the length of rope secured to one of the overhanging trees. If you launched yourself with sufficient momentum, the rope was just long enough to allow you to drop off on the other side. But the timing was critical. Let go too soon, and you landed on the slope of the bank and toppled backwards into the water. Too late in letting go, and you were already on your way back and would land in the water.

I watched a couple of boys do it. It didn't look too hard. Grabbing the rope, I launched myself towards the other bank. I quickly realised I had not given myself enough momentum and was not going to make it. The backward swing was also short of the bank. Slowly, I lost momentum, until I was left hanging in the middle of the canal. Had I had the strength, I could have climbed up the rope and down the tree. But with my puny arms, all I could do was hang there.

'Get me a raft,' I shouted to the crowd of onlookers, all anxious to see how long I could hold on.

They deliberately took their time, so by the time the raft arrived, (excuse the pun) my arms were 'on their last legs'. Then, to add to the fun, I was so anxious to get onto the raft, I tipped it over, sending the would-be rescuer and myself into the canal. He was not amused.

An hilarious uproar from the delighted onlookers could be heard as I waded up the bank. I was told I had now passed my initiation ceremony.

The following day, Sunday, we gathered in the car park to be inspected before going to church. No chance of slinking away to catch tadpoles, like in Exmouth.

I was wearing the only shoes I possessed, which had spent the night in the drying room. Despite me cleaning them, they were beautifully patterned with watermarks. My shirt collar was none to clean, whilst my tie, which I had borrowed, was not tied properly. Not having a blazer, I wore a second-hand jacket which my step-mother had scrounged for me.

'Are those the only shoes you have?' asked the inspecting teacher, looking me up and down as if I was a bad smell under her nose.

'Yes Miss.'

'Where's your blazer?'

'I haven't got one.'

'How on earth did you manage to get into this school without a blazer? I mean, you can't possibly sow a school badge on 'that' jacket.' I had no answer.

She checked the two boys either side of me, smiling in appreciation at their immaculate turnout. She then gave me a look of despair, and joined the other teachers.

We marched off to church. I sat at the back as far away from the altar and the priest as possible, and let the smartly dressed boys sit at the front.

Each Sunday evening, we were expected to write a letter to our parents. Except on the third Sunday of each month, which was visiting day. I used a sheet of paper from my exercise book, and an envelope supplied by the school. All our letters were read before being sent out to make sure they were properly laid out, legible, and with no spelling mistakes. All the boys joked it was to make sure nobody wrote anything bad about the school.

About three weeks after joining the school, I was busy pondering what to write. After writing 'Dear Mum and Dad' I'd run out of ideas.

The headmaster, as he usually did, popped in, and called me out to the front.

'Have you got your towels yet?' he asked.

'No Sir.'

'How do you manage without towels?'

'I just borrow one.'

He said it was an unsatisfactory arrangement and I was to inform my parents that if they did not supply me with a set of towels within one week, I would be expelled and sent home. I was delighted. At least I now had something to write home about. Within a week, my towels arrived. Obviously, the thought of having me back home was a great motivator. I now knew how I was going to get my blazer.

On another occasion, I was again pondering what to write to my parents, when the teacher supervising us called me out to the front of the classroom. It was the same teacher who had remarked on my appearance when we were going to church.

'According to the records, you are a Catholic.' she said. The way she said 'Catholic' I thought she was about to spit. Not knowing where her question was leading to, I just looked at her without comment. She took my silence as a yes.

'So, why don't you go with the *Catholics* to your own church?' Not seeing the relevance of her question; one religion being much the same as the next as far as I was concerned, I continued silently gazing at her.

'Didn't you realise you were in the wrong church?' At last, a simple yes or no question.

'No Miss.' I answered.

'You can't be much of a *Catholic* if you didn't notice the service was different.'

'I'm not.'

'Not what?'

'Much of a Catholic. In fact, I am not even sure I am a Catholic.'

'Well, as far as the school is concerned, you are a Catholic. So, from now on, you had better go to the Catholic Church.'

It was quite obvious my scruffy appearance didn't sit well with her and this was her way of getting rid of me. Memories of Exmouth came flooding back, and I dreaded the thought of going back to the Catholic church.

The following Sunday morning, I teamed up with the other Catholics in the school driveway. There were not that many of us, so we were left to make our own way to church. Given the chance, I would have given it a miss and sloped off somewhere. But the other boys were dead keen, so I followed them. I sat at the back on my own. I also decided that as soon as I had managed to convince my parents to get me a blazer, I would go back to the Church of England.

Once the service was over, we were left to make our own way back to the school. I always took the opportunity to wander around the village, such as it was. None of the shops were open, not that I had any money, so I didn't hang around long, not wanting to miss my dinner. During one of my Sunday morning walkabouts after church, I noticed a ballpoint pen factory.

A Hungarian journalist named Laszlo Biro invented the first ballpoint pen in 1938. The British government bought the licensing rights to Biro's patent during World War 2. The British Royal Air Force needed a new pen that would not leak at higher altitudes in fighter planes the way fountain pens did. The ballpoint's successful performance for the Air Force brought Biro's pens into the limelight.

Ballpoint pens were just becoming popular, but were frowned upon by the education department in the belief they detracted from the development of writing skills. We were still using a nib on the end of a wooden pen, dipped into an inkwell on each students' desk. They did have one advantage over a ballpoint pen. They made a great dart when the nib was broken.

The school did however condescend to allow students to use ballpoint pens for private work. But they were expensive, so few boys had them. I once borrowed one, and knew I just had to have one.

Apart from going to church on Sundays, the only other time we were allowed out was on Saturday afternoons. If you told the duty master you were going rambling, a fine outdoor activity for a young school boy, you were let out. I gave the rambling a miss and headed into Cranleigh to the ballpoint pen company. I'd noticed a bin outside, and figured there was a good chance I could get enough parts to make myself a pen. After several minutes rummaging around, I only succeeded in covering my hands in ballpoint ink. I had never seen this type of ink before, and was surprised at how difficult it was to remove compared to ordinary water-based ink.

I then spotted a bin inside the security fence, which looked a lot more interesting. After a quick check around, I quickly scaled the link fence and dropped into the enclosure. Several minutes later, I climbed back over the fence with enough parts to make several pens.

Back at school, I stashed my loot, got cleaned up, and went for my tea. Later that evening, I found a quiet spot and made up my first ballpoint pen. I showed it to a couple of boys, inviting them write with it. They were so impressed, they asked if I could get them one. Seeing the chance to make a few pence, I told them I'd see what I could do. Over the next few days, I made up three more pens, which I sold for threepence each.

It was a month before I could get back to the factory. I always went on my own, not wanting to share my new-found source of income. I knew if I was caught I would be expelled; but the lure of earning some money too great an opportunity to miss. Back at school, I made up several more pens. One was much better than the one I was using, so I kept it and sold my old one.

Within a few weeks, the novelty of owning a ballpoint pen wore off. Most of them soon ran out of ink, leaked, or just fell apart. At least I was spared the ordeal of breaking into the factory and risking being expelled.

The third Sunday of each month was visiting day. As all the students came from Essex, the parents arrived on coaches from Victoria Coach Station. One or two of the more wealthy ones arrived in cars.

There was always an air of excitement when the coaches were due, with a number of the boys waiting at the end of the drive to see who could spot them first. As soon as the first coach was sighted, they would come scampering up the drive excitedly shouting, 'they're here, they're here.'

I never knew if my parents were coming or not, as they never wrote. But I still joined the excited throng of boys anxiously watching as each coach unloaded its passengers. As the number of waiting boys got fewer and fewer, I hoped I wouldn't be the only boy left with no visitor. Somehow it was more tolerable if other parents hadn't bothered to visit their offspring.

When it was obvious my parents were not coming, I would wander off to the playing fields, anywhere to avoid seeing all the excited boys with their parents. The worst part of being parentless on visiting day was the boredom of trying to fill a day designed for family reunions. Most parents took their sons out for the day, or picnicked in the school gardens. I would pass them, trying to look unconcerned as if I was on my way somewhere. But there was a positive side though. Tea and sandwiches were laid out in the dining hall for the visitors. I always managed to grab a handful, which was my way of placating myself.

On one occasion, my friend Derek's parents invited me to join them. We went to a restaurant in Cranleigh in their car, and his dad bought me dinner. I couldn't picture my dad doing that for Derek. It was a great day.

Sometimes, I was fortunate enough not to be the only boy whose parents hadn't visited. My friend Brian Reece, who had let me use his towels when I had none, often didn't have a visitor. But he only had a mum, his dad having been killed in the war. Apart from not having visitors, we also had one other thing in common. He never had any money either.

So, inspired by our lack of cash, one visiting day, we set up a shoe-shine stand during visiting hours. Using an upturned barrow and a wooden box, we located ourselves so that parents who had visited the allotments or 'Young Farmer's Club', would have to pass us.

It went well for a couple of visiting days, then the headmaster intervened. He said it didn't present the right image for the school, so another of my little entrepreneurial ventures 'bit the dust'.

During my four years at boarding school, my parents only visited twice. On one occasion, fed up with being disappointed when nobody turned up, I didn't even bother going to meet the coaches. They sent someone to tell me my parents were here. I thought they were joking, and refused to go to the car park. I was still unconvinced, until I heard a voice say,

'Couldn't you be bothered to come and meet us then?'

It was my dad and step-mother. They had also brought my brother Frankie with them. As it was their first visit, I excitedly showed them around the school, particularly my allotment and the bee hives. It was customary for parents before leaving to give their children a couple of shillings. My dad had obviously not heard of the custom, or chose to ignore it.

Chapter Sixty-Three

~◦~

All students were expected to go home during the Christmas, Easter, and summer holidays, so the school closed. Transport was provided by Essex County Council, but no transport was provided for the half-term break. As it was normally only a few days, we had the choice to go home, or stay at school.

By lunch time on the first day, all those going home had gone. I preferred to stay behind, not that I had much choice. I had no money for the fare, and my parents were not about to pick me up. Even if I had had the money, I still wouldn't have gone home. One of the benefits of staying behind was that the food was much better, and more plentiful, reason enough to stay.

Some of the more affluent boys had bicycles, which they would leave at the school whilst they were away. Another one of my friends; you can see I chose my friends very carefully, had a bicycle, and let me use it whilst he was away. I loved it, excited at the thought of the fun I would have for the next few days now I had a bike.

Each morning, we had breakfast in the unusually quiet dining hall, cleaned up our dormitory, and by nine o'clock, the rest of the day was our own. This was my time to explore the Surrey countryside. I would ride for miles, always remembering to be back at school for meal times.

One afternoon during the Easter half-term break, I was cycling around and came upon an open-air swimming baths. The pool was open, but despite the spring sunshine, there were no swimmers. I stood for a while admiring the sparkling water, whilst casting my mind back to the scummy water in the creek in Canvey Island. I was about to get on my way, when the man at the pay desk asked me if I wanted to come in for a swim. I told him I had no money or costume.

'It's alright,' he said, opening the gate, 'I can lend you a towel and costume.'

I got changed, and gingerly approached the empty pool. I dipped my toe in and knew immediately why I was the only swimmer. It was freezing. I considered leaving, but felt obligated to the man for lending me the costume. Plucking up the courage, I took the plunge. My skinny, lily-white body shuddered as I hit the cold water. I swam a quick length and climbed out. A combination of the cold water and noticing the time on the clock by the pool, ensured it was time I was on my way. As I was leaving, I handed the man the towel and costume. To my surprise, he told me to keep them, saying people often left stuff behind and didn't come back to claim them. I thanked him, delighted to have a proper swimming costume and an extra towel. *Things are really looking up* I thought, as I merrily rode back to school.

A few weeks later, it was time for our summer holidays. We were all sitting waiting for our coach to pull out from the school grounds, when the School Secretary came on board and handed out the letters that had arrived that morning. She handed the boy sitting in front of me an envelope. I enviously watched as he opened it to reveal a birthday card with a ten shilling note inside. He quickly read the card, gave the ten shilling note a cursory glance, and with not a flicker of emotion, stuffed it into his back pocket. If I had received such a gift, I would have been over the moon. I sat back in my seat, annoyed by his attitude to such a magnanimous gift. More money than I had ever seen in my life. The more I thought about it, the more envious I became.

Throughout the journey, the 'mega rich' boy in front of me was up and down all the time. Each time he moved, my eyes were drawn to the envelope hanging from his pocket.

We had nearly reached Victoria Coach Station in London, our destination, when we would all be going our separate ways. Then, by chance, the backside of the boy in front was inches from my face; and there, staring at me, was the envelope containing all the money in the Bank of England. All the things I could do with ten shillings flashed through my mind. The coach pulled into Victoria Coach Station, and we began disembarking.

My next coach was quite full when we left Victoria, but by the time we reached Canvey Island I was the only student on the coach.

There was as usual nobody home when I arrived. I dumped my bag on the veranda. Only then, perfectly alone, did I examine the ten-shilling note which had come into my possession. Retrieving my trusty 'Golden Virginia' tobacco tin, I headed for the waste land where I had hidden my paper round money.

Later that evening, my dad asked me how I intended spending my time off. I told him I would be catching up with my mates and going to the beach. He pointed out that now I had an allotment at school and knew about growing vegetables, I could dig the vegetable plot; the same plot where I had buried Nunky Bills' underwear. I pointed out the plot was full of weeds and would take forever to dig.

'Just do a little bit each day. You will soon have it done,' he said.

Digging was a punishment, often used by some masters at school for something quite trivial, instead of writing lines, and was why I hated it. The gardening teacher loved it. It was his way of getting the vegetable plots 'double dug'

The following day, I dug up Nunky Bills' underpants and vest. Apart from the burn marks and thick mud, they were still in good condition. I disposed of them in the bins behind the shops.

I waited a day or so before spending my ten shillings. I felt sure with a sum of money this big, someone was going to ask me where I got it. Entering the shop, I chose a cake, and nervously handed over the ten-shilling note. To my surprise, the shopkeeper handed me my cake and my change without a second glance. I breathed easier, and from then on only took a few 'coppers' each day until I had dribbled the ten shillings away.

I suppose I should have felt guilty as I spent my 'ill-gotten' gains. But it never occurred to me that I had stolen the money. I never gave it a second thought. A lifetime of poverty and a-surviving-at-all-costs-attitude saw to that. It was simply a case of, 'opportunity makes the thief', as Francis Bacon said.

I had just turned thirteen when I arrived home that summer holiday. I soon discovered that a new family had moved into the house opposite.

Apart from the mother and father, who went to work each day, there were two teenage daughters, and a younger brother. The older daughter went to work with the parents, whilst the younger daughter, Sheila, who was fourteen, looked after her brother.

She was a slim girl, but with rationing none of us were very fat. A little taller than me, with brown shoulder length hair. I found her quite attractive, and made a point of getting to know her. This didn't suit Pamela. She hated it when I went over the road to Sheila's garden, and would often call out to me. Sheila would grab my arm and say, 'No, don't go.' In an effort to please both of them, I would often go walkabouts.

One fine hot sunny day, Sheila and I were fooling around. I ran, intent on jumping onto the veranda railing, just as she made a grab for me. My shorts were suddenly around my ankles exposing my nakedness. Sheila laughed, as I slowly pulled them up. Later that day I said I was going for a walk. She asked me not to, but I said I was bored and wanted to catch up with my mates.

So she called me into her parent's bedroom to see something. She then sat at the dressing table mirror and brushed her hair.

'Is that what you wanted me to see. You brushing your hair?'

'No,' she replied, standing up and pushing me onto the bed.

She then began brushing my hair. I quite enjoyed letting her form different styles, then ruffle it up and start again. After a while I became bored.

'So is that it? Is that all you wanted. Just to brush my hair? I'm going for walkabouts.'

'No, don't go,' she said. 'I haven't finished yet. What about the other hair?'

'What other hair?' I asked. She indicated with her eyes to my groin area.

'I haven't got any down there.'

'Yes you have. I saw just now.' Pushing me back onto the bed, she quickly pulled my shorts down, not that I put up much of a struggle.

'There, just beginning to grow.' She gave them a quick brush before saying.

'Do you want to see mine?'

'Yeah, I wouldn't mind,' I said.

She lifted her dress, trapped it between her chin and her chest, and pulled her pants down. The hair on her vagina, now right in front of my eyes, put my scrawny growth to shame. Instinctively I reached out to touch her. Giggling, she stepped back, pulled up her pants, and let her dress drop.

'And what about these?' she said, cupping her breasts.

'You haven't got any,' I mocked.

'Yes I have,' she said, sticking her chest out.

'Let me see them then,' I said.

Sitting next to me on the bed, she unbuttoned her cotton dress. Her breasts were just beginning to form, and her nipples were exquisite. I instinctively reached out and cupped one of them in my hand. Smiling, she lay back on the bed and I felt a movement in my groin. It must be the way men are wired, because I instinctively leaned over intent on getting her nipple into my mouth. My lips had hardly caressed her, when she suddenly pushed me away, sat up, and buttoned her dress.

'What you doing?' said her young brother, walking into the room.

'Nothing, just playing a game,' she answered.

'Can I play?' he asked.

'Yes, just a minute.' She straightened her dress and left the room.

I got off the bed and noticed a wet patch on the front of my shorts. Feeling somewhat embarrassed, and not wanting Sheila to see it, I left without a word. As I let the sun dry my shorts, I wondered what would have happened if her brother had not come in when he did. I made a mental note that the next time I was with Sheila, I would try to pick up where we had left off.

Later that afternoon, when I returned home, Pamela asked if I had been in Sheila's house that day, becoming visibly annoyed when I nodded.

'I don't know what you see in her,' she said. I would have loved to have told her, if only to give her a chance to make a counter offer.

At the end of the Summer holiday, I said goodbye to both Pamela and Sheila, and headed back to school. During the term I didn't give much thought to either girl, but as soon as the Christmas holiday came around I found myself excitedly looking forward to seeing Sheila again. Unfortunately, any thoughts of another dalliance with Sheila were soon dashed. Pamela took great pleasure in telling me she and her family had emigrated to Australia.

Apart from the disappointment of not seeing Sheila, the other most eventful thing that Christmas was that my brother got a new bicycle. I was totally surprised, and more than a little envious. When I asked how he had managed to get my dad to part with such a huge sum of money, he told me that my dad had only stood guarantor for the loan. He himself had to make the weekly payments from his wages. So, it was hardly a Christmas present. Never the less, I was still envious of him and his new bike. I returned to school in the middle of January 1950, at which time he was happily riding his bike, even letting me have a go.

Frankie and I didn't write to each other, so you can imagine my surprise when I came home for the Easter holidays and found he had left home. My parents said they didn't know where he was. They didn't appear to be too concerned either. I noticed his bike was gone, so assumed he had taken it with him. Pamela couldn't wait to tell me all the details.

Apparently, she had heard shouting and arguing coming from our house. Not wishing to spy, yeah right, she hid behind her Dad's caravan where she could observe without being seen. The door to our house was thrown open, and my dad grabbed the bike from under the veranda and started wheeling away.

'It's going back, and that's that,' shouted my dad.

Frankie pleaded with him not to take it back, even grabbing hold of the bike and attempting to stop him. His pleading fell on deaf ears and my dad returned the bike to the shop. According to Pamela, although she didn't like to carry tales, Frankie not only lost his bike, but he lost the money he had paid on it as well. Not long after that, he left home, never to return.

I didn't think he could be too far away, so decided to look for him. Despite going to all our usual haunts and asking all our friends, he was nowhere to be seen. Strange really. When he was home, he bugged the life out of me. But now he was gone, I missed him. But on the upside, I had the room and the bed to myself. On the downside, I inherited the jobs he used to do.

That night, I unpacked what few clothes I had and placed them in the old gramophone stand, the only furniture in our room. To my surprise and delight, I found Frankie had left a pair of long trousers behind. This was a tremendous find for me. I was still in short trousers. A lot of schools insisted on short trousers up to the age of fourteen or fifteen. Our school only enforced it for going to Church on Sundays. This led to a lot of the boys having long trousers for casual wear, which I yearned for. I had given up on my parents ever buying me a pair, and resigned myself to leaving school in short trousers, which in fact I did.

I laid the trousers out on the bed, and wondered why he had left them behind. Admittedly they weren't the greatest pair of trousers, but they were in one piece and the crutch was not split. It was always the crutch that split, so what more could I ask for. I had spent many an hour on a Friday evening at school sewing up the crutch of my trousers, and was my way of gauging the condition of the trousers.

I tried them on. It would have been too much to hope they would fit. The legs were too long, and they were baggy around the backside.

It was disappointing, but not off-putting. I was determined to go back to school with a pair of long trousers. So, with the help of a belt, some careful tucking in around the waist, a couple of turn ups in the legs, and I thought I looked quite passable. I hid them in case my step-mother spotted them and threw them in the bin. At the end of my holidays, I sneaked them into my bag unnoticed. The first time I wore them was the last. I was seated at my desk, when the teacher asked me to open the window, which was high in the wall. I unthinkingly climbed onto my desk, bringing my long trousers into full view for all to see, not least the teacher.

'Where on earth did you get those trousers?' he said, causing laughter all round. I told him. He suggested I not wear them in class. I took them home on my next school leave and put them back where I got them.

Christmas holidays were not my favourite, as the weather was bad, which meant that most of my mates stayed indoors. So, if I was not lucky enough to 'con' my way into one of their homes, I spent long, cold, boring days, mooching the streets, or sheltering from the cold on the darkened veranda, while waiting for my parents to come home.

My dad had closed off one end of the veranda with tarpaulin. It was his cheap-jack way of gaining another bedroom. It was never used as a bedroom, and finished up as a storage area for all the junk we filched from the bombed buildings. It also served as a place for me to sit to keep out of the weather. I was still not allowed a key to the house, not since my little incident which I blamed the cat for.

I later learned that the Burton's bought the piece of land next door to us and would soon be demolishing the bombed building on it. I was not too happy, as I would lose a ready-made source of wood and other goodies. I had built my den and made a cricket bat from an old floorboard found on the site. I also had great fun jumping around on the rafters that had survived the bomb blast. I decided to gather as much stuff as I could and store it on our veranda. My step-mother was none too happy, remarking the veranda looked like a junk yard. My dad didn't mind, so the stuff stayed.

Chapter Sixty-Four

June 1950, I arrived home for my Summer holidays. I immediately noticed a bicycle hanging from the rafters in the conservatory. I also noticed, to my surprise, my step-mother was at home. That was a first. She then shattered any dreams I had of a long quiet holiday doing my own thing, by telling me she now only worked part-time. That was not the kind of news I wanted to hear. Finally, she told me that my dad was working in Kuwait. I thought it proper to show some concern, and asked why she hadn't let me know.

'What difference would it make?' she retorted. 'After all, he never writes to you'.

'True. So, if he's in Kuwait, whose bike is that hanging on the veranda ceiling?'

'It's your dads. He brought it down from Middlesbrough just before he went away. He's had it since he was a boy.'

'Did he ride it all the way down from Middlesbrough?'

'Don't be stupid. His brother Bill put it on the train in Middlesbrough, and he collected it in London.'

'So, would it be alright for me to ride it?'

'What do you think? He didn't hang it up for nothing. He doesn't want you touching it.'

'Yeah, but he's not here. So, would it be alright if I rode it?'

'No it would not. Stay away from it.'

I sauntered out to the veranda and she followed. Idly spinning the front wheel, I noticed he had removed the valves. There didn't appear to be a pump either. He really didn't intend for me to ride his bike. I gave my step-mother a look of despair, and walked away.

The next day was one of her work days. I took up my spot on the kerb outside the house and watched her head up the street. As soon as she was out of sight, I returned to the veranda, drawn by the allure of the bike. In my mind, there was no way that a perfectly good bike should hang around on a veranda, when there was a healthy boy willing to ride it.

On inspection, I found my dad had screwed two pulleys into the ceiling rafters of the veranda. He had then passed a rope through the pulleys, around the frame of the bicycle, and hoisted it to the ceiling. Lowering it looked straightforward enough; but it was no good if I couldn't find the valves and a pump.

Spinning the back wheel, I listened to the tantalising tick of 'Sturmey Archer' three-speed, whilst contemplating my next move.

A thorough search of the veranda failed to produce the valves or pump. The only other place he could have put them was in his shed, which was locked. But I knew there was a bunch of keys hanging behind the pantry door, and one of them had to be the shed key. But if I couldn't get into the house, it didn't matter one way or another.

I circled the house on the off-chance she might have left a window open. No such luck. I decided to abandon the bicycle for the time being and went in search of Christopher. I was hopeful I might mooch some food from his mum.

By the time my step-mother arrived home that evening, I had planned my next move. I was waiting for her on the veranda, immediately following her into the house. I knew she always went straight into her bedroom to change her clothes. I was not allowed in the pantry, so I had to be quick. Carefully opening the pantry door so the keys didn't rattle, I checked them out. I was sure one of them was the shed key. Before I had time to remove it from the key ring, I heard her returning. I quickly hung them back up.

The following morning, I put part two of my plan into practice. Just before leaving my room, I quietly slid the bolts locking the door to the outside stairs. My step-mother hardly ever came into my room, so I was confident she wouldn't spot it. Then, to my dismay, she told me she was not going to work that day.

The following day, I had better luck. From my position on the kerb, I again watched until she was out of sight. Just to be doubly sure, as soon as she turned the corner, I sprinted to the end of the road and checked she caught the bus. As soon as the bus was out of sight, I raced home and up the outside stairs. After a quick look around, I quickly stepped inside and closed the door behind me. I hardly breathed, as I stared at the bed I had got out of no more than an hour ago, as if I were an intruder.

Lifting the keys from the back of the pantry door, I tried them in the back door, delighted when one fitted. Within minutes, I had unlocked the shed, located the pump and valves, returned to the house, locked the back door, and left via my bedroom door, jamming it closed with a piece of cardboard.

Back on the veranda, I loosened the rope holding up the bicycle. Before I knew it, the bike came crashing to the ground. It was a lot heavier than I thought.

I immediately set about pumping up the tyres. By the time there was enough air in them for me to ride the bike, my arms were hanging off me. I wheeled the bike out to the street, only to discover the saddle was too high. Not only that, the spanners were in the shed.

Retracing my steps, I returned with a spanner. The saddle hadn't been moved for years and was quite stiff. When I finally got it to move, it left a tell-tale mark on the saddle post. I made a mental note to remember this when I put the bike back. I hid the spanner on the veranda.

I again mounted the bike, riding up and down the road to get the feel of it. But despite all my pumping, the tyres were still too soft. I headed for the bike shop and got a loan of a foot pump. Unfortunately, it wouldn't fit my tyres. He offered to lend me a hand pump, but didn't offer to pump them for me. I told him I already had one. Someone in the shop suggested I take it to the local garage.

I parked the bike alongside the air hose, but couldn't see how it would fit my tyres. I spoke to one of the mechanics, and he showed me how to use the air hose.

'But be very careful,' he said. 'You can easily burst your tyres.'

I spent the whole day riding around, hardly dismounting, intent on getting the maximum pleasure from the bike. Ever wary of the time; I wanted to give myself plenty of time to hang the bike back up before my step-mother came home.

It was just as well I did, as the task of hauling the bike back up to the rafters proved to be harder than I expected. I was just not strong enough to hold the bike up to the rafters with one hand, whilst securing the rope with the other.

With no way of knowing the time, I began to panic. I even looked to see if Pamela was in her garden to give me a hand, even though I really didn't want her to know I was using it without permission. But my situation was desperate. As it was, Pamela was nowhere to be seen.

Due to my near state of hysteria, as the minutes ticked away, I wasted a lot of energy on several fruitless attempts. Finally, I calmed down long enough to think straight. Pulling the bike up to the rafters, I wrapped the rope around my waist. I then took a short length of clothes line, stood on a trestle, and secured it around the rafter and the crossbar. This supported it long enough for me to hop down, and secure the rope properly. Stepping back, the bike looked as if it had never been touched.

I considered leaving the valves in the tyres to save me the hassle of pumping them up each day, but worried my step-mother might notice. Over the following days, I continued using the bike on the days she was working, becoming quite adept at hanging the bike back up.

Then one day, I became a little too cocky. I'd left it to the last minute before hanging the bike up. I'd just returned the valves, and was locking the shed, when I spotted my step-mother. She had obviously come home early, and was virtually in the road just outside the house. Within seconds she would be coming down the path to the back of the house.

A cold panic swept over me as I dashed back into the house, locking the kitchen door from the inside, and withdrawing the key literally as she was inserting her key from the outside. The keys were still swinging on the hook on pantry door as I closed the trap door to my bedroom. Hardly daring to breathe, I listened to her moving around below in her bedroom. Silently, taking the outside stairs two at a time, I ran around to the veranda and checked the bike was hung properly. I then wandered into the kitchen as if I had just come home.

'Where were you?' my step-mother asked as I entered.

'Nowhere, just out,' I replied. She gave me a quizzical look reserved for when she didn't believe me.

'Just going to my room,' I said, easing past her.

I had hardly slid the bolts on the external door, when the trapdoor opened, and her head popped up. Her eyes never left my face, as she asked.

'What are you up to?'

'Nothing.' I replied. She climbed into the room and slowly glanced around.

'There's something going on.' I remained silent. Still not wholly convinced, she left the room, and I breathed easier.

That wasn't the only time I was nearly caught out. Christopher came around on his bike one day and asked me if I was going to the beach. I said I would see him there.

'No, it's alright I'll wait for you,' he replied.

'No, you go ahead, as I will be walking anyway.

'Why? What's wrong with your bike?' he asked.

'I don't have a bike,' I replied, easing him towards the gate before he could say anything else. I wasn't sure if my step-mother had heard him, but as she didn't say anything, I thought I'd got away with it.

The next school holidays the bike was still hanging on the veranda, and I looked forward to continuing where I had left off. Then, as if reading my thoughts, my step-mother told me she had stopped work altogether. So, that put an end to using my dad's bike.

Even though she was no longer working, I still left the house first thing in the morning, normally returning at tea time. I still managed to get a dinner at my old secondary school, which suited both me and my step-mother. On the rare occasions I did go home during the day, I always tried to get in and out without her knowing. It was not too difficult, as I normally only went onto the veranda, got what I wanted, and snuck away.

Then one warm summer afternoon, I went home unexpectedly and sneaked onto the veranda. As I passed the stained-glass window in the front door, my eye caught a movement in the front room. I thought my step-mother had spotted me, and jumped out of sight. The door remained closed, so I thought I was mistaken and prepared to leave. But there it was again. Something was moving behind the stained-glass window. Positioning myself so I could peek in, I looked into the living room. What a shock I got. A man was seated in my dad's armchair and my step-mother was seated on his knee. As I watched, she leaned closer and kissed him passionately on the lips, whilst he was fumbling to undo her blouse. I watched for a while, but soon became uncomfortable with what I was seeing. Silently easing myself away from the window, I coughed loudly as if I was just arriving home. Within minutes, my step-mother opened the door, still straightening her blouse.

'What are you doing home so early?' she said.

'Nothing. I just came to get something from the veranda.'

'I didn't hear you come in, have you been there long?'

'No, I just got here.' Hearing a movement behind her, she turned.

'This is Bill,' she said. 'He's building the house next door and has come in for a cup of tea.' She was surprisingly calm and friendly, not her usual aggressive accusing self. *She's feeling guilty*, I thought. *She never explains her actions to me. She doesn't know if I saw anything or not.*

'While you are here would you like a cup of tea?'

A cup of tea. I thought. *She is offering me a cup of tea. She is either feeling really guilty or trying to impress the new 'Amore' in her life.*

Moments later, she placed a cake on the table, and returned to the kitchen for the tea.

'Nice eh,' said Bill, licking his lips and indicating the sponge cake, no doubt made using the eggs from our chickens. The ones I fed. I hoped her new-found generosity would include a piece for me.

My step-mother, her face a fixed smile for our guest's benefit, handed me a cup of tea and a piece of cake. I enjoyed the moment, but left as soon as I was finished.

Bill continued coming over for his tea each day, at least until I returned to school. With me out of the way, my brother gone, and my father in Kuwait, she could do whatever she wanted. The next time I came on leave, the brickwork on the house next door was finished, and Bill had moved on.

Chapter Sixty-Five

Early in 1950, I was accepted into the 'Young Farmer's Club'. There was a lot of 'hyperbole' from the masters about the merits of being accepted. In truth, it was a source of cheap labour.

Little did I know what I was in for. My first assignment was to look after the pigs, the most arduous section. Every morning; seven days a week, up at 5.45, pick up the swill from the back of the dining hall, light the boiler, cook the food, and pour it into the trough when ready. The smell of the food being cooked always had the pigs going berserk inside their pen. The only safe way to release them without being trampled as they dashed to get their snouts into the trough, was to lie on the roof and reach down for the bolt.

Whilst they were snuffling and snorting, I took the opportunity to clean out the old straw, thick with 'poo', and lay new straw. Just what I needed to sharpen my appetite for breakfast. And, just to rub my nose in it, so to speak, I learned that I would only get paid when I left school in about eighteen months.

Then, I noticed one of the pigs wasn't behaving like a pig, and was getting thinner; so we separated it from the others. We put it on a special milk diet which we got from our own goats, to fatten it up. It also had to be exercised. We placed a chain around its neck and took it for a walk, like a dog. It raised a lot laughs, but the pig recovered, and was soon fat enough to send to market.

A few months later, we were rotated. Over the next eighteen months, I looked after the chickens, nothing new there, the goats, the geese, and even the rabbits.

During the winter months, we used the afternoons for outdoor activities, catching up on our school work in the evening.

The countryside around the school was 'alive' with rabbits. One of the boys was a 'dab hand' at setting snares. He showed me how to identify a rabbit run, the best way to set a snare, and, the worst bit, how to kill a rabbit and skin it. I was not too happy about the killing bit, but soon mastered the art of skinning.

Sometimes, we took a couple of ferrets with us. They didn't belong to the school, but were owned by a couple of students. A collar, with a length of line was attached to the ferret, and it was put down the burrow. Although many of the rabbits avoided capture, several of them would run into the sacks being held over the likely exits. We were happy if we could return to school with a 'brace' or two, which was enough to make a good stew.

Skinning and cleaning them was gross, the contents of their guts really stinking. Afterwards, we took them to the kitchen to be cooked for our supper. They made a welcome change from soup, drawing a lot of envious glances from the not-so-fortunate.

Then there was the potato picking season at a nearby farm. I spent several back-breaking days picking up the potatoes turned out by a tractor. It was hard work, but the farmer's wife always gave us a good lunch. The school received a fee from the farmer for our work, which was supposedly paid into our account, again only to be paid to us when we left school.

Then, there was sewing night. Every Friday evening, I would toddle off to the assembly hall clutching a bundle of rags, which I referred to as my clothing. A woman from the town came into the school to show us how to mend our clothes. Split trousers, or a button off the shirt was a doddle for me. It was the holes in my socks which gave me my biggest problem. They were so big, there was more hole than sock. Undeterred, I took them to the sewing lady. She took one look and told me throw them away, even suggesting I ask my parents to buy me a new pair. I told her it was unlikely they would, and I really needed to do the best I could with the ones I had. The look of despair on my face must have clinched it, because an hour later we had affected a repair. It was not perfect, but was better than a hole, even though the wool I used was a slightly different colour.

Finally, it was my last term at school. My 15th birthday was in May 1951, so I would graduate in the June at the summer break.

Graduation was a bit of a non-event for me. The whole school were assembled in the main hall, with many parents coming to watch their offspring graduate. Needless to say, mine were not there. All the graduates assembled on the stage. Each student's name was called, with those who had represented the school at sports, or were 'high achievers', being called first. The headmaster then said something complimentary about the student, and handed them their certificate.

Then it came my turn. My name was called, and for several seconds he remained silent, just staring at my certificate. I thought he had nothing to say about me. Finally, he said.

'William Green. A likeable student, who could, if he had applied himself, achieved more. I am sure he will do well in whatever he chooses to do.'

He then handed me my certificate, and that was the sum total of my graduation. What he didn't point out, was that all the 'high achievers' had good parental support. I might have fared better if I had spent less time darning my socks, or worrying where my next pair of shoes were coming from, and more on my lessons. At fifteen, the world is your Oyster, so the headmaster's words carried very little importance for me.

A few days later, we were told to collect the money we had earned over the years picking potatoes and working for the 'Young Farmers Club'. I was quite excited as I was called into the secretary's office, not sure how much I had earned.

The secretary already had my money made up in an envelope. Indicating with her forefinger, she showed me where to sign, handed me my envelope, wished me good luck, and called in the next student.

My envelope contained nineteen shillings and sixpence, not even a full pound. And that for eighteen months work on the farm, plus three years of potato picking.

My mate Sid Field had received a similar amount. He said it worked out at about a farthing a day. *But it's not about the money,* the Headmaster had assured us, *it's about the experience!*

Chapter Sixty-Six

~

June 1951, the coach from London to Canvey Island dropped me, the last passenger, at the end of my road. As usual I hadn't heard from my parents, so had no idea if anybody would be home or not. In fact, I was not even sure if my dad was still working in Kuwait.

Apart from my meagre possessions, I carried a 'fire guard', made during woodwork and art classes. The wooden frame was not bad. It was certainly an improvement from my disastrous early woodworking days when I split my brother's head open. But the centrepiece was something else. I made it from cardboard, and stuck a water painting I'd done during art classes on it. To call it 'amateurish' would be too complimentary. In fact, it was a disaster. The art teacher, the one who's skirt I had looked up, gave me a picture of a vase of flowers and told me to copy it. The finished result looked like something a five-year-old would do. Parents were expected to buy whatever we made, so I thought my 'Vincent van Gogh' would be left behind for scrap value. To my surprise, the woodwork teacher told me that even though my parents hadn't paid for it, I could take it anyway. I think he was trying to tell me something.

As usual, when I arrived, no one was home. But pinned to the front door was an envelope with 'Billy' written on it. *So, they know I'm coming home, and they have remembered my name. That's promising,* I thought.

The note inside the envelope instructed me to go to an address, which I didn't recognise, where everything would be explained to me. That was it. Nothing to indicate where they were, or when they would be back.

The address was a bungalow on a concrete road. A woman, whom I had never met before, invited me in and gave me a cup of tea and a sandwich. She told me my parents were on holiday somewhere in England, and thought they were due home the following weekend.

'Come on, I'll show where you will be sleeping,' she said.

I followed her, expecting to be shown to one of the bedrooms, but instead she led me outside into the back garden.

'There,' she said, pulling back the flap on a bell tent. 'I'm sure you will be quite comfortable here. Of course you can come into the house for your meals and to use the bathroom. Much better out here, you can come and go as you like.' The tent contained a mattress and sleeping bag.

She made it clear that all she was providing were meals and somewhere to sleep. Once I had washed and had my breakfast each morning, I was expected to disappear until the next meal. My parents had told her that I liked to get out and about and wouldn't be hanging around. This seemed to be a condition for her accepting the job.

She then handed me an envelope and Ration Books. The envelope contained a list of groceries I was expected to get for my parents returning home.

'Did she leave any money for the groceries?' I asked.

'No, apparently you have money from school. She said she will reimburse you when she gets home.' It was a clever move on my stepmother's part, ensuring I wouldn't spend all my money whilst she was away.

By the time the weekend came, and my parents were due back, I was well ensconced in my tent. It was really quite comfortable. The weather had been kind, I'd slept well, eaten well; so in a way I was a bit sorry to be leaving. I packed my few belongings, said goodbye to the woman, and went back to my own house.

The groceries cost fifteen shillings of my nineteen shillings and sixpence, which equated to about two years of my wages.

It was late evening by the time my parents arrived home. They didn't tell me much about their holiday and I didn't ask. If they hadn't complained how tired they were after their journey from Scotland, I wouldn't have known where they'd been.

'I got the groceries you asked me to get.' I said, hoping my step-mother would give me the money straightaway and not make me ask again for it.

She picked up the basket and began placing the groceries in the pantry. When she didn't ask me how much they were, I said.

'They were fifteen shillings.'

'Don't think you will be getting that back,' she finally said. 'You've left school now and have to pay your way. That will be your first week's housekeeping.'

I felt the tears of anger and frustration welling within me. I could have punched her, but instead walked away. In the privacy of my room I choked back the tears of rage. To her it was a week's housekeeping money, but to me it represented two years' work. And now, in an instant, it was gone. I should have left the groceries and told her I had no money. Lesson learned.

Later that evening, by which time I had come to terms with losing my hard-earned money, my dad called me in for a word. The last time I had spoken to him was when he was on leave from Kuwait. He told me he was going back to Kuwait in a few days' time and wanted to know what I intended to do for a job. I had no idea. I knew he was a welder and seemed to be doing alright in Kuwait, so I suggested that maybe I should become a welder. He said it was a lousy job and suggested I get into something else.

Come the Monday morning, my step-mother wasted no time in taking me to the Youth Employment Centre in Hadleigh, on the mainland.

The Youth Employment Officer glanced at my school leaving certificates and asked me what I would like to do. Over the weekend I had spoken to Pamela's dad. He told me to say I wanted to be an electrician. The Youth Employment Officer rummaged through a small filing drawer and said.

'We don't have any vacancies for electricians at the moment. What about a motor mechanic. You like cars, don't you?' I was fascinated with cars, so said yes.

He then told me he had a vacancy for an apprentice motor mechanic just down the road in Thundersley. I told him I didn't want to be a motor mechanic, I wanted to be an electrician.

'That's the only apprenticeships we have at the moment.'

I was for walking out, but my step-mother told him I would take it. He rang the company and set up an interview. As we got up to leave, he said.

'You'll need long trousers. Can't go for an interview dressed like that. And, if you get the job, you'll need overalls.'

'Yes, we'll get some when we leave here,' my step-mother quickly assured him, desperate that nothing should stop me from getting the job. Once we got outside, I told her that I didn't want to be a motor mechanic.

'Well you'll just have to take it. There's nothing else, and I am not having you hanging around doing nothing,' she replied.

I tried pointing out that if I didn't go for the job, she wouldn't have to buy me long trousers and overalls.

'Doesn't matter what job you go for, you'll need long trousers.'

When we left the clothes shop, I was clutching my first pair of long trousers; light grey, like you would wear to school. They were completely unsuitable as a working trouser, but were the cheapest in the shop.

'What about the overalls?' I asked.

'I don't have money for overalls.'

'The man said I needed overalls.'

'I don't care what the man said. I haven't got money for overalls.'

'If you hadn't taken my money, I could have bought them myself,' I sarcastically suggested.

'Anymore of your lip, and you'll get my hand across your face. You're never satisfied.'

The next day, dressed in my new long trousers and accompanied by my step-mother, I went for my interview. The fact I was the only person being interviewed for the job should have told me something.

It was a building company who serviced their own lorries, dumpers, concrete mixers, and manager's cars.

Despite not putting myself out to impress the interviewing officer, I was still offered the job. I was hoping I would fail the interview, so I could look for something else. They said I could start the next day if I wanted to. As it was already Tuesday, I said I would wait until the following Monday, but my step-mother cut in and said I would start the next day.

I was not at all happy about the job. The garage was dirty, and I didn't like the look of the work they were doing on the lorries. Also, it was quite a trek from Canvey Island to Thundersley. I mentioned this to my step-mother, saying it would be better if I got something on the Island. She was not moved.

'I've been travelling between Canvey and London for years,' she said. Now you'll know what it is to work for a living, so don't complain to me.'

'I'm not complaining about the journey, just how I am going to get there at that time in the morning.'

'By bus of course. You can find out the times when we get to Benfleet.'

It turned out that to get to work by 8am I would have to leave the house at 6.15am and catch three buses. I also needed to take lunch with me, which was another problem. She told me that if I thought she was going to make lunch for me every day, I had another thought coming. Instead, she gave me a shilling each day (5p) and told me to buy something from the shops.

I was expected to work a forty-four-hour week. Five eight-hour days, plus four hours on a Saturday, which was not classed as overtime. My pay was eight pence ha'penny (halfpenny) per hour, rising to ninepence farthing after six months, a whole three farthings an hour increase. For those who don't remember farthings, (derived from the Anglo Saxon fourthling), they were small copper coins about five eights of an inch in diameter. There was four of them to a penny, two hundred and forty pennies to a pound, making it nine hundred and sixty farthings to one pound. So my increase, for those mathematically inclined, was three 960ths of a pound per hour.

Fred Horner, the foreman mechanic, pointed out that my light grey trousers were more suited to working in an office, and asked where my overalls were. I explained my situation, and told him I would have overalls by next week.

My first job was to wash down a truck engine with paraffin and a paintbrush. Within minutes, my new trousers were spattered with oil and paraffin stains.

My step-mother gave me one hell of a row, accusing me of deliberately ruining the trousers because she had not bought me any overalls.

'Well, if I didn't work in a garage they wouldn't get dirty,' I pointed out.

'Nice try. But you're not getting out of it that easy. Anyway, you can take them off now you're home. I don't want you going out to play in them. In future, as soon as you get home, change your trousers.'

'But I'm working now, I can't go out to play in short trousers,' I protested.

So, each evening when I got home from work, I changed into short trousers, and went outside to play.

Chapter Sixty-Seven

Come the Thursday, to my surprise, I received my first pay packet; all of three days' wages. It came in a brown paper envelope with the payslip stapled to the top. I undid the staple, read the slip, and was surprised to find I'd been paid 12 shillings. I put my pay packet into my pocket.

'Better check it's right,' advised the yard foreman.

I opened the packet and found a ten-shilling note plus a two shilling coin. When I got home my step-mother wasted no time in taking it off me.

'This packet has been opened,' she pointed out.

'I know, I had to check it.'

'Well in future I don't want you to open it.'

'But what if it's wrong?'

'I'll tell you if it's wrong.'

'But you've got the pay slip, so you'll know if take any money out.'

'Listen. I've had it with you. No matter what I say you've got an excuse. Just bring the pay packet home unopened. Now that's it. I don't want to hear another word.'

I knew it was futile to argue as I patiently waited whilst she checked the pay slip. I was anxious to see how much she was going to give me. She deliberated for a while, before reaching for her handbag and taking out five shillings. Two half-crowns, (one quarter of one pound). I was delighted.

Over the weekend, I told my step-mother that if I didn't have overalls for my work the foreman said I would have to leave. On the Monday evening she brought a pair home from work which she had acquired from one of her customers. They were not new, but I didn't care. Also, when I went in on the Monday, Les, one of the mechanics had brought me in a pair of his old overalls. They were a bit long in the leg, and the backside was a bit baggy, nothing new here, but now I had overalls, I was able to work properly, and at least I looked like a mechanic.

The following Thursday, I excitedly looked forward to the yard foreman bringing the payslips. I had worked a full week of forty-four hours, and wondered how much I would get.

I checked the amount, and told the yard foreman that my mum had forbidden me from opening my pay packet, and that she would check it.

On my way home I calculated that if she had given me five shillings for just three and a half days' work, I should receive at least six shillings and sixpence for a full weeks work.

I handed her my pay packet, unopened. She was delighted to see that for a full weeks work I had been paid one pound eleven shillings and sixpence; a king's ransom in my estimation, and certainly more than I was paid for three years work at school.

She checked the money, and handed me my pocket money. My face dropped when I saw it was five shillings, the same as the previous week. She spotted the look on my face.

'What's up?' she asked. I told her that I expected more because I had worked more hours.

'That's typical of you. Last week I gave you five shillings, even though you only worked half a week. You should only have got three shillings and sixpence. But out of the goodness of my heart I gave you a full week's pocket money, and you're still not satisfied.'

'So, am I only to get five shillings a week no matter how many hours I work?' I asked.

'No. If you work overtime I'll give you extra. Or, if you get a pay rise then we will see. Now that's it. I don't want to hear any more about it.'

Feeling the anger welling up inside me, I left the kitchen and went into the garden muttering too myself.

'Five miserable shillings. For working in a stinking garage covered in grease and muck all week. I might as well work for nothing. Well here's what I think of your five shillings.'

Before I knew it, I had flung the two half-crowns into the garden and stomped off up the road, my anger only subsiding when I reached the High Street. Only then did I realise the stupidity of my actions, and quickly turned back, but in the diminishing light I had no chance of finding them.

I was up early the next morning hoping to find my money before I left for work, but it was still too dark. As soon as I got home that evening, I tried again, but still no luck. Come the Saturday morning, as soon as the first rays of daylight filtered through my room window, I was up and sneaking down the outside stairs into the garden. I needed to find my money before my step-mother was awake. I certainly didn't want her knowing what I done.

The grass and weeds were long and wet on my bare legs. Because I was in a temper when I threw the money, I was not too sure where they had landed. Standing roughly where I was standing when I threw the coins, I threw a stone and watched where it landed. With one eye on the kitchen window watching for any movement that might suggest my step-mother was awake, I desperately searched the area where the stone had landed. After several minutes with no luck, I sneaked back up to my room and sat on the bed.

Bugger. What if I don't find the money, then I will really have worked all week for nothing. I thought. *And if she finds out, I'll never live it down.* After a while, I heard my step-mother pottering around and went downstairs.

'Were you outside just now?' she asked.

'No, I've just got up,' I replied.

'I could have sworn I heard someone on the outside steps.'

'No, don't know what it was, but it wasn't me.'

Later that morning, my step-mother left to go shopping. As soon as she was out of sight, I began the search again. With her out of the way and the early morning sun giving me more light, I was better able to focus on what I was doing. Then, to my delight, glinting in the morning sunshine was one of my lovely half-crowns. Quickly pocketing it, I reasoned the other one must be close by. I kept going back to the spot where I had found the first half-crown, even though there was nothing. I then stuck a stick in the ground to mark the spot and went to the top of the outside stairs, hoping I might spot it from a height. I was sure I saw something glint in the sunshine, but when I got close to it, it was nothing.

I was on my knees crawling in the grass, when Gyp, who had been for his morning run around the neighbourhood, came into the garden. Seeing me on my knees, he immediately came over and licked my face. I playfully pushed him away, and he responded. Soon the two of us were rolling around in the grass. Then, as I twisted out of his way, something caught my eye. There, lying on the grass, was the other half crown. I grabbed it. I was so delighted I kissed Gyp on the top of his head, and told him what a good boy he was.

Chapter Sixty-Eight

November 1951. I'd been travelling on the bus to work for about six months. Then one pay day, I handed my step-mother my wages and she decided to talk finance. According to her, by the time she gave me my lunch money and bus fare each day, I was not contributing anything to the housekeeping.

'So, I was thinking,' she said. 'If you had a bike, you could ride to work instead of getting the bus.' For once I agreed with her. I hated the bus journey each day.

My dad's bike was still hanging on the veranda beams. I was still not allowed to ride it and felt sure she was going to tell me to take it. But no. A few days later, I arrived home to find an old clapped out bike on the veranda.

It was not anywhere near as good a condition as my dad's bike. I pointed this out to my step-mother.

'You're a mechanic, I'm sure you can fix it,' she said.

I took it for a test ride and found the three-speed kept slipping. No matter how I adjusted the cable, I couldn't get it to work properly. The pedals would slip without any warning, usually when I was applying the most pressure. But one thing was for sure. Come rain, hail, or shine, this piece of junk was my transport to work.

Next morning I left for work early. I had calculated that the journey should take less time on a bike than on the bus. But that was a bike with no problems. I was not sure how long it would take on the piece of junk I was riding. Part of my journey, after crossing to the mainland, was up a long steep hill called Church Hill. I knew it as 'Bread and Cheese' hill. It seemed only professional and dead keen cyclists managed to ride their bike to the top. The rest usually dismounted and pushed their bike.

Always up for a challenge, I was determined to ride my bike all the way up to the top, even if it meant standing up on the pedals. Given the way the three-speed gear kept slipping, I was taking a risk riding my bike this way. But nothing ventured, nothing gained.

Although my speed was not much faster than walking, I'd probably reached the half way mark. Standing on the pedals, leg muscles burning, I applied maximum downward pressure. Then, 'wham', the three-speed slipped. The pain as my nuts crushed onto the crossbar does not bear thinking about. Squealing like a stuck pig, I jumped from the bike and threw it into the side of the road. Slowly sinking to my knees, I gently cradled my scrotum as I held back the tears. Several other cyclists, sensibly pushing their bikes, asked me if I was alright.

'Fine,' I managed to say through the pain, in no mood to elaborate. It was several minutes before the pain had subsided enough for me to continue my journey. I pushed the bike to the top of the hill, fiddled with the three-speed, and gently cycled the rest of the journey. My nuts ached for the rest of the day, but I didn't share my experience with anyone.

That night, when I got home, I stripped the three-speed gear down to see if there was any way I could fix it. In truth, all the gears were completely worn out. So, despite dressing them with a file and carefully rebuilding the hub, it was just as bad.

Come the weekend, I took it to the bicycle shop for a second opinion, as if I needed one. He confirmed the three-speed was beyond repair. Only a new one would fix the problem, which would cost more than the bike was worth. I enlightened my step-mother of the situation. She immediately blamed me, convinced I had deliberately stuffed up the bike.

'It's the way you ride it,' she said.

No matter how I explained the situation to her, she was not interested. In the end I had no other option but to continue using the bike. I spent more time fixing the bike than riding it. But over time I became a little wiser. I discovered that as long as I kept an even pressure on the pedals, the three-speed remained engaged. But as soon as I freewheeled, like slowing down for traffic lights, it disengaged. To fix it, I had to dismount, fiddle with the three-speed until it engaged, then re-mount, and slowly pedal away. I was off and on the bike every few minutes; as if riding a bike was not exercise enough.

Then, an unforeseen but somewhat fortuitous event changed things. One really dark night; one when you can hardly see your hand in front of you, I was on my way home. I was taking a short cut across the 'Winter Gardens', a single concrete path about six feet wide, which cut a huge chunk off the road journey. It was not illuminated, so not many people used it at night. But I did. The front light of my bike did little to light the path, but ensured anyone coming in the opposite direction could see me. However, not everyone else was so considerate. I was making good progress, and for a change the three-speed was behaving itself. Then, out of the dark, I heard a voice say 'ding-ding'. Before I had time to react, a numbnut on a bike with no light came zooming out of the darkness. Before I knew it, my bike, with me desperately clinging to the handlebars, had left the concrete path and was zooming down the pitch black embankment. Moments later, I came to an abrupt halt when I met a garden wall. For several moments I just lay there, nestled in long grass and stinging nettles.

'You alright?' the other cyclist called out. I looked up, and could just make out the silhouette of the cyclist, standing there with one foot already on the pedal.

'I think so, but I've landed in a bunch of stinging nettles.' I called back.

'Oh well, as long as you're alright I'll leave you to it.' With that, he cycled off.

After extricating my legs from the bicycle frame, I lugged it up the embankment. Even before I mounted it, I knew the three-speed didn't work. No amount of fiddling worked. By the time I'd pushed the bike home, I'd had it with the piece of junk, flinging it onto the veranda with such anger, my step-mother came out to see what all the noise was about. I angrily told her the bike had finally given up. Despite showing her my bruised and nettle stung legs, she was still convinced I had manipulated the situation.

It took her a full hour before she condescended to let me take my dad's bike, even giving me a hand to lower it to the ground.

'Where's the valves for the tyres?' I innocently asked.

'In the shed, as if you didn't know.' Handing me the key she said.

'You can stop your games now.'

'What games?' I asked, in all innocence.

'You know what. You're not going to stand there and tell me you haven't been riding this bike?' It was obvious she knew, and I thought I had been so clever.

A few weeks later, my dad came on leave. He was not a 'happy chappy' when he learned I was using his bike for work. My step-mother explained to him how much it cost to get the bus each day. The thought of money being saved soon convinced him.

He inspected the bike and complimented me on how clean and well maintained it was. I thought for one moment he was going to tell me to keep it. Some hope!

A couple of weeks later, his leave finished and he went back to Kuwait. He left me in no doubt that although he agreed to me riding the bike, it was still his.

Chapter Sixty-Nine

~~~

April 1952, and my sixteenth birthday was fast approaching. I was told I needed a medical examination, a pre-requisite to signing my apprenticeship papers. I was instructed to be at the company's doctor on the Monday morning. Fred Horner, the foreman mechanic, told me to make sure I took a bath and that I was wearing clean underwear.

A simple enough request one would think. But for me it presented a couple of problems. One, we didn't have a bathroom at home. Two, I was not sure if I could get clean underwear. That evening I shared my news with my step-mother. She sorted me out a pair of clean underpants, which could either have been my dad's or one of her lover's.

When I asked her what I should do about taking a bath, she just told me to flannel myself down like I usually did, only be a bit more thorough. Once a week, whether I needed it or not, I gave myself an all over wash with a basin of hot water and a flannel. It was an attempt to be hygienic, but I must have been stinking. Not that I noticed, but Fred probably did. I had not had a bath or shower since leaving school.

During the warmer months I went swimming in the creek, or in the River Thames that flowed around Canvey Island. But we were just coming out of winter, and I had not had a swim for some time. I checked my knees, and they were ingrained with dirt and oil. I was desperately in need of a bath.

Canvey Island didn't have a public baths, but Southend on Sea, some twelve miles away, did. So, come the Saturday afternoon, I was on my bike and heading for Southend on Sea. Gives a whole different meaning to going for a 'long hot bath'. The only thing 'long' about it was the cycle ride.

By mid-afternoon, stinking and sweaty, I entered the baths. Only then did I wonder if I should have brought a towel and soap. I had no idea how much a bath cost, but if it was more than a shilling I wouldn't bother.

'How much is a bath?' I asked the attendant.

'Sixpence.'

'What about soap and towel?'

'Thruppence.'

Nine pence altogether. I pondered if it was worth it. I could do a lot with nine pence. Buy some food; go to the pictures. Both appeared to be better options than wasting it on a bath. I cursed my stupidity for not sneaking a towel and soap from the house. It would have saved me thruppence.

'Well, do you want it or not?' he said.

'Yeah okay,' I answered.

Reluctantly I handed over a precious sixpenny piece and three pennies. He handed me a rough towel and a sliver of soap, which was a cross between floor soap and washing soap. He showed me to the bathroom, took a small turncock from his pocket, and turned on the hot tap.

'I'll be back in a minute,' he said.

I watched the bath fill, and hoped he would take his time so that I would get the maximum amount of hot water. When he finally turned the hot tap off, the bath was well filled. There were no restrictions on the cold water, so by the time I had cooled the bath sufficiently to get in, it was nearly brimming over.

I eased my manky body into the glorious hot water and laid back until only my face was clear. As I luxuriated in the hot water, I cast my mind back to bath night in Exmouth. Then I longed for a bath to myself. I may have had to share a bath with other evacuees, but at least I got a bath each week.

Before the water got too dirty, I knelt in the bath and washed my hair with the sliver of soap. The dirt that came from my hair as I dunked my head was unbelievable. But if that was bad, by the time I had scrubbed my knees and legs, the water was so filthy you could have walked on it.

The pants my step-mother gave me were not too bad a fit. A bit baggy around my skinny back-side, and lots of ball room. But at least the elastic was still good.

When the attendant came in to clean the bath and saw the ring of scum around the bath he said, 'Looks like you needed that.'

I felt really good as I cycled back home. The hot water had done wonders for my body. I thought it would be nice to live in a house with a proper bathroom.

Chapter Seventy

~~~

November 1951, and my dad returned from Kuwait. His contract was finished, so he went back to his old job in Tilbury Docks.

He had sold his Norton motor bike before going to Kuwait, so was without transport. But within a couple of weeks he bought a black Morris Oxford four door saloon. It reminded me of the car in the back alley in Exmouth. He parked it on the concrete strips he had previously put in for the Wolseley.

During the week, the car was covered with a large tarpaulin, only to be removed at the weekends. If he had petrol, he would take it out for a run. If not, he just sat in it and fiddled about.

Then, one Saturday morning, I heard a lot of activity in the kitchen and garden. I looked out the window and was surprised to see my dad was already up and loading stuff into his car. Normally on the weekend he had a lie in. Quickly dressing, I dashed into the kitchen and asked my step-mother where he was going.

'We're moving,' she said, matter of factly.

We were moving to the mainland – just like that! Neither of them had bothered to tell me. I wondered if they intended sneaking out whilst I was asleep. Then when I got up I'd find them gone. Many a true word spoken in jest.

When the car was loaded, my dad told me to get in. I was delighted to be getting a ride in his car, but I was even more delighted when we drew up outside the new home. It was a restaurant on Parkfields

Parade, adjacent to London Road, Hadleigh, about a ten-minute cycle ride to Hart Road, Thundersley, where I worked. On one side of the restaurant was a chemist, and on the other a newsagent. This was a real step up in the world. From the back and beyond of Canvey Island, to the throbbing metropolis of Hadleigh.

Apart from the restaurant itself, there was a large kitchen and a living room on the ground floor. Upstairs, there were three bedrooms, a bathroom, and separate toilet. At the back was a small garden with a gate to the rear access.

Whoopee I thought, *now I can get a regular bath and no more cycling to Southend.* What a dreamer I was.

I managed just two baths during the two years I lived in that house. I was told by my step-mother that electricity costs money, and I didn't earn enough to justify all that hot water.

I also had visions that now I was living in a restaurant, I would be eating better and could expect to get a packed lunch each day. Some hopes.

Come the Monday morning, my dad was already up when I entered the kitchen.

'I thought you would be working in the restaurant,' I casually remarked.

'Don't be such a galoot, what would I do here all day?' he scoffed.

As I readied myself to leave for work, I hopefully looked around to see if my step-mother was going to give me any lunch. She just handed me my usual shilling. A packed lunch would have been nice, but by eating frugally I was able to pocket a couple of coppers by not spending the full shilling.

The ride to work that morning was less arduous now I lived closer. I told everybody at work about the restaurant, and it wasn't long before some of our lorry drivers began using it. One even remarked on how good the food was, pointing out how lucky I was to have a mum like that. I just smiled, fingered the shilling in my pocket, and kept a low profile when I nipped around to the fish and chip shop to buy my lunch.

Six months after signing my apprenticeship papers, November 1952, I developed an ache in my left shoulder. Every day, at about the same time, my left shoulder would ache. It went away when I rested it, but returned each day about the same time, usually early afternoon. I could get some relief if I massaged my shoulder on the door frame. I thought it was a temporary condition and would eventually right itself. If anyone asked me what was wrong with my shoulder, I told them I had pulled it. But it didn't improve, and I finally told my dad. To my surprise, he set up an appointment and took me to the doctors.

The doctor told me to strip to the waist. He then moved my arm through its full range of movement whilst listening to my shoulder with his stethoscope. After due deliberation, he diagnosed that I had an extra bone in my shoulder. His conclusion was based on the grating sound my shoulder made when he rotated it. He suggested I do pull-ups, which would build up my arms and might alleviate the pain in my shoulder. But he was more concerned with how thin I was. He asked how my appetite was and if I got enough to eat. My dad didn't look to happy when I said no, and that I was always hungry. As we walked back to the restaurant, my dad said.

'I thought you were quite well built until you stripped off. It must be your overcoat. It makes you look bigger than you are. And what's the problem with the food then? Don't you get enough to eat?'

It turned out that my step-mother led him to believe that by the time he got home at night I had been fed, and had gone out.

'But there's always plenty of food in the restaurant. If as you say you are always hungry, why don't you take some of that?'

'I'm not allowed to touch any food in the house.'

'Are you hungry now?'

'Starving,' I replied.

We entered the house, and my dad went straight to the kitchen and cut a couple of slices of bread. He was rummaging through the pantry when my step-mother came in from the lounge.

'What's going on?' she asked.

'I'm getting him something to eat, he says he's starving.'

'He always starving, that's nothing new,' she replied.

'Well, he's obviously not getting enough to eat. The doctor said he is severely undernourished. And why do you give him money to go to another café to eat?'

'After cooking all day, sometimes I don't feel like cooking in the evening.'

'But you cook for me.'

She didn't answer. Pushing him to one side, she made a sandwich and handed it to me, before making tea for all of us. The look she gave me left me in no doubt she was not happy with me. I sunk my teeth into my sandwich.

'Right, so starting tomorrow night he can get his dinner here?'

My step-mother nodded as she mumbled, 'I suppose so.'

When I had finished my sandwich, my dad and I went upstairs where he showed me how to do pull-ups. There was a small window above each bedroom door. The sill provided an excellent hand grip, which was ideal for pull-ups. My dad did two or three quite effortlessly, and invited me to have a go.

'Is that the best you can do?' he said, when I was only able to lift myself a couple of inches from the floor.

'Yes, that's it.'

'You are weak. You've a lot of work to do. I want you to practice every day. In fact, every time you go in and out of your room, do a pull-up. Then do one when you go into the toilet, another when you go into the bathroom, and so on. I'll check your progress. I want to see you doing ten by the end of the week.'

'Ten. You only did three.'

'Yeah, but I haven't got a dodgy shoulder, your need is greater than mine.'

Later on, as I lay in bed, I wondered if I should have kept quiet about not getting any dinner. I knew my step-mother would give me a hard time after my dad left for work the next morning. Not only that, I would miss the one shilling and sixpence she gave me each evening.

Chapter Seventy-One

A few weeks after my visit to the doctor, I was still doing my pull-ups, but my step-mother had stopped giving me an evening meal and I was back to getting my one shilling and sixpence. In truth, it suited me. It meant I didn't need to hang around in the house each evening. Also, I could save a couple of pence to supplement by miserable pocket money.

Weekends were the same. I often left home on the Friday morning, and didn't return home until the Monday night. It was not unusual for me to go days without seeing my dad.

One Friday, I was staying with Les, the other apprentice, for the weekend. He lived in Westcliff on Sea. On the way to his house we called into the restaurant.

Les spotted the cakes on display behind the counter. He pointed out the one he wanted. My step-mother served him and took his money without batting an eyelid. His parents fed me all weekend, gave me a packed lunch on the Monday morning, and she couldn't give him a cake.

But that's not the best bit. Minutes later, we left the restaurant with Les eating the cake my step-mother had made him pay for.

'Where's your cake?' he asked.

'I haven't got money for cakes,' I replied.

'It's your mum's shop. You don't need to pay. She should give you one for nothing.'

'You would think so. But she made you pay. That's just the way she is.'

'Do you want me to buy you one?' he offered. I wouldn't give her the satisfaction of virtually selling me a cake.

'No, it's alright. Come on, let's go.'

Les came from such a kind and loving family he was unable to grasp just how mercenary my so called 'mother' could be.

Every other weekend, Fred the foreman mechanic who was an avid 'Spurs' fan, took Les and I to White Hart Lane. When Spurs were playing away, Les and I would watch Southend United. Often, after the football, we went to 'Rayleigh Rockets' in the evening. Les was more keen on the speedway than I was, but I went with him as it was hard not to when I was staying at his house and his dad was paying.

So, one Saturday evening, Les and I were wandering around the speedway track trying to get the best vantage spot. As we passed the viewing window of the bar, I heard knocking on the glass. It was Nunky Bill, beckoning to me to come into the bar. I had never been in a bar before and felt a little self-conscious, especially when I spotted my step-mother at his table. If I had known she was there, I would have kept walking.

'Sit down,' he said. 'What are you drinking? He bought me and Les an orange juice just as the next race started. By the time the race finished, I had drunk my orange juice. I thanked Nunky Bill for the drink and made a move to leave. He caught my arm.

'Before you go. Have you heard from your dad yet?' he asked. I looked at him somewhat puzzled.

'What do you mean, have I heard from him? Why would I hear from him?'

'Well, when did you last see him?' he asked.

'I don't know. I'm not home that much.'

It was not something I gave much thought to. If I saw him, I saw him; if not, so be it.

Not only did I not see my dad, normal conversation between my step-mother and me was minimal. She never asked me where I was going, or where I had been when I came in, only too happy I was not hanging around the restaurant lowering the image as she called it.

On one occasion, I came in the front door of the restaurant in my working clothes and asked a customer to move so I could get upstairs. The tirade of abuse I received from her was no one's business, as she warned me to never to come through the restaurant again.

'So, you don't know where he is do you?' said Nunky Bill. My step-mother sat silently watching me.

'No. I suppose he's at work. I haven't been home since yesterday morning.'

'He doesn't know does he?' he said, directing his question towards my step-mother. She remained silent.

'He's in Jamaica,' he finally announced.

'Jamaica!' I said.

'He's been gone for some weeks and you didn't even know he was gone.'

'No.'

'So he didn't say goodbye to you?'

'No.'

'Some father you've got. Didn't you miss him when you didn't see him around?'

'No. I never see him much anyway. I just thought he was at work.'

'Well that's because you are never in,' my step-mother finally interjected.

I thought about saying that if I got fed and my home life was more pleasant, I might be more inclined to stay in. Now I knew why my evening meal had stopped.

'So, where is his car?' I asked.

'Where do you think? It's in the garage where it always is. Heaven forbid we should go for a run in it.' my step-mother sarcastically replied. My dad rented a garage from an old lady several streets away.

I thought about volunteering to run the engine and check the tyres whilst he was away. Then I thought. *If he was concerned, he could have asked me. He couldn't even be bothered to say goodbye.*

Each month my dad wrote to my step-mother, but I never got to read the letters. As soon as my step-mother read the letter she ripped it up, so I had no idea what he was doing or if he ever mentioned me.

I still had my old bike from Canvey Island lying doing nothing in the back garden. My friend Peter suggested I should use it to take up cycle speedway. Between us we sorted out a wide back wheel. Speedway motorbikes always have a much broader rear wheel for grip, and we fashioned our bikes to look the same. We called ourselves the Rayleigh Racers, and competed against other teams, usually in a clearing in the nearby woods. Each race was run over four laps like the motor cycle speedway. I always left my bike at Peter's house so my step-mother wouldn't know, in case she stopped me using my dad's bike.

Apart from cycle speedway at the weekends, I did two evenings a week at Technical College and one evening at the ATC (Air Training Corps).

During the summer we were given the chance to go to an RAF base to see what life was like in the air force. We were there for a week, living in tents on an operational airfield. What a rude awakening we got each morning when the bombers warmed up. The noise was deafening, but I enjoyed the flight we got in them, the leather helmets reminding me of the wartime heroes. We also got the opportunity to fly in a Tiger Moth. Now that is an experience that should be on everyone's bucket list.

The de Havilland DH.82 Tiger Moth is a 1930s bi-plane designed by Geoffrey de Havilland and built by the de Havilland Aircraft Company. It was operated by the Royal Air Force and many other operators as a primary trainer aircraft. There are two open cockpits. The pilot sits in the rear, and the trainee sits in the front. Wikipedia.

I felt like a wartime ace about to engage the enemy as I climbed into the front seat and was strapped in by the ground crew. The pilot gave the thumbs up, the ground crew member swung the propeller, and moments later we were bouncing across the grass towards the runway.

'Everything alright?' The pilot's voice came through my headphones.

'Yes fine,' I replied.

'Turn your mike on, I can't hear you.' I clicked the switch.

'Now turn it off. Turn on to speak, off to listen, got it. Right, pay attention. We'll be going to the end of the runway and lining ourselves up as I wait for permission to take off. You won't hear any of the conversation between me and the control tower. I'll speak to you again when we are airborne.'

Within minutes of reaching the runway, the propeller, only a few feet in front of me, revved so hard it was a wonder it didn't fall off. We quickly gathered speed as we raced along the runway. Before I knew it, we were airborne.

'Everything alright?' asked the pilot. I assured him I was well.

'Are you well fastened in? Don't want you falling out,' he chuckled.

Before I could answer, the front of the plane dropped and we were heading at breakneck speed towards the ground, the force pushing me hard against my seat back. As I stared in terror at the ground rushing towards me, I thought the pilot was never going to pull out. Then, just as I thought I was about to meet my maker, he pulled the plane up, and seconds later I was looking at the blue sky above me.

The pressure on my face and body was enormous as the plane climbed out of the dive. I tried to re-adjust myself in my seat, but before I could move we went into another dive, the pilot again leaving it to the last moment before pulling out. The ground disappeared and the next thing I know I am hanging from my straps staring at the ground below. We had just done a 'loop-the-loop'. As we levelled out, the pilot said.

'Something fell out, what was it?'

'I've no idea,' I replied.

'It looked like your hat.'

I suddenly remembered I had thrown my hat on the floor of the cockpit when I put on my leather WW2 helmet.

If we had landed then, I might just have got away with it. But the pilot was enjoying himself. Several more manoeuvres saw the huge fry up I had for breakfast deposited into my mouthpiece. I'd never felt so ill in my life. It was revolting. I couldn't remove the mouthpiece and had to endure several more minutes of cold vomit stuck to my face, whilst the pilot continued enjoying himself, showing me just how good he was, whilst giving me a running commentary. In the absence of any complaints from me, he thought I was also enjoying it.

When we finally landed I was so ill I just wanted to die. The ground crew undid my shoulder straps and was disgusted with me when he saw the state of the mouth piece. No sympathy; just clean it up and return it to the stores.

Thankful to be back on terra firma, I staggered off to find a quiet corner, hoping my stomach would be back to normal by lunchtime. It was a shame I was sick, as the experience of flying in a Tiger Moth was awesome.

I enjoyed being at camp and was sorry when we had to go home. But the experience put me off joining the RAF.

Chapter Seventy-Two

~~~

Canvey Island is a small island in the River Thames off the Essex coast, and lies below sea level.

On the night of January 31st 1953, a tidal surge came down the Thames from the North Sea, flooding low lying lands in its path. Canvey Island was badly hit with the sea wall being washed away in the Tewkes Creek area. Fifty-eight people lost their lives and the Island was evacuated.

Nunky Bill and his wife Vi were flooded out, so came to stay with us until the sea wall was fixed.

A flood relief centre was set up. Clothing was still rationed and very hard to come by, so the victims were thankful for whatever they could get. During his stay with us, Nunky Bill often came home with clothing which didn't fit him. He passed it on to me. Being worse off than most of the flood relief victims, I was thankful for anything I could get, irrespective of size, colour, or condition.

One day he came home with a brand new pair of brown shoes which were too small for him. They were stamped with the utility mark CC, so they were not a pair of 'Crockett & Jones'. My step-mother asked him why he had taken them. He said he didn't want to pass up the chance of getting a pair of shoes.

'And anyway, anything that doesn't fit me will fit Billy. What size shoe do you take?' he asked me.

'Size nine,' I answered, spotting the size written inside.

'You're not a size nine, you're only a seven,' chipped in my step-mother.

'No, my feet have grown,' I quickly added.

I was not about to lose the opportunity of getting a new pair of shoes, not when I looked at what I was wearing. A little thing like not being my size was a minor detail. I quickly put them on and tightly tied the laces. They were a bit big, but not so big that I was prepared to let them go.

'Well, if you're happy with them,' said Nunky Bill, 'keep them'.

The Utility Clothing Scheme was a rationing scheme introduced in the United Kingdom by the British government during World War 2. In response to the shortage of clothing materials and labour due to the requirements of the war, the Board of Trade sponsored the creation of ranges of 'utility clothing' meeting tight regulations regarding the amount of material and labour allowed to be used in their construction. Utility clothing was marked with the CC41 tag, which stood for Civilian Clothing and 41 for 1941, the year it was introduced.

But hey, this was my first pair of new shoes in years. The fact that they were from the flood relief shop was a mere detail. I was delighted. However, a few days later, because they were too big, the toes of the shoes turned up like Ali Baba's shoes.

A few days later, Nunky Bill and his wife Vi came home with more stuff from the relief shop. This time he'd picked up a brown corduroy cap. When he tried it on, my step-mother and Vi burst out laughing. He took it off and threw it at me. When I put it on they laughed even more, saying I looked like one of the 'Dead End Kids'.

Pride was never a problem with me, so I took it anyway. My workmates gave me a ribbing, but I ignored them, the pleasure I got from my cap far outweighed their remarks, which soon wore off.

That was the last thing I got from Nunky Bill. The sea wall was fixed, and everybody returned home to start the big clean-up.

Chapter Seventy-Three

May 12th, 1953. My seventeenth birthday, and I applied for my provisional driver's licence. Fred the foreman was delighted, as he would be able to send me out to the various building sites as soon as I got my licence. He told me to get some practice around the large builders yard we had, before I went out onto the road.

I was delighted. I had learned the basics by moving the vehicles around the large garage where we parked the lorries each night. I thought he knew nothing about it.

'I know you have been driving the lorries and vans already, so now you can do it in the open,' he said, a sneaky smile creasing his face.

I was given a Jowett van to learn in, affectionately known as 'a two-lung lizzie' because of its two-cylinder horizontally opposed engine.

It was always a problem finding a qualified driver to go out with me on the road. So, the foreman bricklayer's dad, who was semi-retired and did a bit of part-time work, was assigned to go with me. He hadn't driven for years, but his licence was intact. He continually grumped about my driving, which did nothing to improve my driving skills.

I applied for my test almost as soon as I received my provisional licence. I figured that all the driving I had done around the yard, including driving a road roller on a road works job, and a tractor on the farm, would stand me in good stead and I'd have no problem in passing my test. I failed.

Some months later, I again went for my driving test. However, my trusty little Jowett van was not available. Instead, I was given a Trojan van, which was twice the size of the van I normally drove, and I had never driven it before. So I failed.

It didn't dampen my enthusiasm and I continued driving as much I could. But it was my enthusiasm for driving which finally got me into trouble.

I'd been given the job of fitting a new exhaust system to a large Dodge truck. It had been modified to right hand drive and was a wartime vehicle, part of the lend-lease agreement Britain had with the USA. I was working on it outside in the space between the garage and outside perimeter fence.

One of the bricklayers came to get his concrete mixer which had been in for repairs and was parked in front of the truck. There was not enough room to get it past the truck, so he asked me to move it. I knew the truck would run without a silencer, albeit rather rough and noisy. So, in an effort to impress the builder with my driving skills, I decided to reverse the truck out of the way. I checked the rear-view mirrors, started the truck, put it in reverse, and shuddered backwards. It didn't feel right, but I put it down to there being no silencer.

The bricklayer pulled the mixer clear and I pulled forward. When I stepped down from the cab, I noticed a crowd of workers gathered around the back of the lorry. Curious, I went to see what was going on. What a shock I got.

A small car had been parked behind the truck completely out of sight of my mirrors. Had I done the sensible thing and walked around the back I would have seen it. As it was, I had pushed the car into a pile of scaffolding, turning it sideways and pushing the body half way off the chassis. Worse still: it was a '1932 Swift' with a wood and fabric body, a collector's item.

I was speechless as I helplessly looked for something or someone for support. I looked for the bricklayer who had taken his mixer, but he didn't want to know and was already disappearing up the road. Eric the yard foreman, and Fred the foreman mechanic were soon on the scene.

After I explained what had happened, Eric was all for sacking me. But Fred intervened, saying the decision should come from Cyril, one of the owners of the business.

I knew the car belonged to the new mechanic who had only been with us a couple of weeks. He looked a hard nut and I didn't relish having to tell him I had stuffed up his car. Eric was really enjoying my predicament.

'Where is he now? You'll need to tell him straightaway.' he said, desperate to see me squirm. I was delighted when I heard he was out on a job.

By the morning tea-break, everyone knew about it. A couple of the carpenters tried to wind me up, suggesting I should do a runner as he was bound to beat me up. At least they got a laugh out of it.

As soon as the tea-break was over, Eric, the yard foreman, sauntered over with a smirk on his face and told me Cyril the boss wanted to see me. I was half hoping I would get the sack, then I could grab my things and be away before the owner of the car returned. I didn't get the sack; just a lecture on being more careful when backing up large trucks. He also mentioned that I should thank Fred for me not being sacked.

As soon as Tom, the owner of the car returned to the yard, Fred told him. I was so glad. Now by the time I faced him he'd would have had time to digest the bad news.

Sneaking a look around the side door of the garage, I saw him working at the bench. I pulled back, and rehearsed what I was going to say. My biggest worry was that he might tell me I had to pay for it. The damage probably amounted to more than I earned in a year.

Finally, plucking up the nerve, I approached him. Keeping my distance just in case he really was a hard-nut and I needed to run, I said.

'Tom.'

No response. The silence unnerving. I was about to repeat myself when he suddenly turned catching me off guard. I momentarily stepped back.

'Yes.'

'You know your car.'

'Yes.'

'I did something to it,' quickly adding, 'but it was an accident, honest.'

I explained that because he had parked his car so close to the truck, even using the rear-view mirrors, I was unable to see his car.

'So it was my fault then, was it?' The sarcasm in his voice tinged with more than a small degree of anger.

'No…I didn't say that,' I quickly replied, not wanting to upset him.

'You were the driver,' he snarled. 'Why didn't you check it was clear before you reversed?'

'The builder was seeing me back, and he didn't see it either.'

'So it's his fault then.'

'No…I didn't say that.' He wasn't making it easy for me. 'What I'm trying to say is…'

'Shut up. I know exactly what you're saying. You stuffed up, and now you're trying to blame anything or anybody but yourself. Take responsibility for your actions you useless little shit. Well, I hope you've got plenty of money to fix it.'

'No, I haven't got any money at all.'

All of a sudden, he leapt forward and grabbed me by the front of my overalls. Lifting me off my feet, he brought his face close to mine.

'I should beat the shit out of you, you useless little git. But then I would probably lose my job. Just fuck off and stay out of my way.'

He threw me away like a soiled rag. Stumbling to get my footing, I headed for the door, tripping on the doorstep in my haste to get out of there.

As it happened, things turned out well for him. Cyril, the boss, gave him permission to use the garage resources to fix his car. After that, I overheard him telling one of other mechanics that I had done him a favour. His car needed refurbishing and he was not sure how he was going to afford it.

That incident passed, but I was soon involved in another issue. I was working with Eric, Fred's brother. We were both lying under a Commer truck using two jacks to manoeuvre a leaf spring into position. Without warning, the jack I was operating developed a fault, and the chassis began lowering towards me. I tried tightening the jack handle, but to no avail. We were in real danger of being crushed. I yelled to Eric and started rolling out from under the truck. He told me to stay where I was and shut off the jack.

'I can't,' I shouted, rolling clear. He was livid as he quickly followed, accusing me of endangering his life.

'Why didn't you shut the jack off?'

'I couldn't, it just wouldn't stop. And anyway, I didn't just leave you. I told you the chassis was coming down.'

'Right, get back under there and fix that jack before I put my tongue up your arse.' *Tongue up my arse,* I thought. 'And about six lace holes with it,' he continued.

'I'm not going under there, it's not safe.' I said, walking away.

'Don't you walk away from me,' he shouted. Ignoring him I kept on walking. The next thing I was propelled forward, stumbling to the ground as his fist exploded in the middle of my back. I cried out in agony, the pain so severe.

'Don't be such a baby, I hardly touched you,' he said.

He left me lying there and went back to fixing the truck. When I didn't move, he called out.

'If you don't get under here, I'll really give you something to cry about; now get under here.' I joined him under the vehicle. Les, the other apprentice, had witnessed what had happened, and said I should report him. I didn't. After all he was Fred the Foreman's brother, and Fred had been so good to me. I just put it down as another learning curve.

Apprentices, according to the union rules, were only allowed to work a forty-four hour week. Because we always had lots of work, I always exceeded them as I needed the money. Despite my pleas that my overtime money should be mine, my step-mother still took a cut of it. I asked Fred the foreman if there was any way I could do any extra work without it going into my pay packet.

Not long after I asked him, as the summer months approached, I got the chance. The company I worked for also owned a farm. I was asked if I would like to do some overtime on the farm.

Each evening, as soon as I finished in the garage, I hopped onto my bike and cycled to the farm, about six miles away. My job was to drive a tractor from 6.00pm until it got dark, around 10.00pm. The farm foreman paid me ten shillings cash in hand. On top of that, I was given a huge supper by the farmer's wife, who was a fabulous cook and handed out generous servings. For a few short months I was in seventh heaven. A full stomach, and money in my pocket. What more could I ask for. Unfortunately, the summer months ended, and with it my job and delicious free supper.

Chapter Seventy-Four

~~~

Soon after I learned my dad was in Jamaica, I arrived home to find my step-mother sprucing up the spare bedroom. Fresh curtains on the windows, clean sheets and pillow slips on the bed, and the carpet well swept.

'Thanks, when can I move in?' I jokingly remarked, moving towards the room.

'It's not for you,' she said, barring my way. 'You don't earn enough to get a room like this, so stay out.'

She closed the door and disappeared down the stairs. I returned to the stinking mattress and bare boards of my own disgusting bedroom.

The following day, I arrived home and was introduced to the new occupant of the room.

'This is Bill. He will be staying with us for a while,' said my step-mother. Bill was a bricklayer working on a new development being built at the back of the restaurant. She must have had a thing for bricklayers named Bill.

Within days of him moving in, my step-mother took on a new lease of life. Pity her ebullience didn't extend to me.

Then, to my delight, I arrived home from work one evening to be greeted by the delicious smell of dinner being cooked. This was a new occurrence. Since my dad had been away my step-mother had stopped cooking in the evening. Passing through the kitchen on my way upstairs, I paused and made a show of sniffing, like the 'Bisto Kids' advert.

'Don't know what your sniffing for, there's none for you,' she remarked.

Surely, I thought, as I headed upstairs, *she wouldn't cook a meal without making some for me; or would she?* My mouth watered, the smell of food playing havoc with my empty stomach. She was without doubt a miserable bitch, but if nothing else, she knew how to cook. Normally, I would leave the house within minutes of arriving home, but decided to hang around just in case there was a chance I would get fed.

To while away the time, whilst I hopefully waited to be called for dinner, I wandered onto the landing. The lodger's bedroom door was as usual closed. I had been told to stay out of it. Not knowing if the lodger was in his room or not, I grabbed the door frame and silently pulled myself up until I could see through the window above the door. It was vacant. Easing the door open, I silently entered. For a room that was supposed to be being lived in, something was not right. No shoes or personal possessions lying around, not even a brush or comb on the chest of drawers. And the bed; so pristine it couldn't possibly be being slept in. If my step-mother hadn't been cooking a meal, I would have sworn our lodger had moved out.

My step-mother's bedroom was also out of bounds to me. This was nothing new. I'd never been allowed into my parents' bedroom, even when my dad was at home. I couldn't resist taking a peek.

No attempt had been made to hide the fact she was sleeping with the lodger, the indentations in both pillows a dead giveaway. That explained her new lease on life.

Suddenly, I heard voices in the kitchen below and knew the lodger was home. The silence that followed was obviously them 'swapping spit' as my step-mother put a lip-lock on him. I gave it a few more minutes, and as I had not been called for dinner, went downstairs. I cautiously stuck my head around the door of the lounge, another room I was not allowed in. 'You'll only make it dirty and I want to keep it nice' my step-mother had insisted. On seeing me, Gyp, our little Fox Terrier, bounded over wagging his tail. Sometimes he wagged his tail so vigorously his whole bottom sashayed. I gave him

364

a huge hug and kissed him on the top of his head. At least he was allowed in the room.

My step-mother and the owner of the other indentation in the pillows were seated at the dining table. His smug face and masticating jaws peered at me over his full plate. It was obvious there was nothing for me.

In truth, I hadn't really expected anything, but felt compelled to say something. I knew I was pushing my luck when I dared to step in the room and ask.

'If you cooked for him, why couldn't you have cooked some for me too?'

Her displeasure at my impertinence was immediately evident. Deliberately placing her cutlery down and smiling at the 'new love' of her life, she indicated for me to follow her into the kitchen. As soon as we were out of sight, she grabbed the front of my grubby shirt and pulled my face within inches of hers. I knew she was not about to kiss me.

'Who do you think you are?' she hissed, her teeth clenched tight in a grimace. 'How dare you question me? I had enough of it when your father was here. I'm not taking it from you. Here, buy something.' She pushed me away and thrust one shilling and sixpence into my hand.

I left the house and headed for my favourite little café. As I munched my sausage and mash, I thought about my future. I knew one thing. I needed to get away from her. But with no money, and a poorly paid job, my options were limited.

The following week, on the day I should have been at technical college, I went through to Tilbury to enquire about joining the Merchant Navy. As soon as they learned I was seventeen, they thought I was trying to dodge National Service.

In 1953, all males were required to do National Service when they reached eighteen years of age. However, if you were in a registered apprenticeship, you were exempted until you finished your apprenticeship, normally at age 21.

I'd gone to Tilbury on the spur of the moment without really thinking things through. All I wanted was a way out of my miserable existence, and thought this was my answer. I had lost interest in my job, and even technical college, which I normally enjoyed, had lost its shine.

Over the next few days I made the decision to join the Royal Navy. I was keen to get away, and the thought of a life at sea appealed to me.

After my initial interview in Southend on Sea, I was sent to the Royal Navy recruiting office in Leicester Square, London. When I arrived, it was crowded with new recruits. There weren't enough seats, so I sat on the floor. I was wearing my brown corduroy cap, the one Nunky Bill had given me, which was a still a tad on the large side. The recruiting Chief spotted me and good humouredly remarked. 'Don't kick that cap, there's someone under it.' For the rest of the day he called me 'Cappy'.

After the written exams, we were given tea and sandwiches. I was impressed as I was not used to getting food for free.

We were then told to strip and form a line for the medical examination. I'd continued doing my pull-ups at home, and my arms and shoulders were now much stronger.

When you're naked with a bunch of other recruits it's difficult to know where to look, as it seems your eyes keep getting drawn to the other guys tackle. And, what to do with your hands. The cold room didn't help either, making our 'willies' smaller than we would have liked. I mean, you're with a bunch of naked guys and you want to look like you are 'hung'.

After the medical officer checked we had two of everything, we were given various exercises, like step-ups, and standing on one leg, all very basic. Then came the pull-ups. This was the exercise to sort the men from the boys. We were told to chin the bar, and whilst holding this position rotate our legs as if riding a bicycle. Not a pretty sight when you are naked. One recruit was a little overweight, though for the life of me I had no idea where he got his rations from. He also had weak arms. He'd obviously had a soft upbringing. After several attempts to pull his chin up to the bar, even giving a little jump, he just couldn't make it. I watched, fascinated, as every time he jumped his 'little willie' bounced up and down. It was too much for me, and I couldn't help having a chuckle.

'All right 'Cappy', so you think it's funny do you? Well let's see how smart you are,' said the Chief.

I stepped up, gripped the bar just as I had been doing for months, and in one swift pull my chin was level with the bar. I easily rotated my legs, watched by the rest of the recruits. After 30 seconds or so and with nothing from the Chief, I slowly lowered myself to the floor.

'Hold it. Did I tell you to lower yourself?'

I quickly pulled my skinny frame back up. The pull-ups I had done every day at home proved their worth.

My eye test was not so straightforward. On the black and white scale my vision was twenty/twenty, but my colour perception was poor. This immediately closed off some of the branches where good colour perception was critical.

We were given a scrumptious lunch, which made me even more determined to join. Afterwards, we mustered in the classroom to learn if we had been accepted or not.

'If I call out your name you have not been accepted and you can leave,' said the Chief.

I'd not given any thought to not being accepted. Not being accepted was not in my plans. I just had to get in, failure was not an option. I then began to worry that my poor colour perception might prevent me. I was sure I had passed all the other tests, including the physical. Finally, the Chief said.

'That's it, the rest of you have been accepted.' I was still sitting there.

Breathing a sigh of relief I shook hands and congratulated the person next to me as if we had just won something. I was to be sent to HMS *Raleigh* to train as a stoker. I thought stokers shovelled coal into boilers and wondered where the connection was with my 'apprentice motor mechanic' background. The Chief assured me that was just a name, and nobody did any 'stoking' these days.

I didn't care. I was so delighted to be accepted I would have gone in as anything. We were told we would get a letter in the next week or so confirming our draft.

Now that I had been accepted, I could tell my step-mother. She was ecstatic, making no attempt to hide her delight that I was getting out of her life. I thought that once I told her, it might improve our relationship, it didn't.

A few weeks later, my letter arrived instructing me to report on the 8th of December to the Royal Navy recruiting office in Leicester Square, London. I was delighted, knowing I would be in the Navy before Christmas. I could not imagine what Christmas would have been like stuck with my step-mother and the smug bastard who was shagging her.

A few days later, I left the house for what would be my second last working day in the garage, and my last pay. I normally left the house each morning without saying goodbye. I'd stopped when my step-mother never returned my gesture. I was looking forward to getting my pay as I knew it would be more than my usual wages. I would be receiving my leave pay and Christmas bonus. And, as I was within days of joining the navy, I planned to give my step-mother my usual pay and keep the rest.

I silently opened the back door, and had just stepped outside when her words cut through me like a knife.

'When you get your pay, I want you to bring it to me at the bus stop near your work, do you hear?'

'I can't.' I said. 'I have to go out on a job this morning. So, I won't be there.' I continued out the door without looking back.

'I knew you would have some excuse. You just make sure you're there. Do you hear?'

'I can't. If I'm out on a job I won't even be in the garage. I could be anywhere. And anyway. What difference does it make? You'll get it when I get home.'

'Just you be there…right! Tell the foreman you have to meet me there.'

I knew it was futile to argue and continued pushing my bike towards the back gate. A sound behind me had me instinctively tensing my back muscles. The inevitable punch landed between my shoulder blades.

'Don't turn your back on me when I'm talking to you. Now just make sure you are at the bus stop at eleven o clock. Do you hear?'

Ignoring her, I continued towards the back gate. I was seething inside. Her punch was quite sore, but I didn't want to give her the satisfaction of knowing she had got through to me. Mounting my bike, I headed for work, her last words going around and around in my head.

Each week my step-mother took my pay packet, unopened at her insistence. On a good week, if I had worked overtime, my wages could be as much as three pounds ten shillings. She would take the three pounds and grudgingly hand me the ten shillings.

Eleven-o-clock came, and the foreman handed me my wages. I could hardly contain my excitement as I saw the amount. Twenty-eight pounds; more money than I had ever seen in my life. Now I knew why my step-mother was so keen to meet me at the bus stop. I was still undecided what I was going to do, so asked Les, one of the mechanics, if he would check the bus stop. He confirmed that both she and the lodger were there.

'You're not going to give her your pay, are you?' he asked, when I asked him to drive me to the bus stop.

'I really don't know.' I replied, as I entered the van.

The closer we got to the bus stop, the more uncertain I became. I really didn't want to give her my pay packet, but wasn't sure I had the balls to defy her. A life time of being coached and disciplined to respect adults made it difficult for me to defy her. Occasionally, in a moment of bravado, I might answer her back, but I always came off worst.

Les began slowing the van down, and my step-mother, recognising the company name on the van, moved towards the kerb.

Suddenly, I heard myself yelling, 'Keep going, keep going'.

Les quickly accelerated past the bus stop, as I ducked below the level of the windscreen. Cautiously raising my head, I looked out the rear window, nervously giggling as I caught the look of disbelieve on my step-mother's face.

'Good for you,' said Les.

Alright for him to say, but I was the one who would ultimately have to face her. We later passed the bus stop on the way back to the garage, and they were gone. Fred told me she had called into the garage and asked where I was. He told her I was out on a job.

Chapter Seventy-Five

Before leaving work that evening, I removed all but three pounds ten shillings from my pay packet, and left the rest with Fred. The nearer I got to the house, the faster my heart beat, and the more I worried about my moment of bravado. I parked my bike several yards up the road, and walked. By the time I reached my back gate, I had taken several deep breaths and had steeled myself for the impending confrontation.

'Bugger', I muttered, seeing the house in darkness. Now I would have to worry about it until my step-mother came home, and I was desperate to get it over.

Wandering around to the front of the restaurant, I sat on the saddle of my bike and propped my foot on the window ledge of the newsagents. I pretended to read the papers and magazines in the window, but my mind kept returning to my present predicament.

I was really worried how I was going to explain to my step-mother that I had only brought home a normal weeks wage. I knew she would take it all, but decided I could live with that provided I kept the rest. I only had to stall her for a few days, then I would be off to join the navy. But what about her vile temper. She was no stranger to lashing out with whatever came to hand. *If she tries that tonight,* I thought, *I'll do a runner. I can always stay with my mate Les.*

'What are you doing here?' a voice asked, so startling me I completely lost my balance. Just as I was about to land in a heap on the pavement, I jumped from my bike, did a bit of a tap dance, grabbed my bike just before it hit the ground, and regained my balance. I hoped it looked like this was my usual way of dismounting. Then I saw the smile on Alexis' face. At least I had amused her.

Alexis was the girl from the chemists shop next door to us. My attitude changed immediately, and I afforded her my best smile. She was an attractive girl, about my age, but in the two years I had lived there I had hardly exchanged more than half a dozen words with her. I would like to have dated her, but never asked as I was always shabbily dressed and stunk of oil. She, on the other hand, was always clean and fresh, with a hint of the perfumes she sold in her mother's chemist shop.

'Hi Alexis,' I said. 'How are you?'

'Fine, but I didn't expect to see you here.'

'Why not. Did you think I'd joined the navy already?'

'No. I didn't know you were joining the navy.'

'Oh. Okay. Well I am, in a few days' time. So why did you ask what I was doing here? I mean, I live here.'

'I know, but I thought you had moved,' she replied.

'Moved !!! What made you think that?'

'Well, there was a removal van here this morning which took all your furniture away.'

'Took all our furniture away!' I peered through the restaurant window. Everything looked normal, tables and chairs in their usual place.

'You sure?' I said, turning back and facing her. 'Only everything seems alright. Take a look yourself.' I indicated the restaurant window.

'No, I don't need to. I know what I saw. I watched it all being loaded into the van. Furniture, beds, dining room suite, everything. I couldn't miss it. Have you been in the house yet?'

'No I haven't. But I'm confused. What time was this?'

'About ten o'clock.'

'Right. Did my mum go with it?'

'No, she followed in your dad's car.' I knew my step-mother couldn't drive.

'So who was driving?'

'That man, your lodger. Didn't she tell you she was moving?' It was obvious I knew nothing about it and Alexis sensed it.

'So, she moved without telling you?'

'Yeah. It looks like it.'

'And don't you know where she's moved to?'

I desperately racked my brains for an answer. It sounded so stupid to have to admit that your mother, so to speak, has moved home whilst you were at work and you knew nothing about it. But unable to think of anything that would justify my situation, I mumbled,

'No.'

'My mum said there was something fishy going on. Wait till I tell her.'

She gleefully dashed into the chemists shop to share the news with her mum, who was serving behind the counter.

For some minutes I just stared at the darkened front window of the restaurant, unable to get my head around what I had just been told. Finally, I returned to the back garden and looked through the French Door windows. Alexis was right. The living room was bare. I then checked the kitchen. Apart from the fixed cupboards and gas stoves, there was nothing.

Retrieving my German 'SS' dagger from its hiding place in the coal bunker, I approached the French door and inserted the dagger between the catch and the door frame. Seconds later the door swung open. I was well practiced in this method of entry, having used it many times in the past. Often, when I returned home to find nobody in and the coal bunker offering the only shelter from the weather, I would sit inside and wait until I heard the key being inserted into the front door. I would then nip outside, close the door, and pretend I had been waiting outside for them to come home.

Nerves jangling, as if I was a burglar, I silently stepped into the empty lounge, pausing in the doorway whilst I listened. I didn't trust my step-mother one little bit, and was still not fully convinced she had gone. After several seconds, and my rapid heartbeat pounding in my chest the only audible sounds, I quickly moved through the rest of the house. She had cleared everything, even my old iron bed.

Fortunately, she had thrown my filthy mattress and army blanket onto the floor. Stinking as they were, at least I knew I had somewhere to sleep. Her bedroom was empty, the dust and marks in the fitted carpet where the bed had been still prominent; not surprising given all the shagging that had taken place in that room.

Back on the landing, I sat on the top stair and stared into the semi-darkness as I let the day's events slowly unfold.

So, I thought. *She's left my dad and run off with the lodger, taking all the furniture, plus his car.* Well, I suppose it was inevitable. After all, my dad will return to England at some time and she might have a hard time explaining the lodger.

The more I pondered the situation, the more my face creased into a smile. Then, before I knew it, I began nervously giggling as the realisation my step-mother was out of my life hit home. It was like a huge burden had been lifted from my shoulders. I headed down the stairs, my laugher now so hearty I nearly missed my footing. By the time I set off on my bike for my favourite café, I was laughing like a man possessed. Passers-by must have thought I was 'touched'. By the time I reached the café I was fully composed, now all the pressures I'd been worried about were gone.

'Usual Billy?' asked the café owner as I entered.

My usual was one sausage, mash, and gravy with onions through it. This was the best bulk value for my one shilling and sixpence. With me, it was more to do with quantity than quality. I fingered the unopened wage packet in my pocket.

'No...give me two sausages,' I replied. *After all,* I thought, *I'm a millionaire.*

'Two sausages!... you come into the money then?' he joked.

I savoured every mouthful of food. For the first time in my life I felt really free. The thought of not having to face her ever again so satisfying I wanted to tell the world. Not only that, I had more money in my pocket than I had ever had in my life. The yoke of my step-mother had finally been removed.

As I sipped my mug of tea, I again mulled over the day's events. To say it had been an interesting day was an understatement. 'Her', leaving the way she did, once again proved what a heartless bitch she was. Not only had she moved house without telling me, effectively, as far as she was concerned, leaving me homeless, but she had also intended leaving me penniless as well. Now it made sense. She had obviously supervised all the furniture into the removals van, then, with her fancy man at the wheel, driven in my dad's car to the bus stop. No doubt they parked the car out of sight in case I spotted it. What a bit of luck I'd yelled 'keep going' that morning. Why, I wondered, didn't she wait another few days until I had joined the Navy. Then she could have taken my money, moved, and I wouldn't have known anything about it.

It was ten-o-clock by the time I got back to the restaurant. Parking my bike out of sight, I took up a position across the road in the shadows. For several minutes I watched the darkened restaurant for any signs of movement. I still didn't trust my step-mother had altogether left. It was out of character for her to walk away from the chance of taking my money. After several minutes, I was satisfied the restaurant was still deserted. Grabbing my dagger from the coal bunker, I opened the French Door and let myself in.

Not wanting to get trapped upstairs if she came back whilst I was sleeping, I brought my oil stained mattress into the kitchen and laid it on the floor. The kitchen was not only the warmest room in the house, thanks to the oven, it was also closest to the back door.

The noise of a car door slamming startled me into life. I was on my feet in a second. Heart thumping like a steam hammer, I grabbed my clothes and opened the back door ready to run. When nobody entered, I sneaked a look into the restaurant. Through the front window I saw the van delivering the morning newspapers to the Newsagent's shop next door.

Before leaving for work, I lugged my mattress back upstairs. If my step-mother returned whilst I was at work, I didn't want her to know I could get into the house. Satisfied everything was as she had left it, I went to work.

That evening, I said goodbye to the people I had worked with for the last two and half years. I was not sad to be leaving, knowing that my future couldn't possibly be any worse than my present situation. I did however have a tinge of sadness when I watched my mate Les ride off on my dad's bike. He had still never said that I could have the bike. Well, too bad now, because I had sold it to my mate Les, the other apprentice, for two pounds. The money kept rolling in!

As I shook hands with Fred, he asked me if I wanted a lift home, but I said I would walk. I would miss Fred, he had taught me many things and was more of a dad to me than my father ever was.

I refused the offer of a lift because I didn't want a company vehicle drawing up outside the restaurant, just in case 'the bane of my life' had returned. Also, if I walked, I could use a short cut through the bushes which would bring me to the back of the restaurant where I could approach unseen.

It was a cold December evening. On a night when I would have welcomed the darkness, the moon was bright in a clear sky. Standing silently, I carefully observed the darkened restaurant over the back fence. After some moments, I was satisfied it was empty and entered the back garden, wedging the gate open. Sticking close to fence, I silently edged my way towards the back of the house. Suddenly, a voice called out.

'Billy, Billy.' I stopped dead in my tracks, unable to locate the voice.

'Billy, up here.' It was Alexis. She was leaning out of her upstairs bedroom window.

'Are you looking for your mum?' she asked.

'No,' I angrily replied, annoyed she had nearly caused me to soil my already grubby underpants.

'Well anyway, she was here this morning, but she's gone now. Thought you'd like to know.' Realising it was good of her to let me know, I waved and called out 'thanks'.

So, my instincts had been right. She had returned. Alexis continued watching me from her window. Not wanting her to see how I got into the house, I turned and headed out the gate.

'Thanks for letting me know,' I called over my shoulder.

A few minutes later I returned. Alexis was gone and her bedroom in darkness. The news my step-mother had been back had put me on my guard. Stealthily approaching the darkened house, I again retrieved my dagger and inserted it between the door frame and snib. Only then did it occur to me that she could have slid the dead bolt from the inside. If she had, I had no way of getting in. I smiled as the French door silently opened allowing me to step into the lounge. Leaving the door open, I again stood for several minutes listening, before stealthily making my way through the house. Upstairs, I was delighted to find my oil stained mattress and blanket were still where I had left them that morning.

Chapter Seventy-Six

Early the next morning, I was outside Post Office in Hadleigh. I wanted to make sure my money was safely deposited in my Post Office Savings Account, the account my dad had hassled me into opening.

'Even if it is only sixpence a week, it all mounts up,' he had insisted, when I pointed out I didn't earn enough to save.

Back home later that afternoon, I felt confident enough to risk taking a bath. Up till now I had refrained from putting any lights on, and wasn't sure if the electricity had been cut off. Making up the power switch in the cupboard under the stairs, I was delighted to see the meter whirring. An hour later, I stretched out in a bath that had not seen my backside too often over the last two years. I would have liked clean underwear, but that was a little too optimistic.

That evening, being a Saturday, I went to the pictures. There were plenty of empty seats, so I was surprised when a girl came and sat next to me. Given my scruffy appearance, accompanied by the unmistakable aroma of engine oil, this didn't happen too often.

I was soon in conversation with her. She told me her name was Belinda, and no, she didn't have a boyfriend. As soon as the lights went down, I chanced putting my arm around her, delighted when she cuddled in. It was nice to feel the closeness of another human being, especially the young female kind. I was really glad I had taken a bath.

During the interval, she asked me what I did for a living. Hoping to impress her, I told her I was on leave from the navy. It wasn't too far from the truth, and sounded far more glamorous than, 'apprentice motor mechanic'. Believing sailors were more generous than motor mechanics, and again hoping to impress her, I bought her an ice cream. I couldn't normally have afforded to do that. But what the heck, I had all my pay, plus my two pounds bike money to myself. My generosity must have overwhelmed her, because when I asked if I could walk her home she agreed. As we walked, I casually mentioned I lived by myself, and would she like to see it.

Everything was going well, and I was sure it was my lucky night, until we reached the restaurant. She became suspicious when I told her to wait whilst I ran around to the back. It took me longer than usual to open the door, my excitement getting the better of me. I was relieved to see she was still waiting when I eventually opened the front door. She was reluctant to come in, unable to understand why I didn't have a key, convinced I had broken into an empty restaurant. After a lot of smooth talking, I convinced her to come inside. As I'd not expected to meet anybody that evening, never mind bring them home, I hadn't really thought things through. My hastily put together plan was that we could 'romp and frolic' on the fitted carpet in my parent's bedroom. She took one look at how I was living, and quickly left. That was the last time I saw Belinda. Pity, she was really quite attractive.

Three days later, for the last time, I arose from the oil stained mattress on the floor of the kitchen where I had spent the night. Using the side of my hand I cleared the condensation from the front window and peered out for any signs of life. I had looked forward to this day for some weeks, and I didn't want to be late for my appointment.

The icy cold water from the kitchen tap quickly brought me to life, as I stood shivering in my grubby underwear. Picking up the crumpled heap of clothes from the floor, I carefully eased myself into my trousers. The masking tape holding the split crotch together had lost most of its stickiness, so snagging my toe could see my only pair of trousers rent asunder.

Having safely navigated myself into my trousers without any major mishaps, I shivered myself into my grubby cream shirt complete with matching 'frayed' collar and cuffs. A handful of cold water from the kitchen tap flattened my hair, before donning my brown corduroy cap. To keep out the winter chill, I pulled on my well-worn blue Melton overcoat, which over the years had become a tad too small, but fitted if I didn't do all the buttons up.

Re-reading my call up letter for the umpteenth time, I smiled at the part instructing me not to bring too many personal possessions. Apparently, once our uniforms were issued, all civilian clothing would be parcelled up and sent home. It appeared people actually wore clothing worthy of being sent home. It also appeared that they also had homes to send it to. Alright for some. As I had neither, I knew exactly where my rags were going as soon as I received my uniform.

My worldly goods amounted to my Post Office Savings Book, containing twenty-six pounds and one shilling, a soiled towel, a well-worn toothbrush, and a sliver of soap. I packed them into my 'suitcase', an ex-war department respirator case I was using as a shoulder bag.

Slinging it over my shoulder, I stepped out into the cold morning air and headed off to catch my train.